NORTHLANDERS

BOOK THREE: BLOOD IN THE SNOW

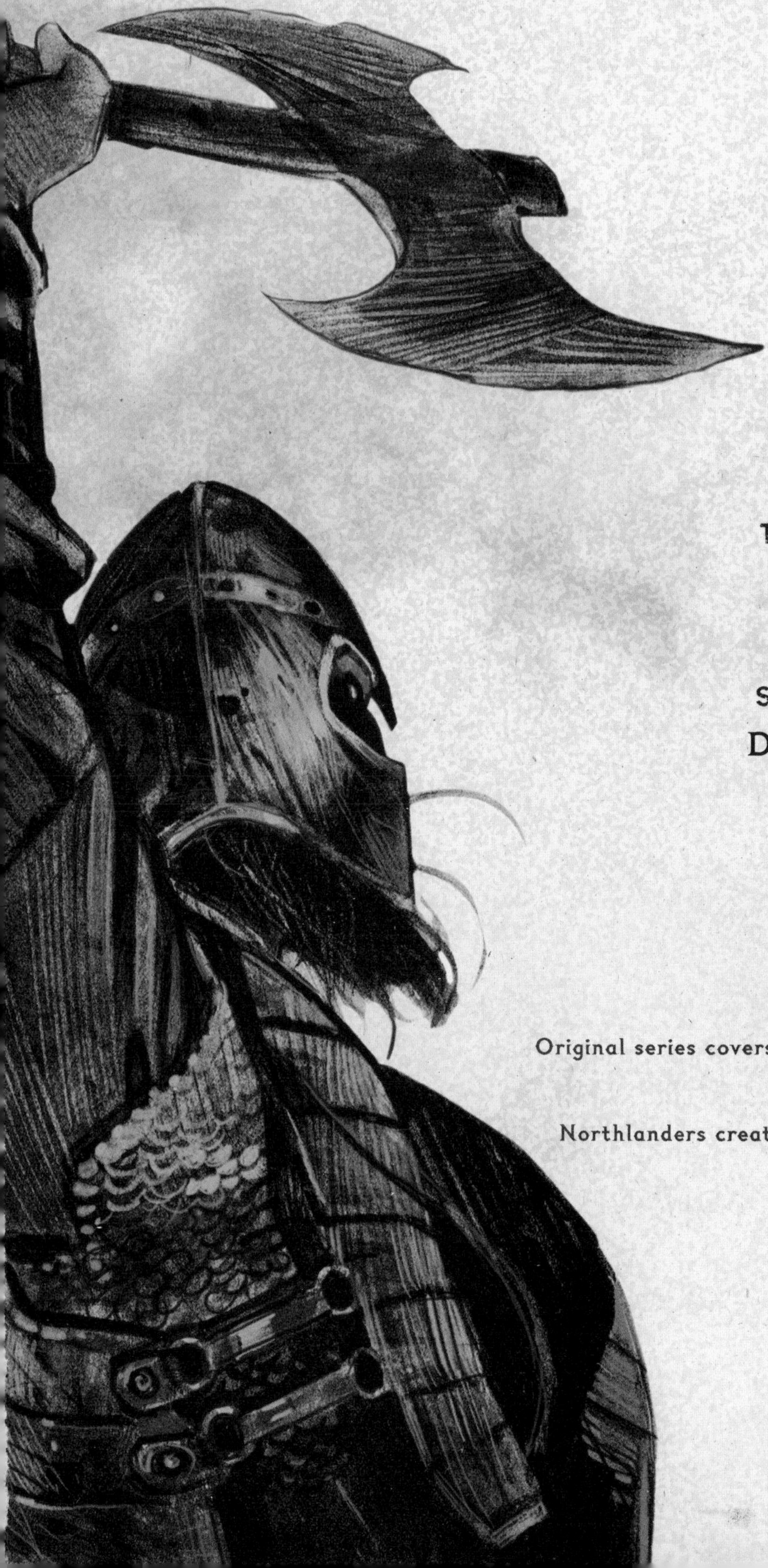

Brian Wood
Writer

LINDISFARNE
Dean Ormston
Art & Colors

THE VIKING ART OF
SINGLE COMBAT
Vasilis Lolos
Artist

THE SHIELD MAIDENS
Danijel Zezelj
Artist

SVEN THE IMMORTAL
Davide Gianfelice
Artist

Dave McCaig Colorist
Travis Lanham Letterer
Original series covers by Massimo Carnevale

Northlanders created by **Brian Wood**

Karen Berger SVP-Executive Editor
Will Dennis Mark Doyle Editors – Original Series
Casey Seijas Assistant Editor – Original Series
Georg Brewer VP – Design & DC Direct Creative
Bob Harras Group Editor – Collected Editions
Robbin Brosterman Design Director – Books
DC COMICS
Paul Levitz President & Publisher
Richard Bruning SVP – Creative Director
Patrick Caldon EVP – Finance & Operations
Amy Genkins SVP – Business & Legal Affairs
Jim Lee Editorial Director – WildStorm
Gregory Noveck SVP – Creative Affairs
Steve Rotterdam SVP – Sales & Marketing
Cheryl Rubin SVP – Brand Management

Cover illustration by Massimo Carnevale
and design by Brian Wood

NORTHLANDERS: BLOOD IN THE SNOW
Published by DC Comics. Cover and compilation
© 2010 DC Comics. All Rights Reserved.

Originally published as NORTHLANDERS 9, 10,
17-20. Copyright © 2008, 2009 Brian Wood and
DC Comics. All Rights Reserved. VERTIGO and all
characters, their distinctive likenesses and related elements
featured in this publication are trademarks of DC Comics.
The stories, characters and incidents featured in this
publication are entirely fictional. DC Comics does not
read or accept unsolicited submissions of ideas,
stories or artwork.

DC Comics
1700 Broadway, New York, NY 10019
A Warner Bros. Entertainment Company
Printed in the USA.
09/09/2011. Second Printing.
ISBN: 978-1-4012-2620-6

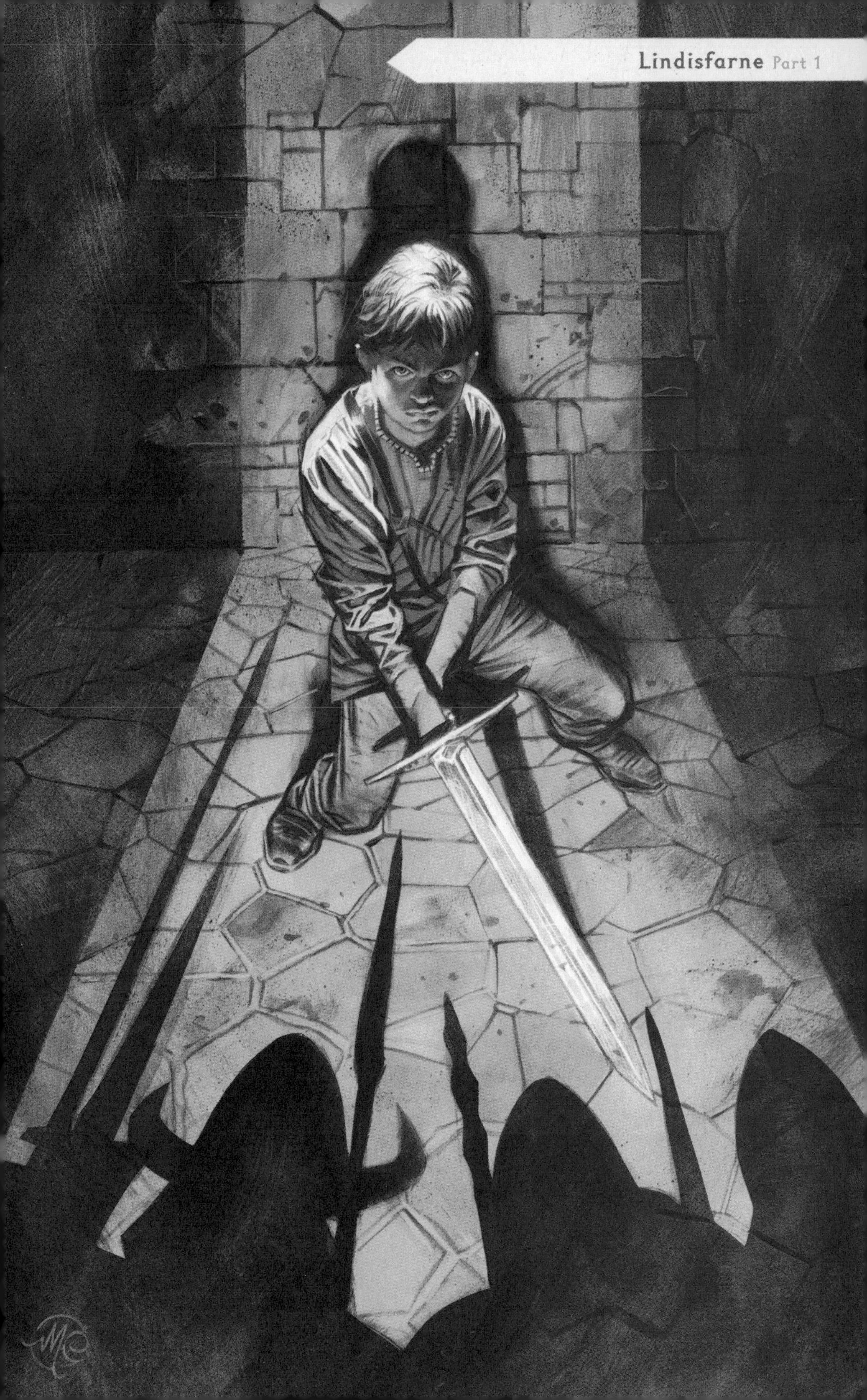

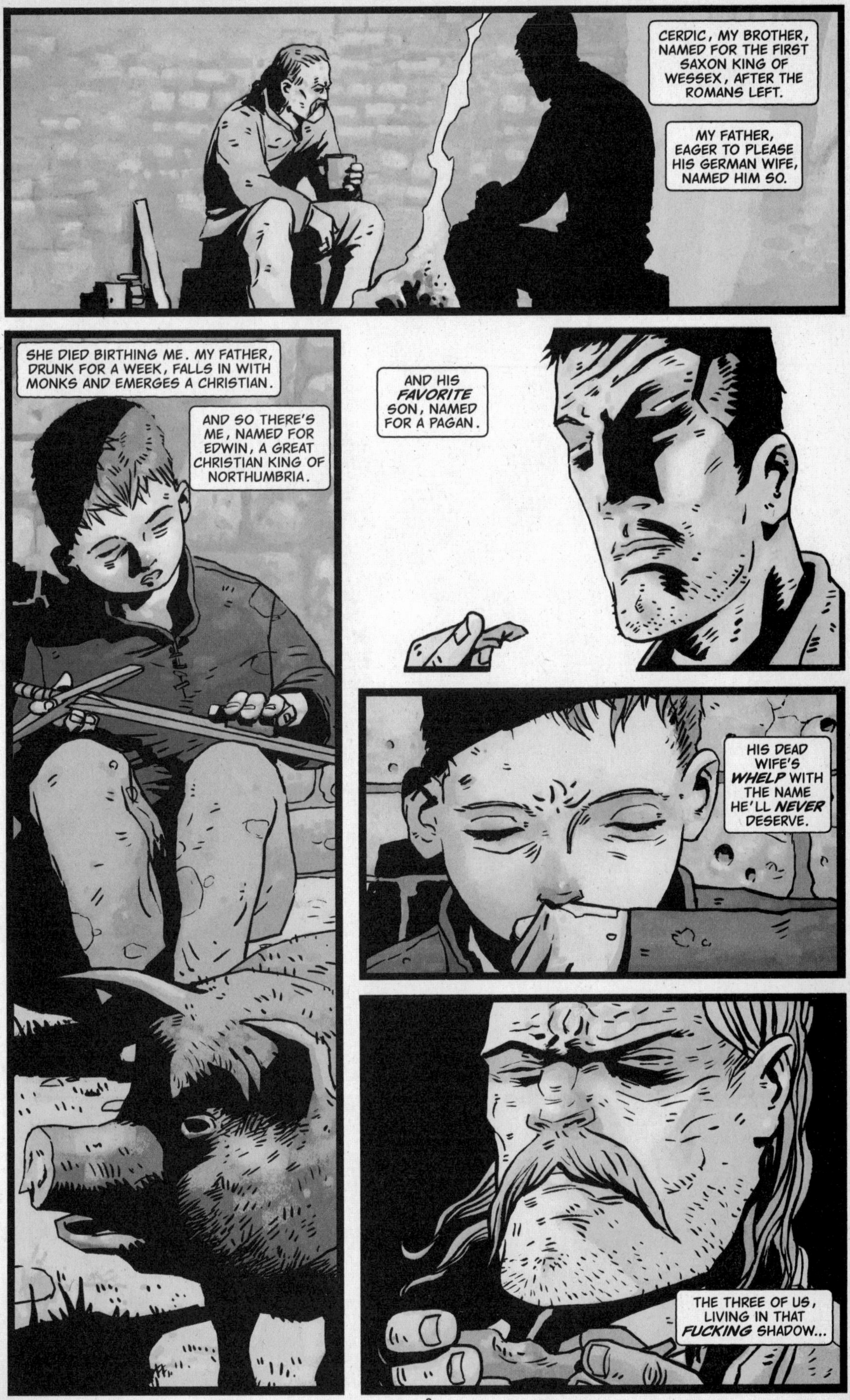

CERDIC, MY BROTHER, NAMED FOR THE FIRST SAXON KING OF WESSEX, AFTER THE ROMANS LEFT.
MY FATHER, EAGER TO PLEASE HIS GERMAN WIFE, NAMED HIM SO.
SHE DIED BIRTHING ME. MY FATHER, DRUNK FOR A WEEK, FALLS IN WITH MONKS AND EMERGES A CHRISTIAN.
AND SO THERE'S ME, NAMED FOR EDWIN, A GREAT CHRISTIAN KING OF NORTHUMBRIA.
AND HIS FAVORITE SON, NAMED FOR A PAGAN.
HIS DEAD WIFE'S WHELP WITH THE NAME HE'LL NEVER DESERVE.
THE THREE OF US, LIVING IN THAT FUCKING SHADOW...

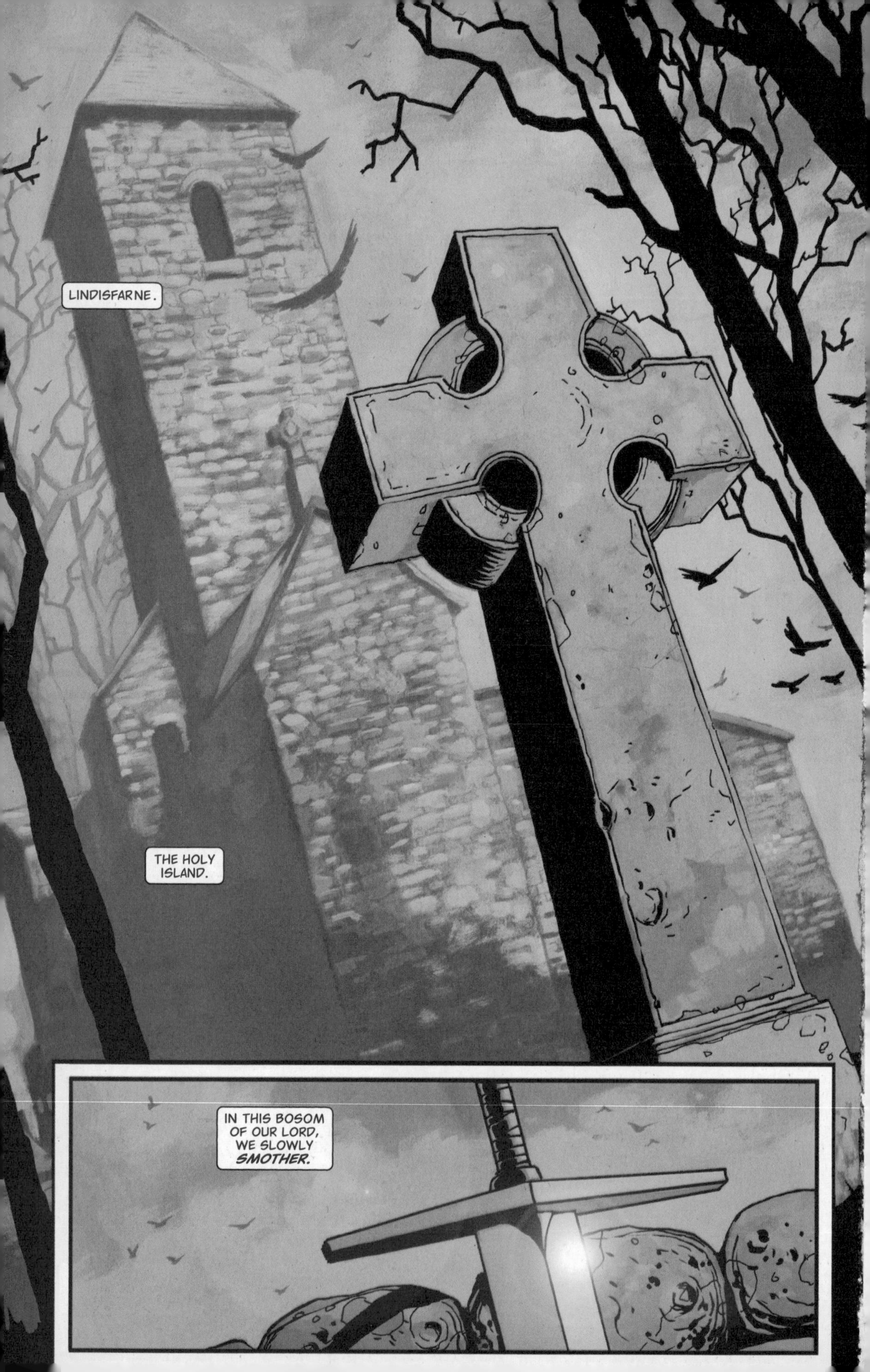
LINDISFARNE.
THE HOLY ISLAND.
IN THIS BOSOM OF OUR LORD, WE SLOWLY *SMOTHER.*

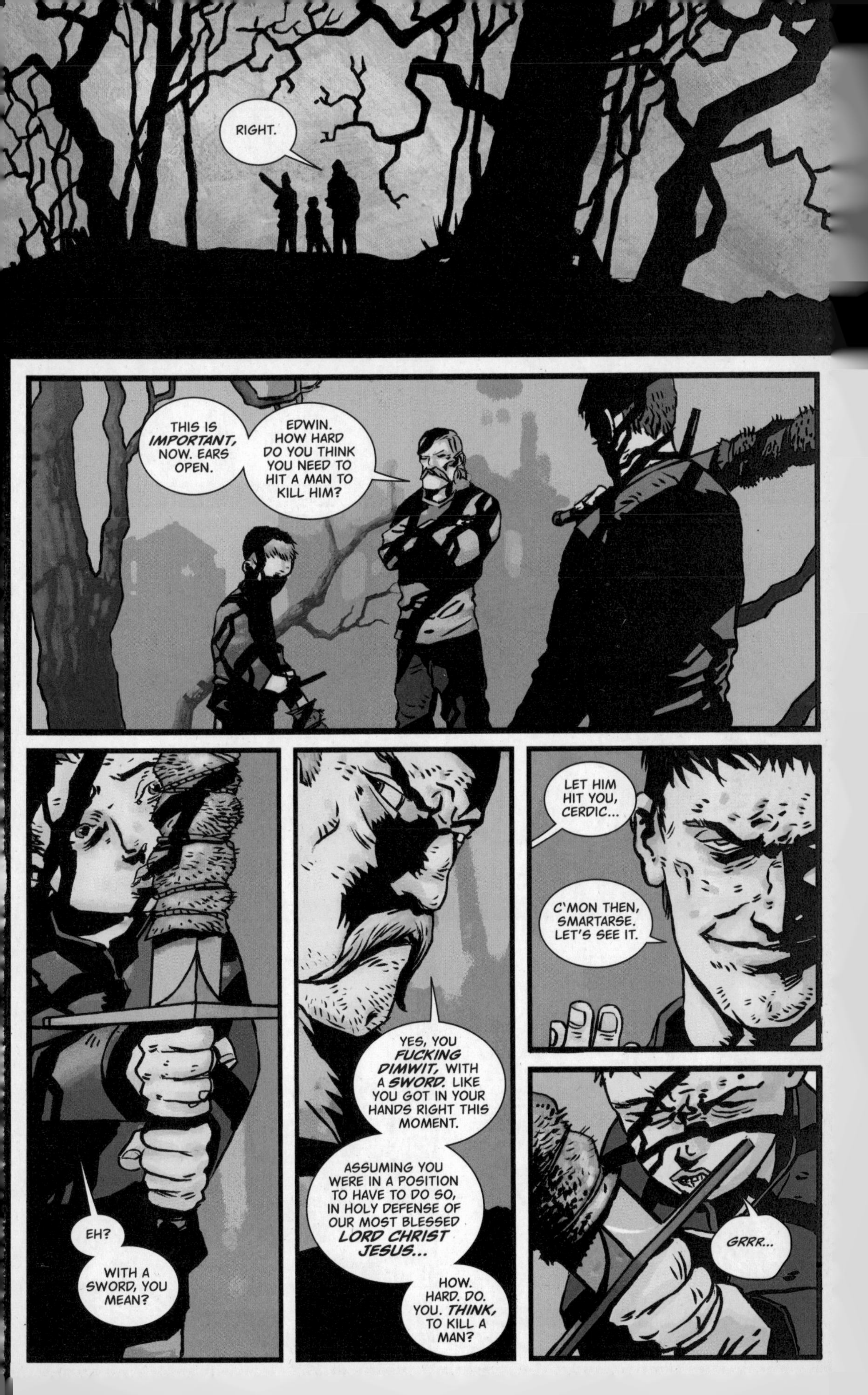
RIGHT.
THIS IS IMPORTANT, NOW. EARS OPEN.
EDWIN. HOW HARD DO YOU THINK YOU NEED TO HIT A MAN TO KILL HIM?
EH?
WITH A SWORD, YOU MEAN?
YES, YOU FUCKING DIMWIT, WITH A SWORD. LIKE YOU GOT IN YOUR HANDS RIGHT THIS MOMENT.
ASSUMING YOU WERE IN A POSITION TO HAVE TO DO SO, IN HOLY DEFENSE OF OUR MOST BLESSED LORD CHRIST JESUS...
HOW. HARD. DO. YOU. THINK, TO KILL A MAN?
LET HIM HIT YOU, CERDIC...
C'MON THEN, SMARTARSE. LET'S SEE IT.
GRRR...

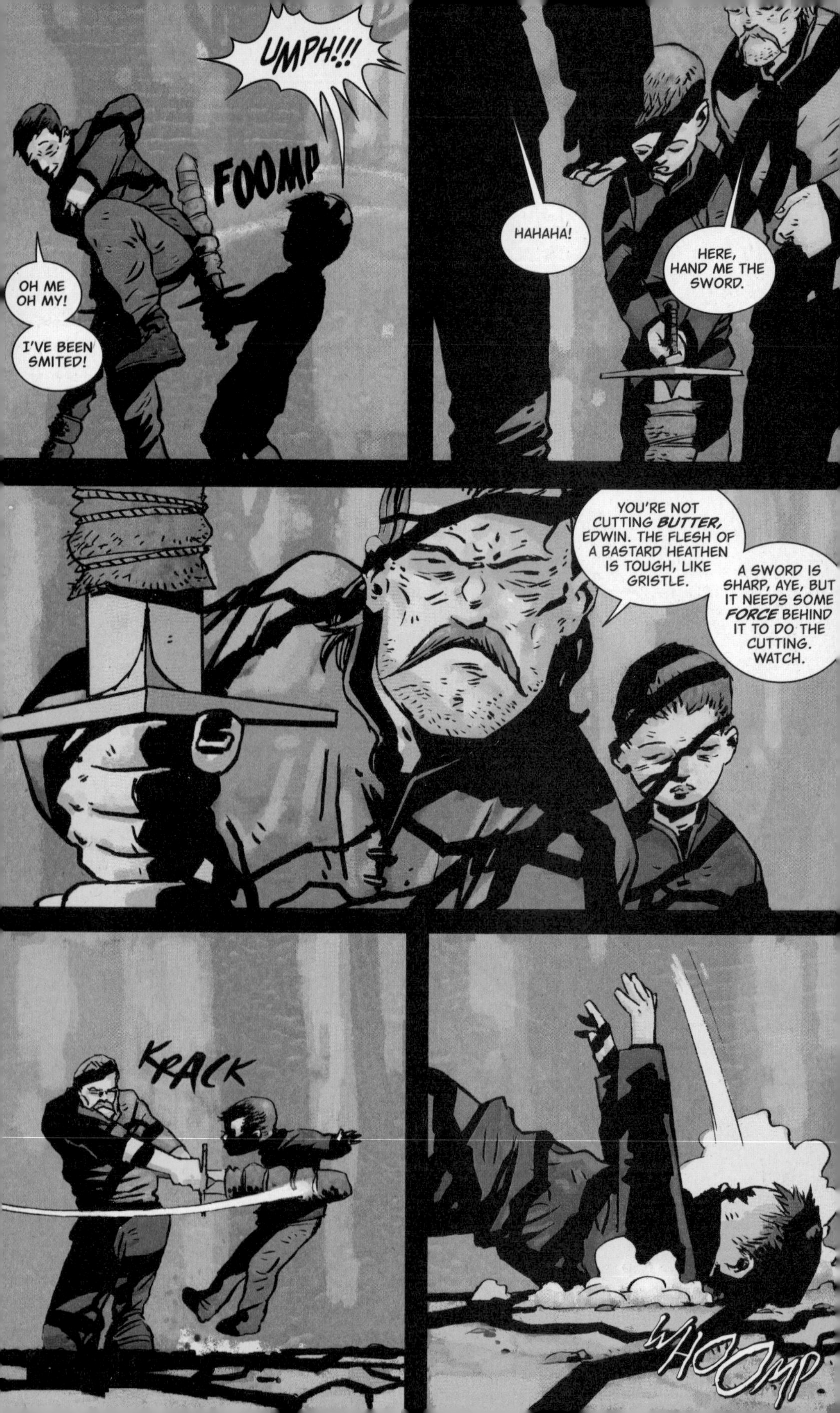
UMPH!!!
FOOMP
OH ME OH MY!
I'VE BEEN SMITED!
HAHAHA!
HERE, HAND ME THE SWORD.
YOU'RE NOT CUTTING BUTTER, EDWIN. THE FLESH OF A BASTARD HEATHEN IS TOUGH, LIKE GRISTLE.
A SWORD IS SHARP, AYE, BUT IT NEEDS SOME FORCE BEHIND IT TO DO THE CUTTING. WATCH.
KRACK
WHOOMP

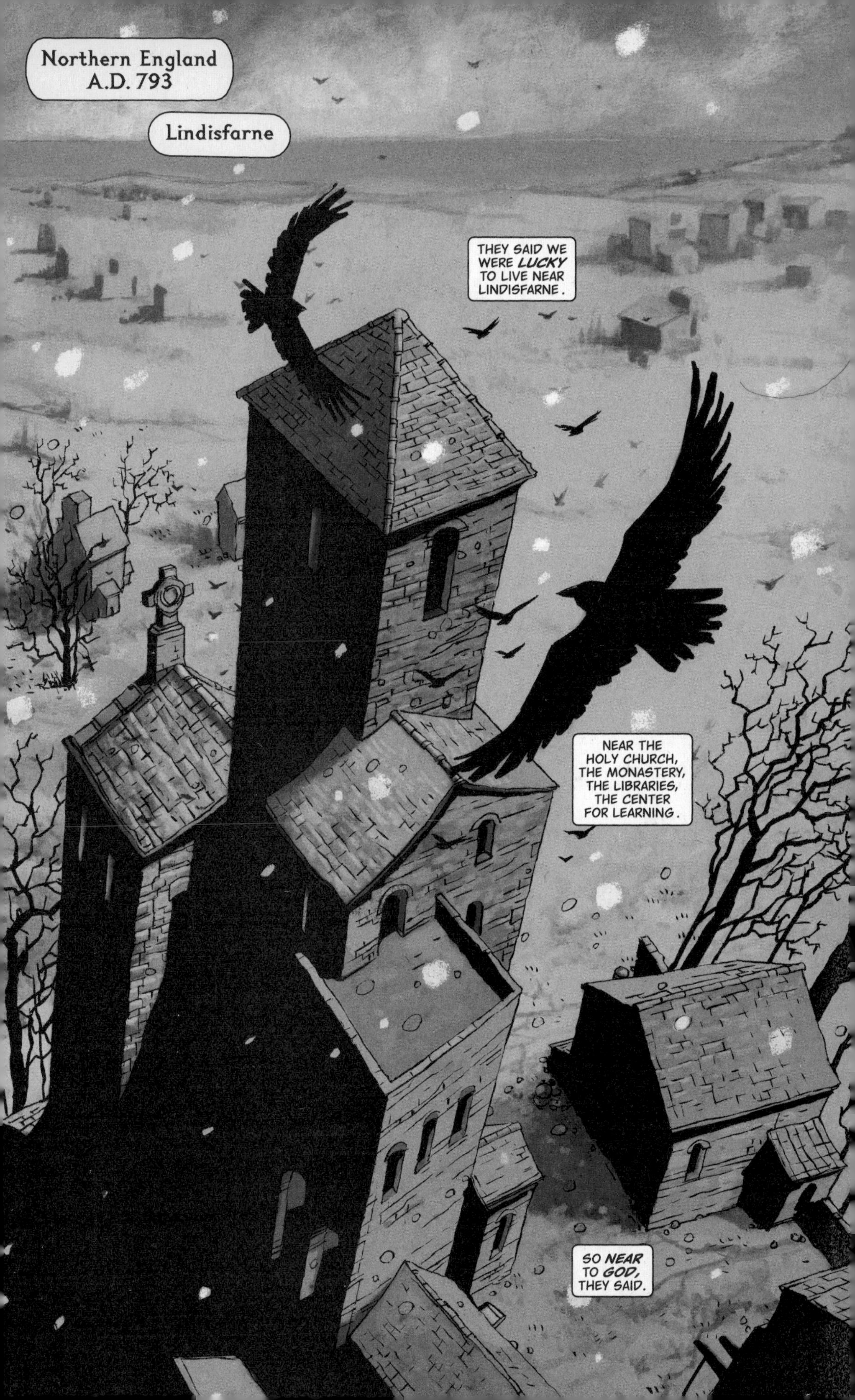

Northern England A.D. 793
Lindisfarne
THEY SAID WE WERE LUCKY TO LIVE NEAR LINDISFARNE.
NEAR THE HOLY CHURCH, THE MONASTERY, THE LIBRARIES, THE CENTER FOR LEARNING.
SO NEAR TO GOD, THEY SAID.

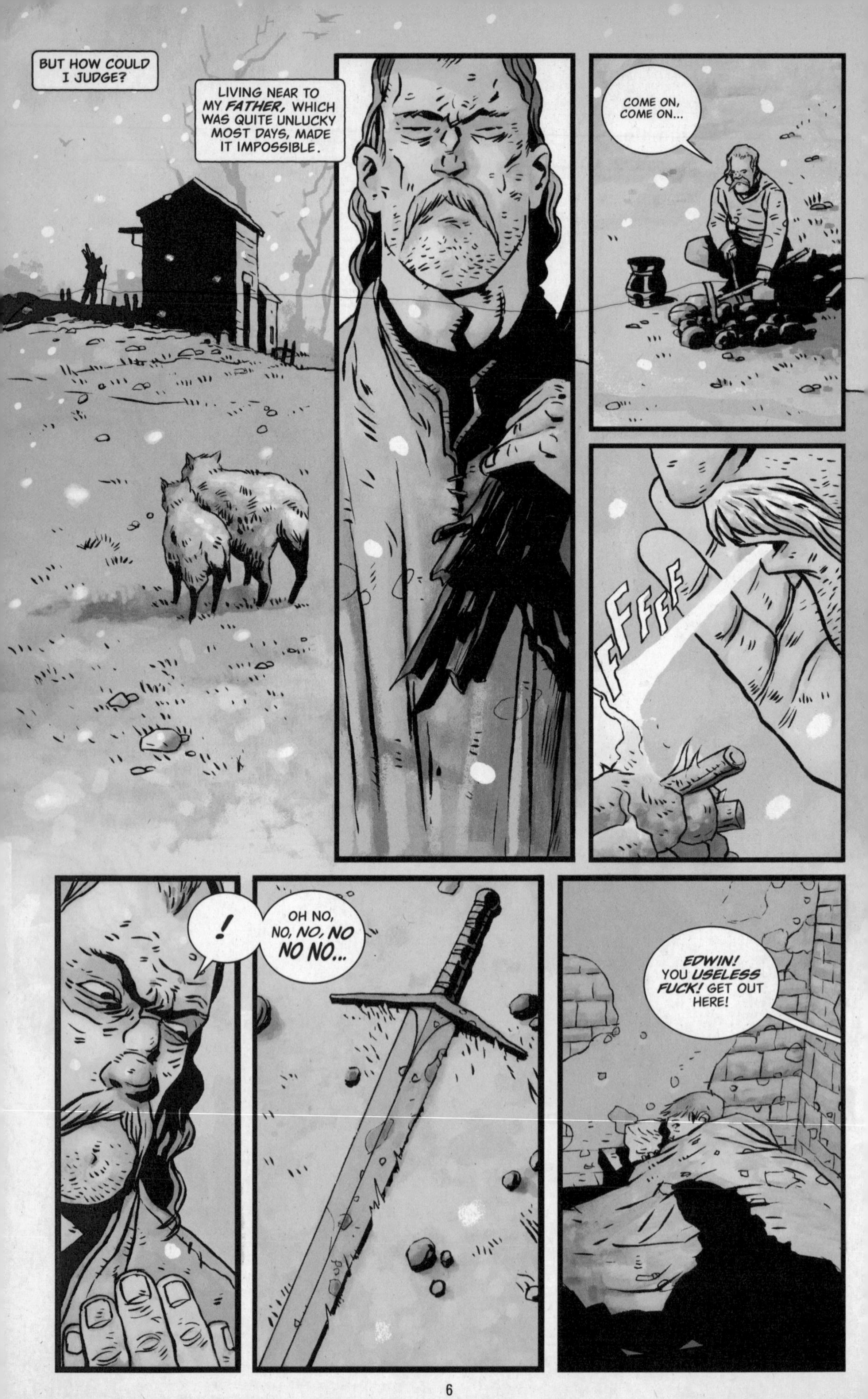
BUT HOW COULD I JUDGE?
LIVING NEAR TO MY FATHER, WHICH WAS QUITE UNLUCKY MOST DAYS, MADE IT IMPOSSIBLE.
COME ON, COME ON...
FFFF
!
OH NO, NO, NO, NO NO NO...
EDWIN! YOU USELESS FUCK! GET OUT HERE!

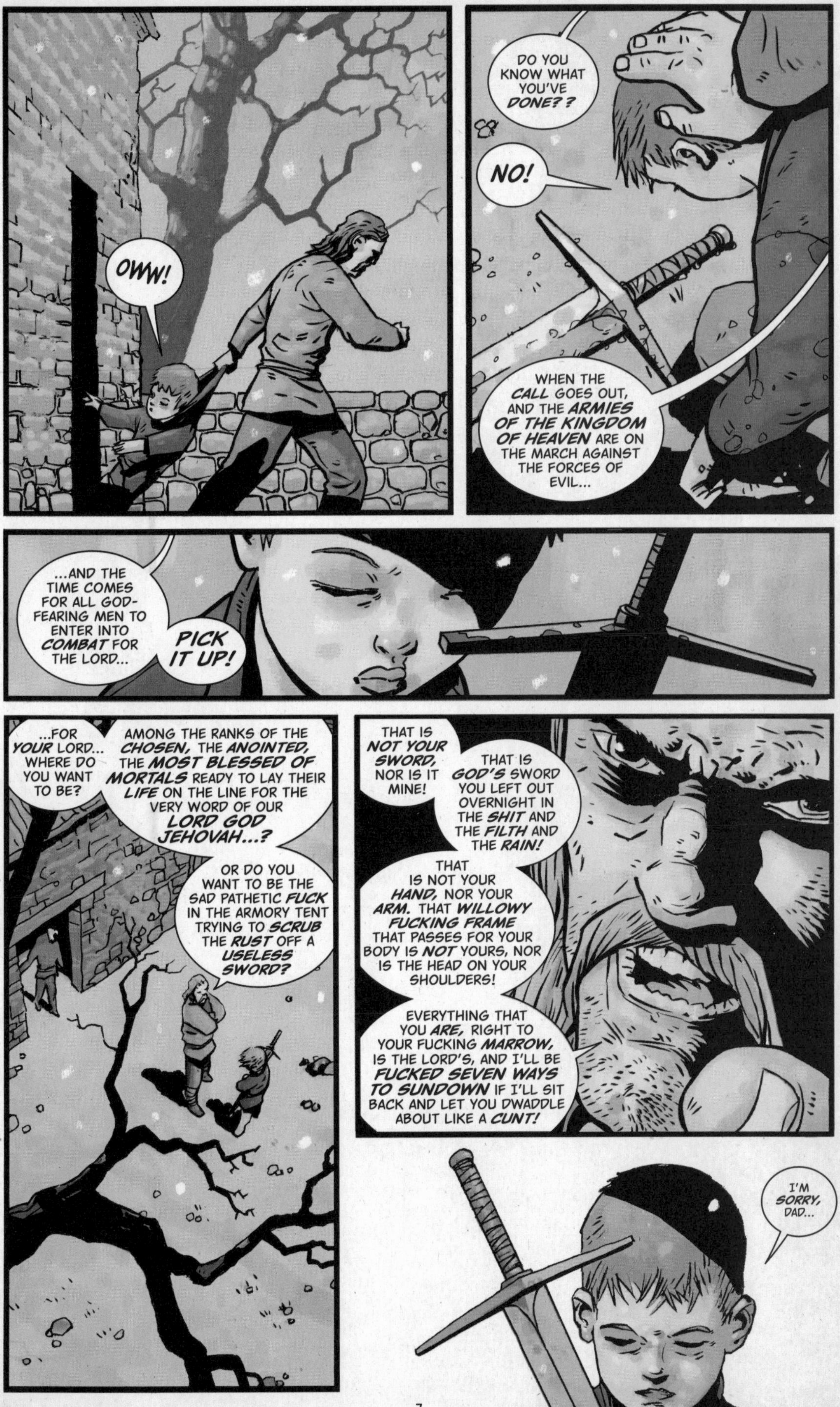
OWW!
DO YOU KNOW WHAT YOU'VE DONE? ?
NO!
WHEN THE CALL GOES OUT, AND THE ARMIES OF THE KINGDOM OF HEAVEN ARE ON THE MARCH AGAINST THE FORCES OF EVIL...
...AND THE TIME COMES FOR ALL GOD-FEARING MEN TO ENTER INTO COMBAT FOR THE LORD...
PICK IT UP!
...FOR YOUR LORD... WHERE DO YOU WANT TO BE?
AMONG THE RANKS OF THE CHOSEN, THE ANOINTED, THE MOST BLESSED OF MORTALS READY TO LAY THEIR LIFE ON THE LINE FOR THE VERY WORD OF OUR LORD GOD JEHOVAH...?
OR DO YOU WANT TO BE THE SAD PATHETIC FUCK IN THE ARMORY TENT TRYING TO SCRUB THE RUST OFF A USELESS SWORD?
THAT IS NOT YOUR SWORD, NOR IS IT MINE!
THAT IS GOD'S SWORD YOU LEFT OUT OVERNIGHT IN THE SHIT AND THE FILTH AND THE RAIN!
THAT IS NOT YOUR HAND, NOR YOUR ARM. THAT WILLOWY FUCKING FRAME THAT PASSES FOR YOUR BODY IS NOT YOURS, NOR IS THE HEAD ON YOUR SHOULDERS!
EVERYTHING THAT YOU ARE, RIGHT TO YOUR FUCKING MARROW, IS THE LORD'S, AND I'LL BE FUCKED SEVEN WAYS TO SUNDOWN IF I'LL SIT BACK AND LET YOU DWADDLE ABOUT LIKE A CUNT!
I'M SORRY, DAD...

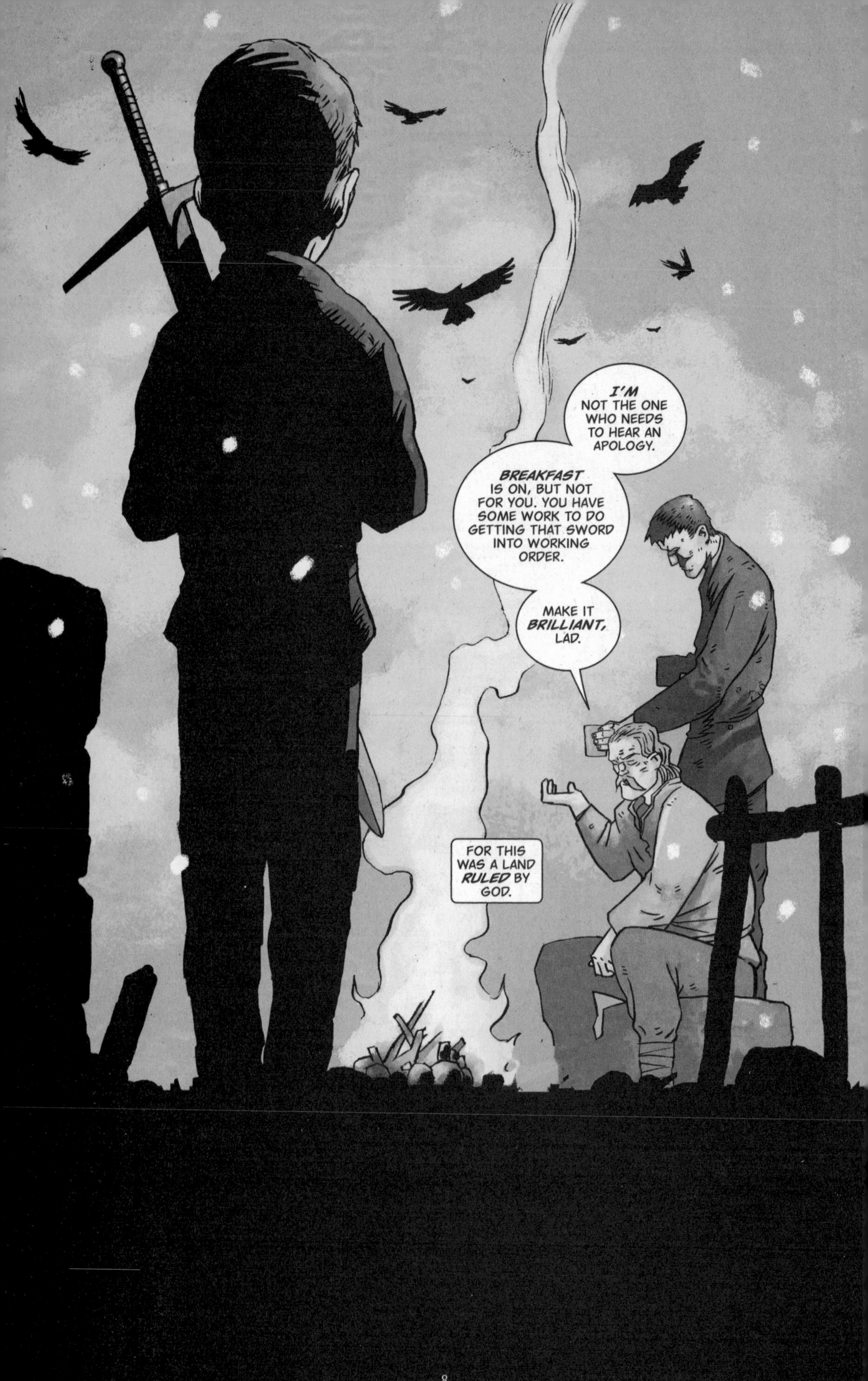
I'M NOT THE ONE WHO NEEDS TO HEAR AN APOLOGY.
BREAKFAST IS ON, BUT NOT FOR YOU. YOU HAVE SOME WORK TO DO GETTING THAT SWORD INTO WORKING ORDER.
MAKE IT BRILLIANT, LAD.
FOR THIS WAS A LAND RULED BY GOD.

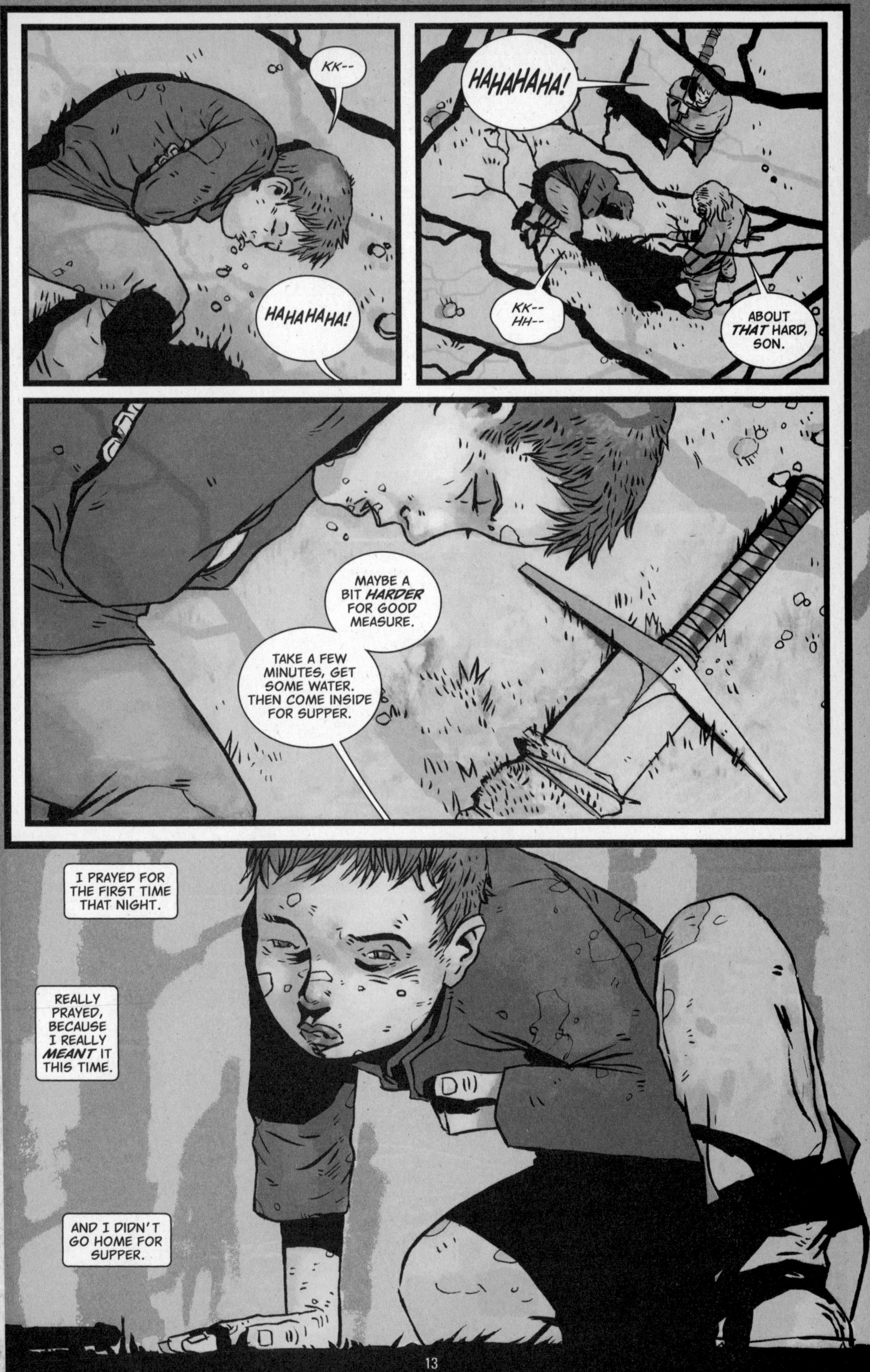
KK--
HAHAHAHA!
HAHAHAHA!
KK-- HH--
ABOUT THAT HARD, SON.
MAYBE A BIT HARDER FOR GOOD MEASURE.
TAKE A FEW MINUTES, GET SOME WATER. THEN COME INSIDE FOR SUPPER.
I PRAYED FOR THE FIRST TIME THAT NIGHT.
REALLY PRAYED, BECAUSE I REALLY MEANT IT THIS TIME.
AND I DIDN'T GO HOME FOR SUPPER.

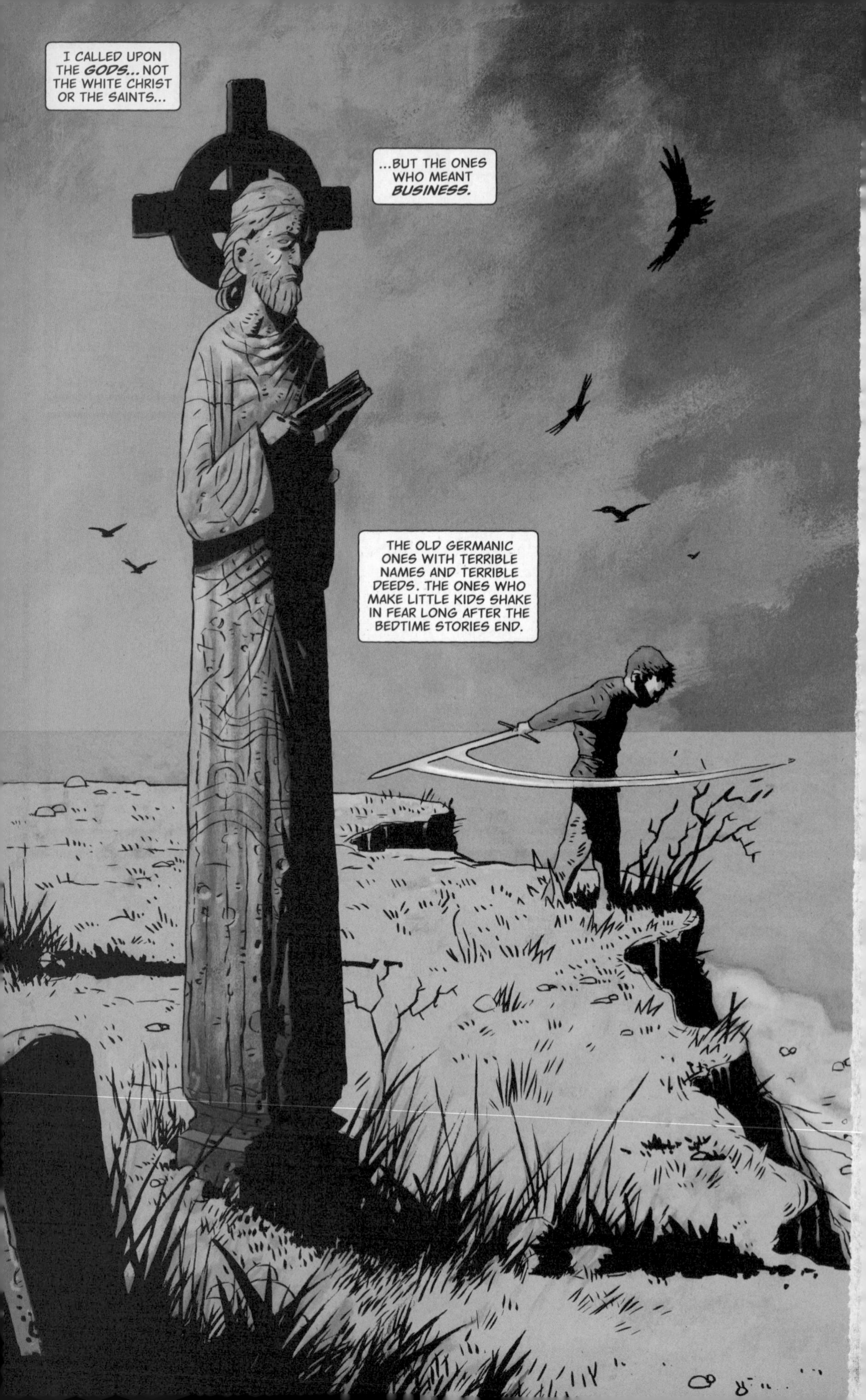
I CALLED UPON THE *GODS*... NOT THE WHITE CHRIST OR THE SAINTS...
...BUT THE ONES WHO MEANT *BUSINESS.*
THE OLD GERMANIC ONES WITH TERRIBLE NAMES AND TERRIBLE DEEDS. THE ONES WHO MAKE LITTLE KIDS SHAKE IN FEAR LONG AFTER THE BEDTIME STORIES END.

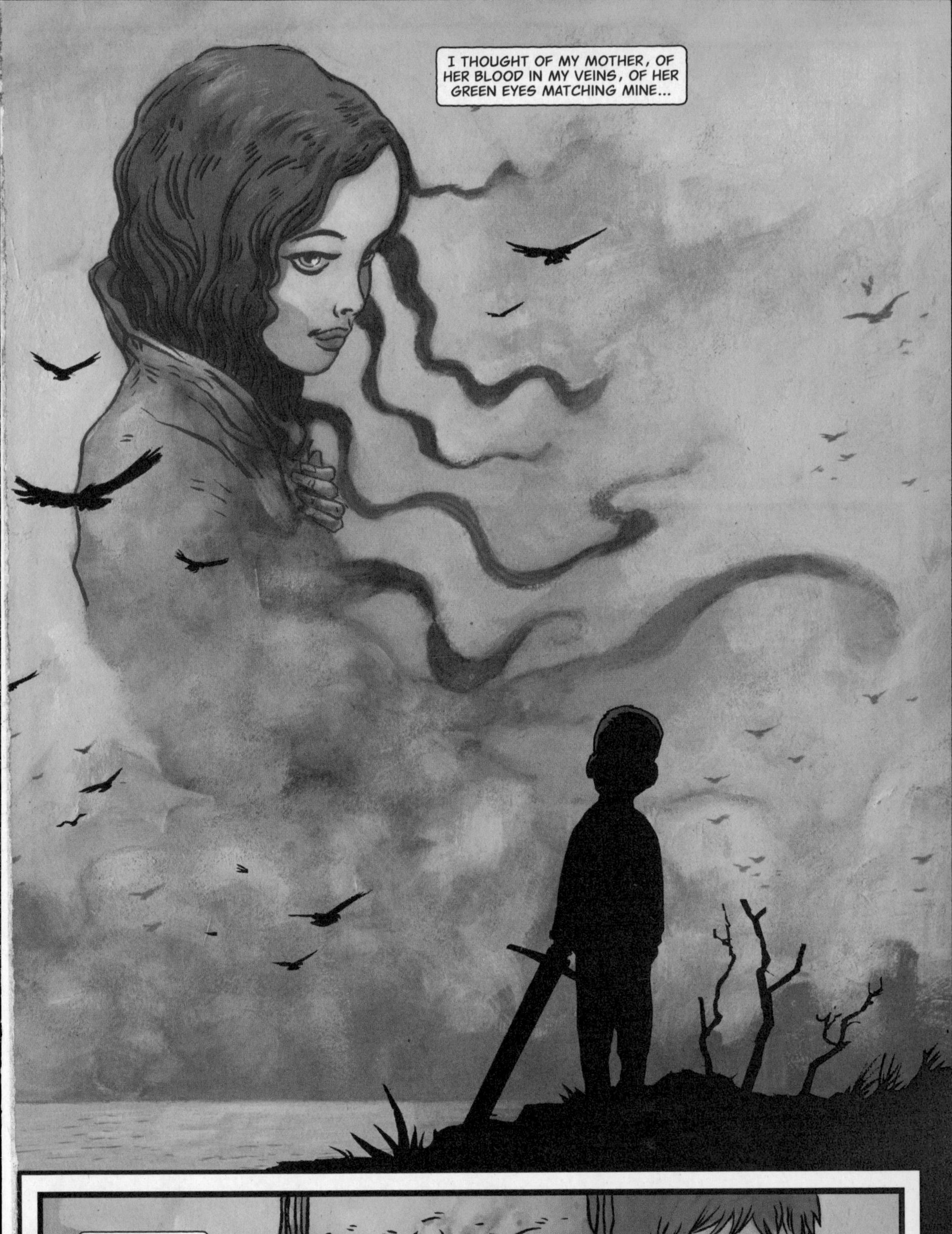
I THOUGHT OF MY MOTHER, OF HER BLOOD IN MY VEINS, OF HER GREEN EYES MATCHING MINE...

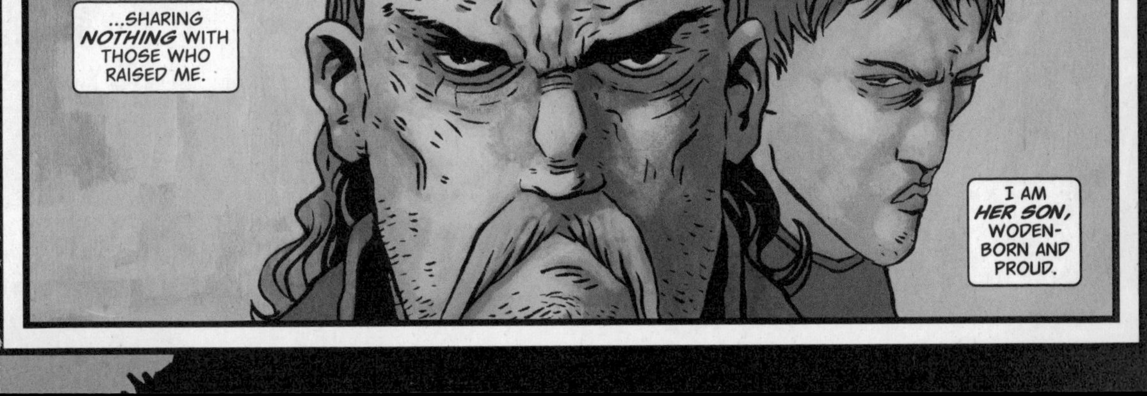
...SHARING NOTHING WITH THOSE WHO RAISED ME.
I AM HER SON, WODEN-BORN AND PROUD.

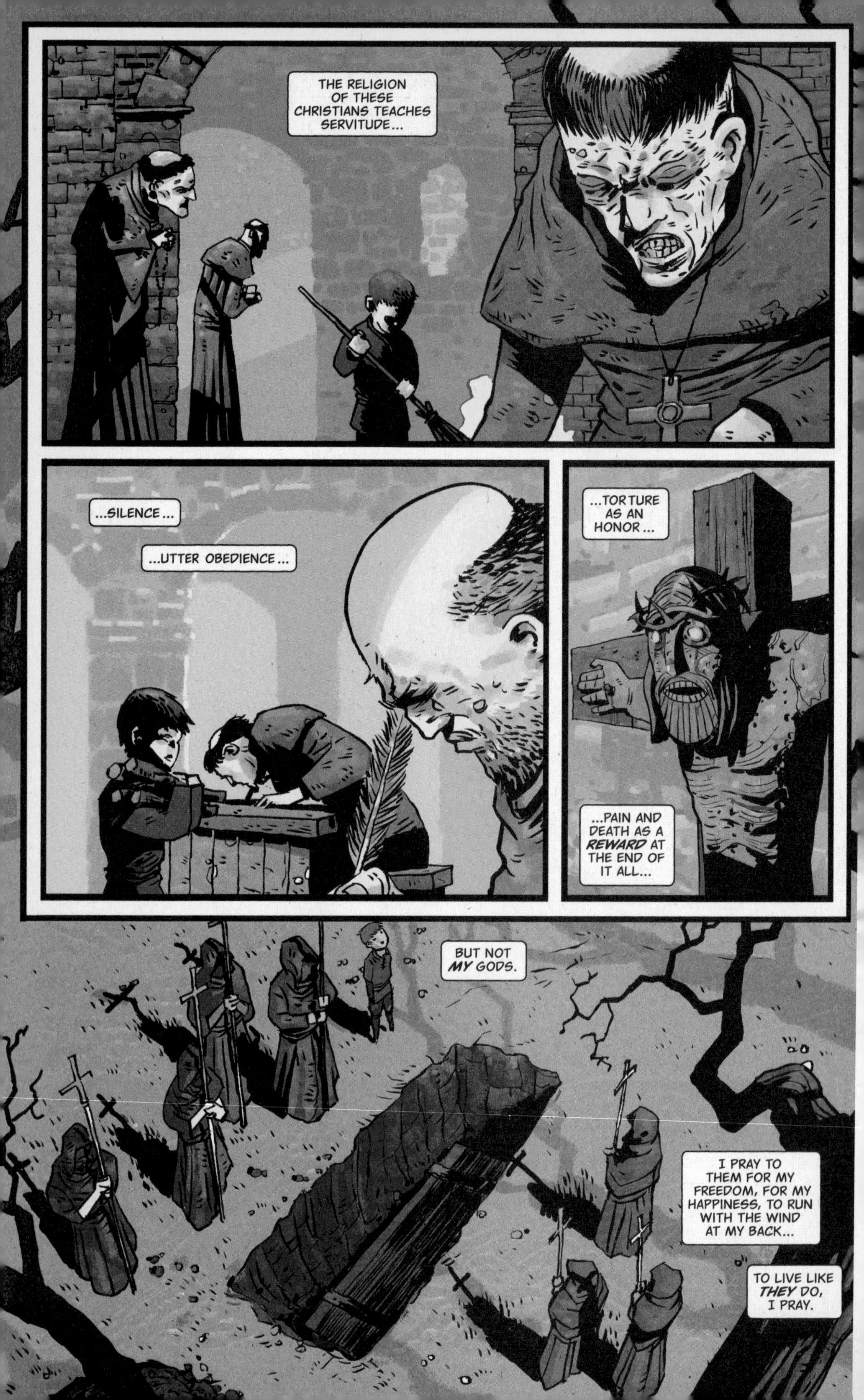
THE RELIGION OF THESE CHRISTIANS TEACHES SERVITUDE...
...SILENCE...
...UTTER OBEDIENCE...
...TORTURE AS AN HONOR...
...PAIN AND DEATH AS A *REWARD* AT THE END OF IT ALL...
BUT NOT *MY* GODS.
I PRAY TO THEM FOR MY FREEDOM, FOR MY HAPPINESS, TO RUN WITH THE WIND AT MY BACK...
TO LIVE LIKE *THEY* DO, I PRAY.

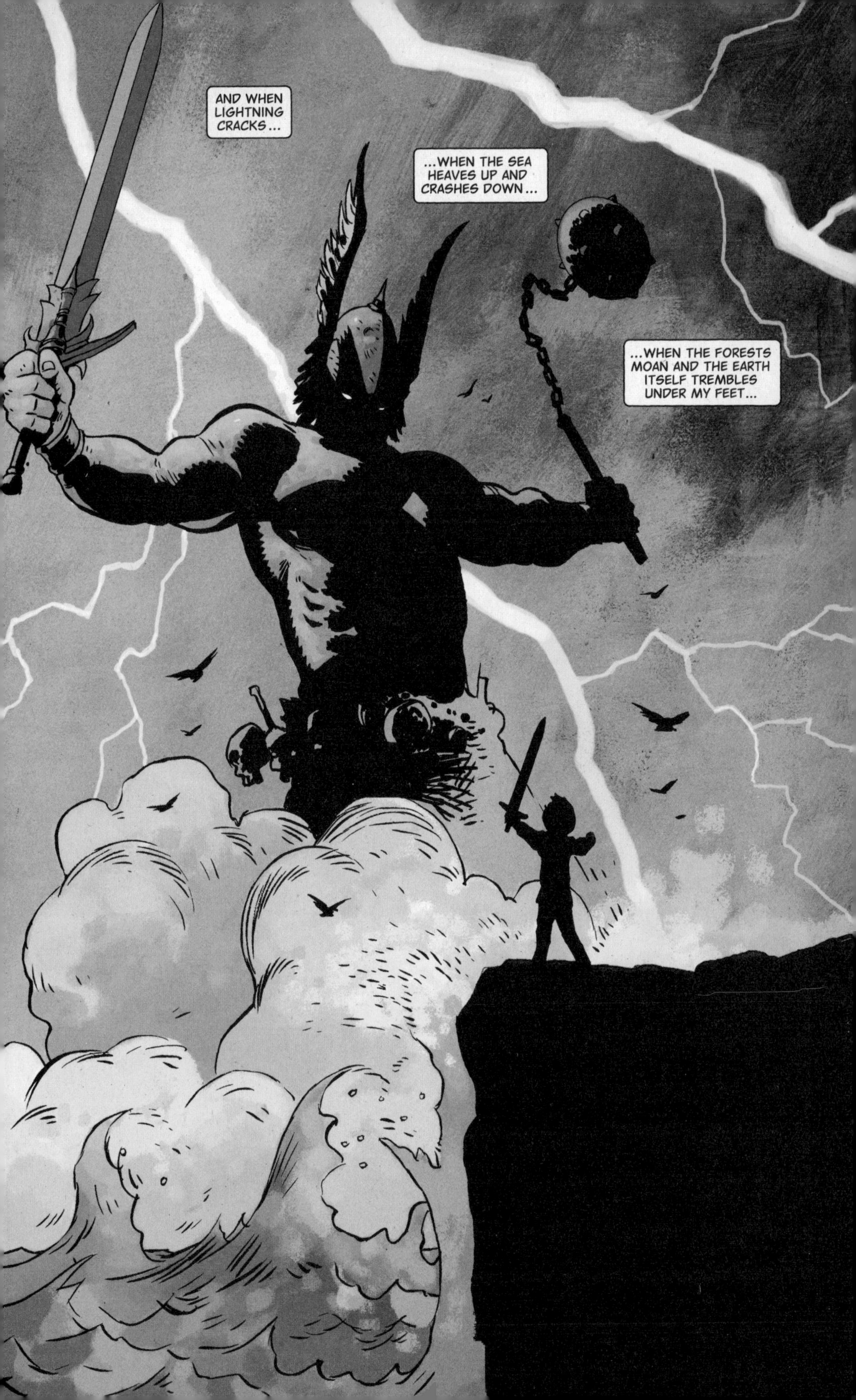
AND WHEN LIGHTNING CRACKS...
...WHEN THE SEA HEAVES UP AND CRASHES DOWN...
...WHEN THE FORESTS MOAN AND THE EARTH ITSELF TREMBLES UNDER MY FEET...

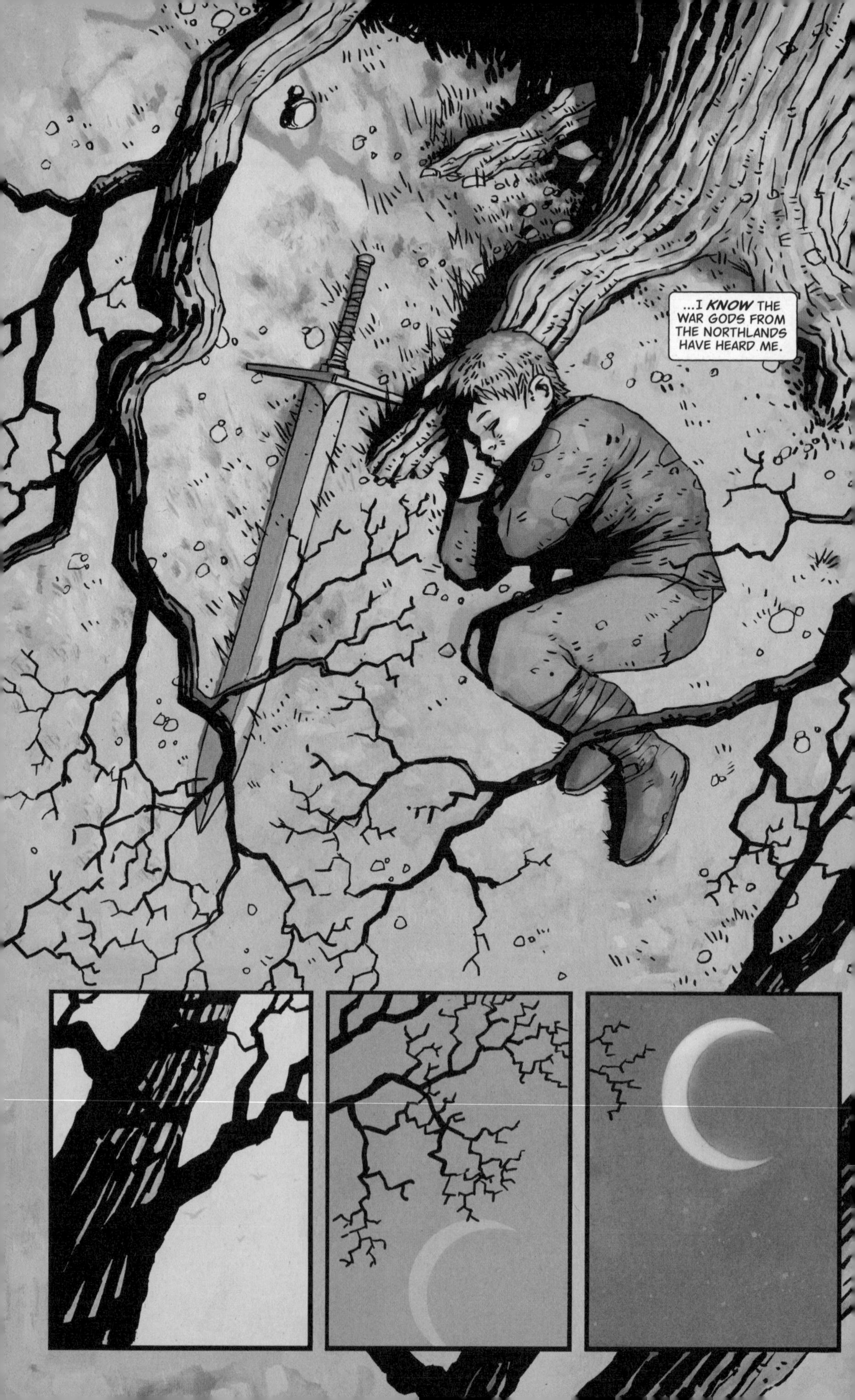
...I KNOW THE WAR GODS FROM THE NORTHLANDS HAVE HEARD ME.

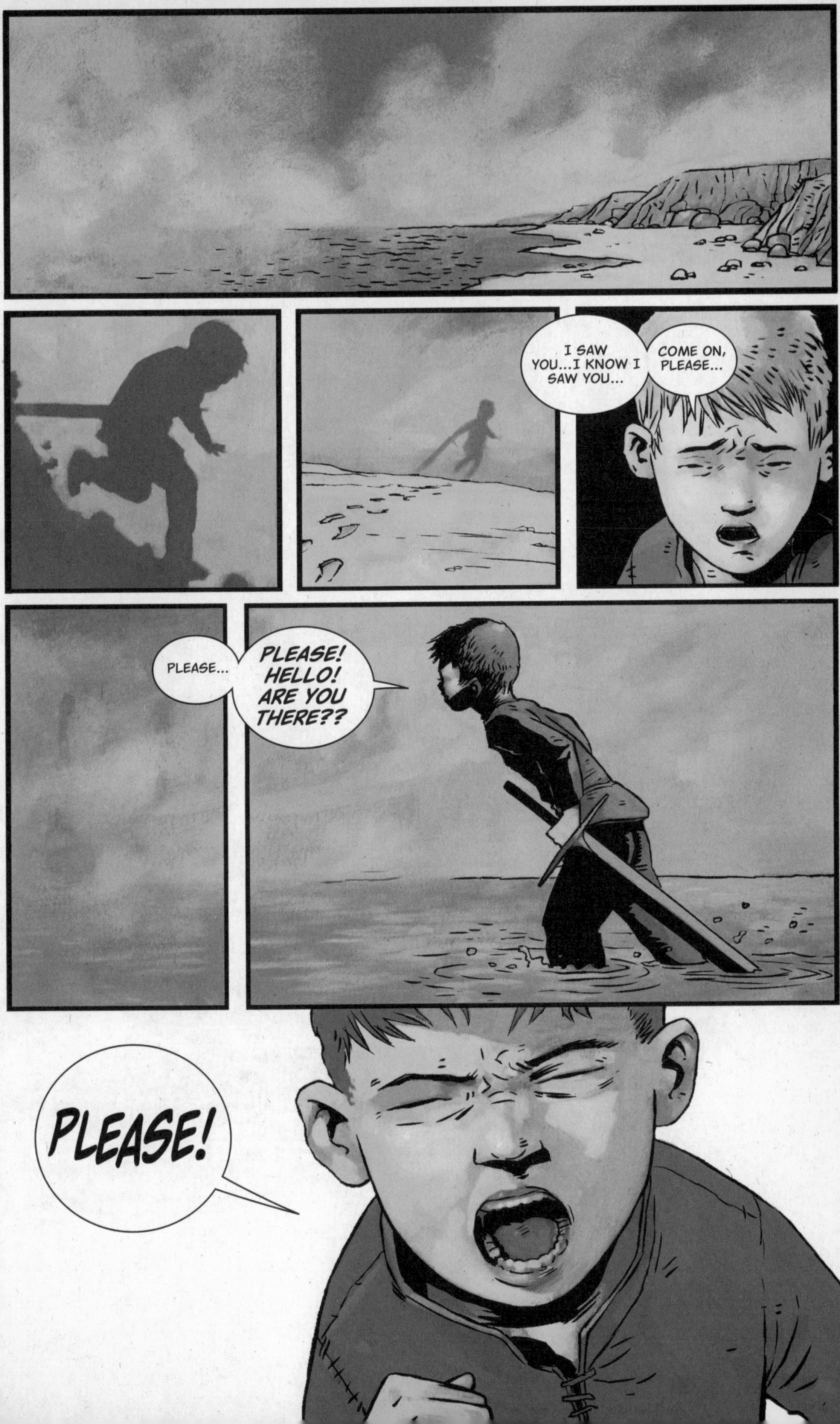
I SAW YOU...I KNOW I SAW YOU...
COME ON, PLEASE...
PLEASE...
PLEASE! HELLO! ARE YOU THERE??
PLEASE!

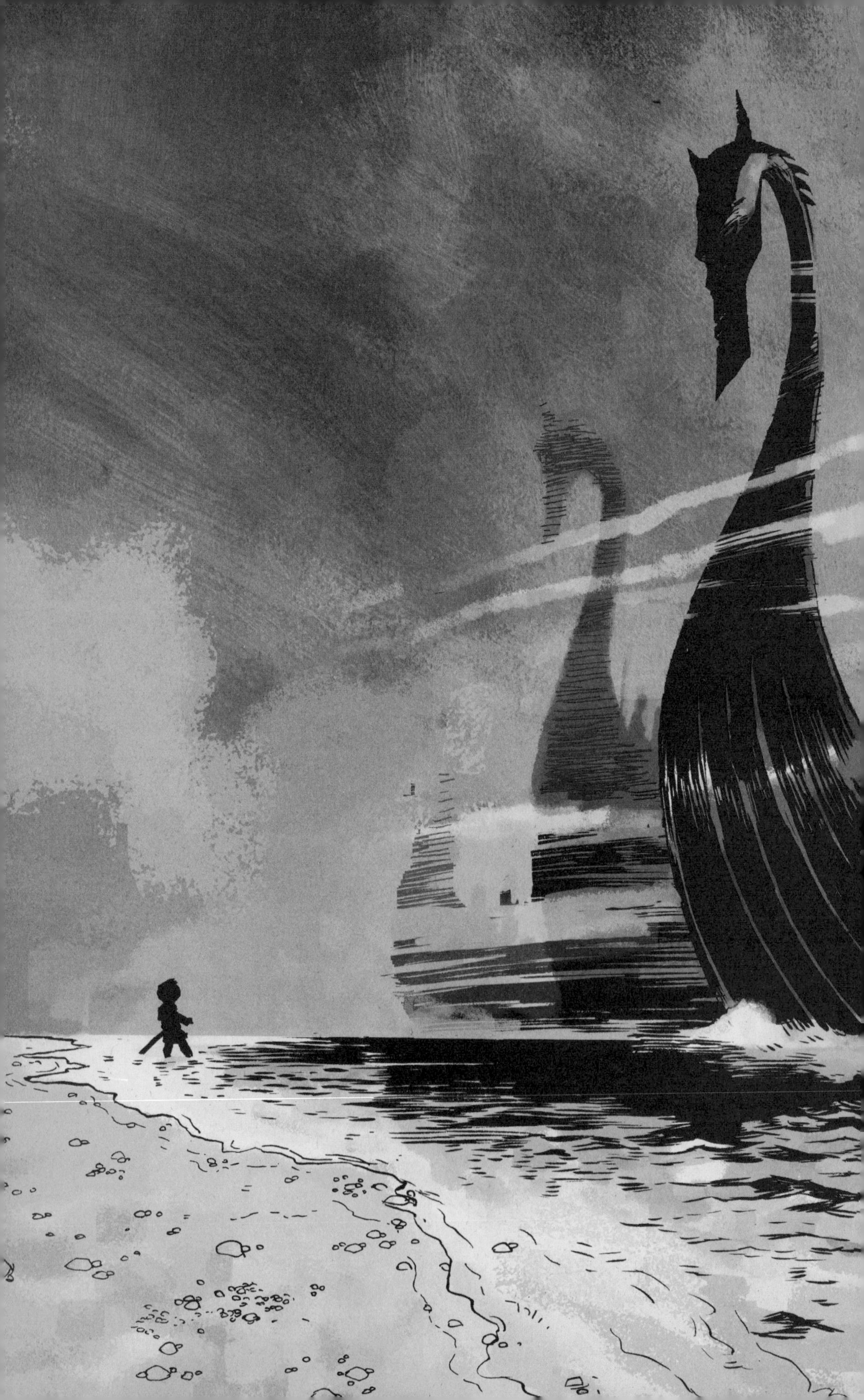

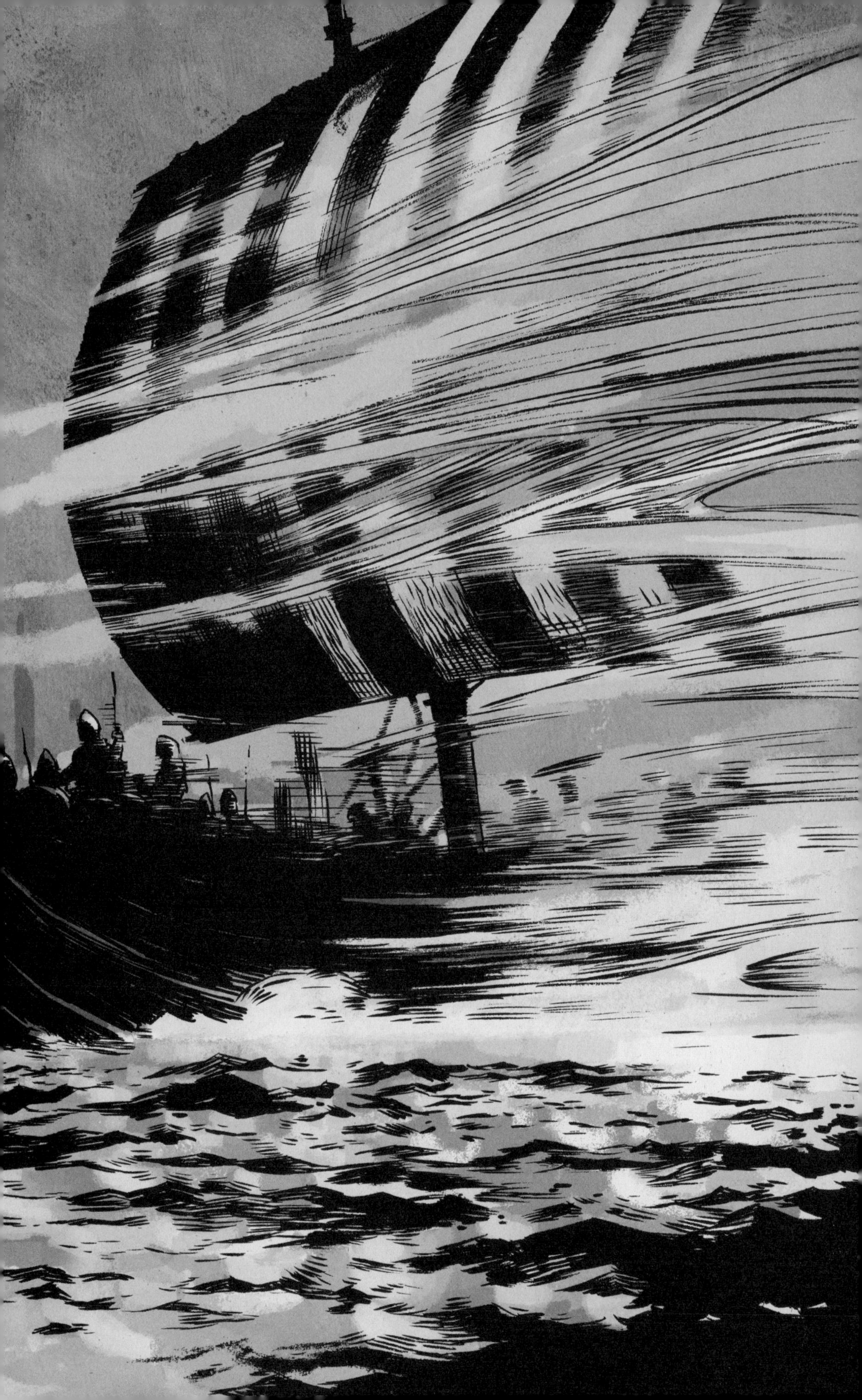

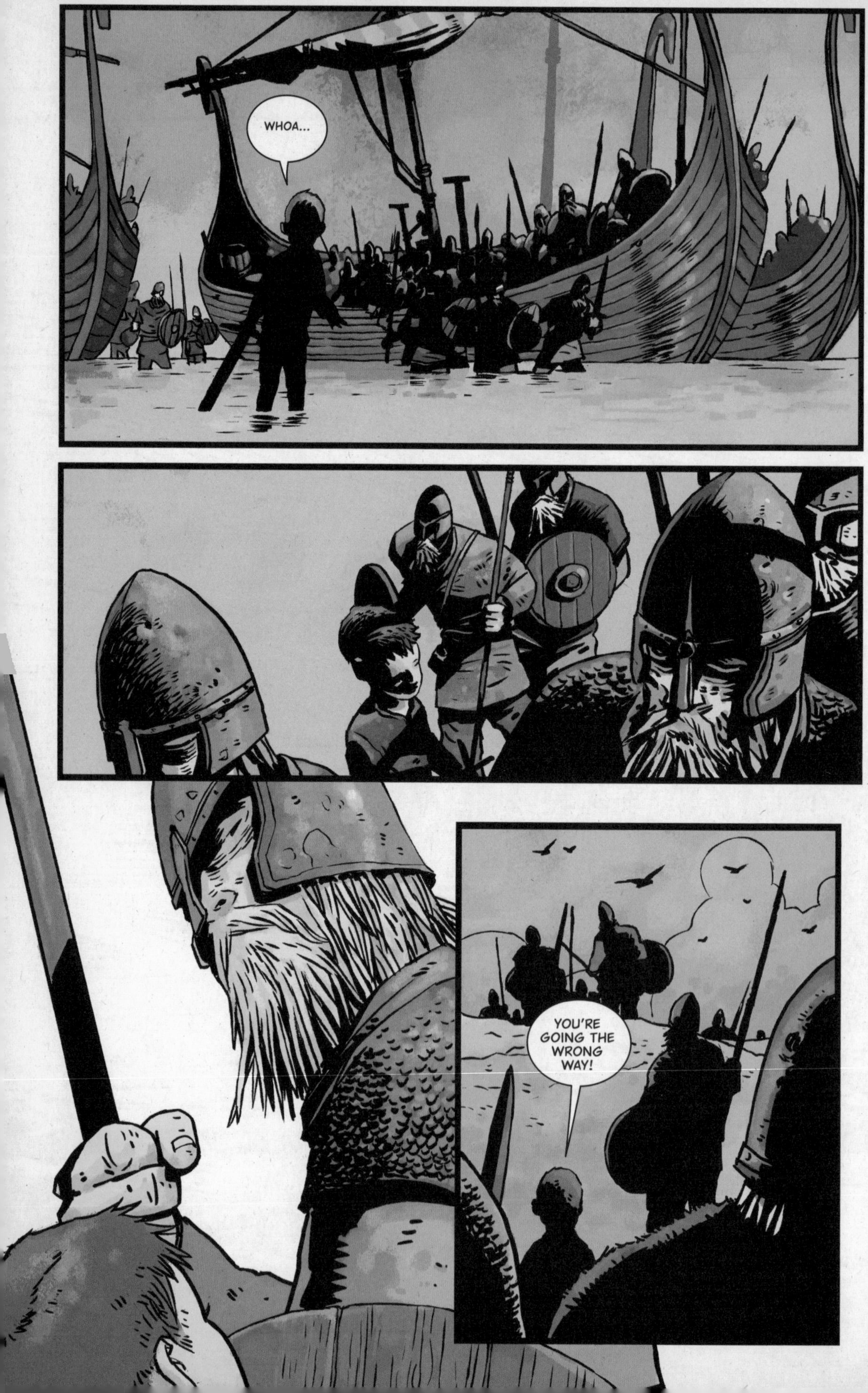
WHOA...
YOU'RE GOING THE WRONG WAY!

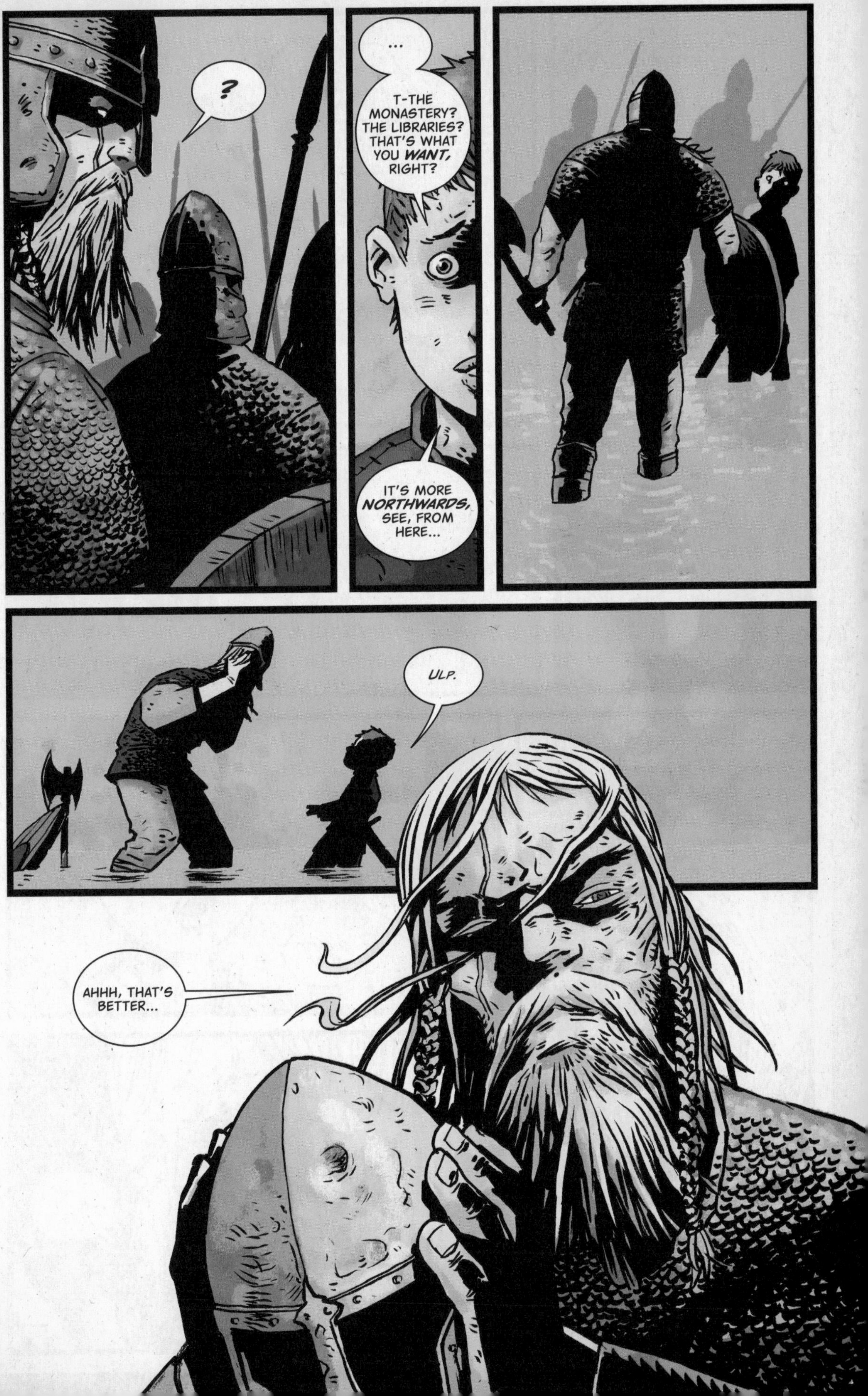
?
...
T-THE MONASTERY? THE LIBRARIES? THAT'S WHAT YOU WANT, RIGHT?
IT'S MORE NORTHWARDS, SEE, FROM HERE...
ULP.
AHHH, THAT'S BETTER...

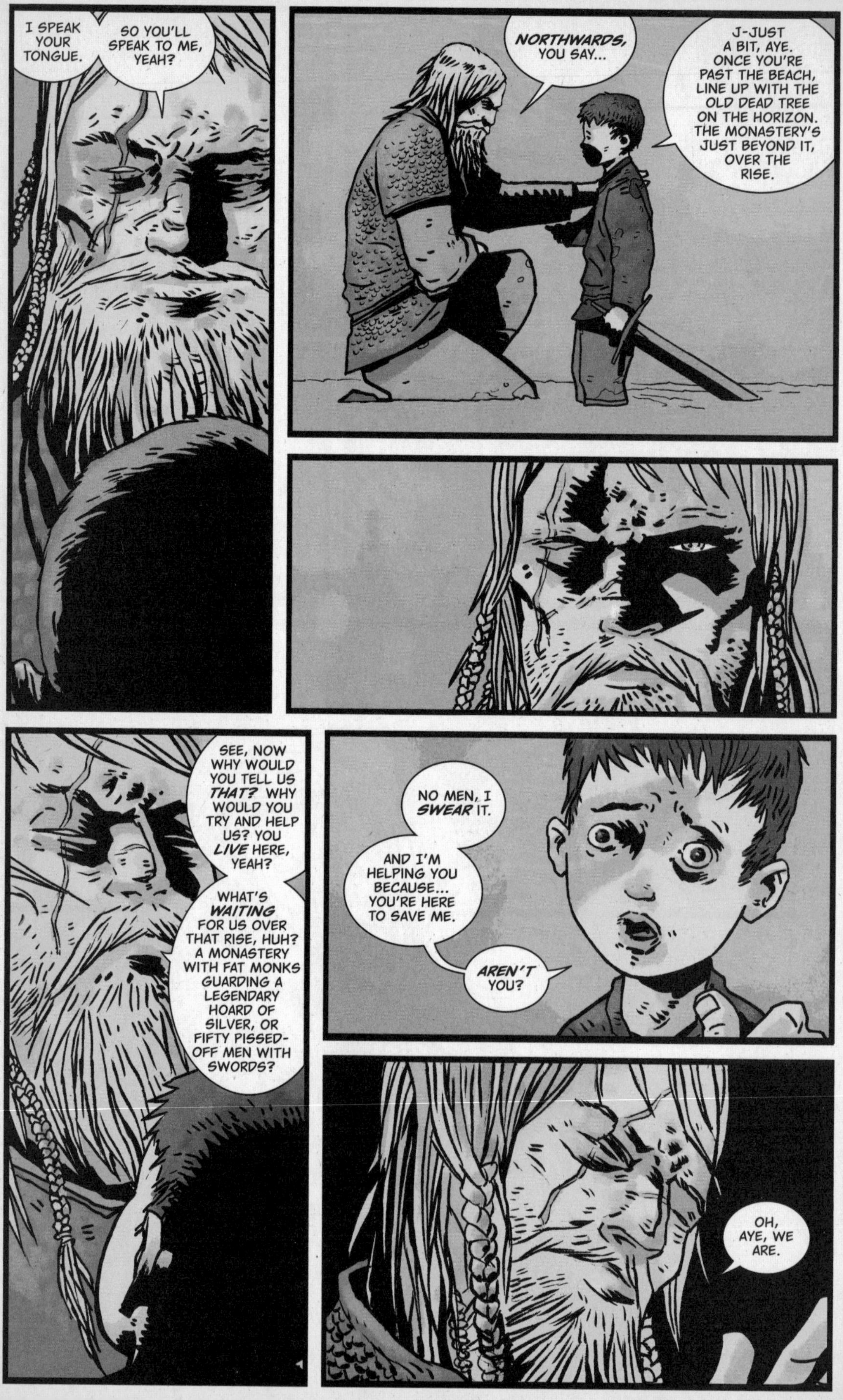
I SPEAK YOUR TONGUE.
SO YOU'LL SPEAK TO ME, YEAH?
NORTHWARDS, YOU SAY...
J-JUST A BIT, AYE. ONCE YOU'RE PAST THE BEACH, LINE UP WITH THE OLD DEAD TREE ON THE HORIZON. THE MONASTERY'S JUST BEYOND IT, OVER THE RISE.
SEE, NOW WHY WOULD YOU TELL US THAT? WHY WOULD YOU TRY AND HELP US? YOU LIVE HERE, YEAH?
WHAT'S WAITING FOR US OVER THAT RISE, HUH? A MONASTERY WITH FAT MONKS GUARDING A LEGENDARY HOARD OF SILVER, OR FIFTY PISSED-OFF MEN WITH SWORDS?
NO MEN, I SWEAR IT.
AND I'M HELPING YOU BECAUSE... YOU'RE HERE TO SAVE ME.
AREN'T YOU?
OH, AYE, WE ARE.

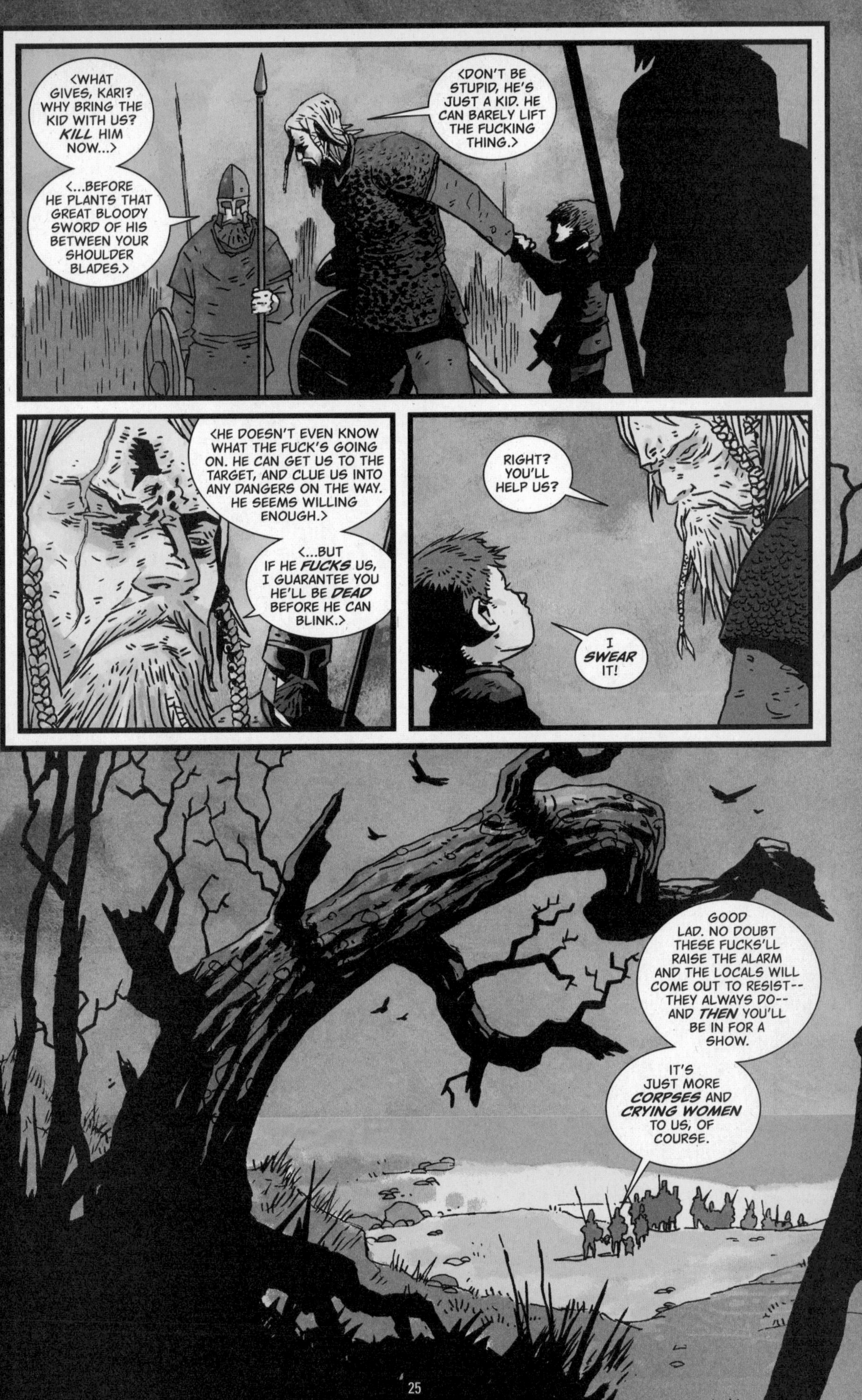
<WHAT GIVES, KARI? WHY BRING THE KID WITH US? *KILL* HIM NOW...>
<...BEFORE HE PLANTS THAT GREAT BLOODY SWORD OF HIS BETWEEN YOUR SHOULDER BLADES.>
<DON'T BE STUPID, HE'S JUST A KID. HE CAN BARELY LIFT THE FUCKING THING.>
<HE DOESN'T EVEN KNOW WHAT THE FUCK'S GOING ON. HE CAN GET US TO THE TARGET, AND CLUE US INTO ANY DANGERS ON THE WAY. HE SEEMS WILLING ENOUGH.>
<...BUT IF HE *FUCKS* US, I GUARANTEE YOU HE'LL BE *DEAD* BEFORE HE CAN BLINK.>
RIGHT? YOU'LL HELP US?
I *SWEAR* IT!
GOOD LAD. NO DOUBT THESE FUCKS'LL RAISE THE ALARM AND THE LOCALS WILL COME OUT TO RESIST-- THEY ALWAYS DO-- AND *THEN* YOU'LL BE IN FOR A SHOW.
IT'S JUST MORE *CORPSES* AND *CRYING WOMEN* TO US, OF COURSE.

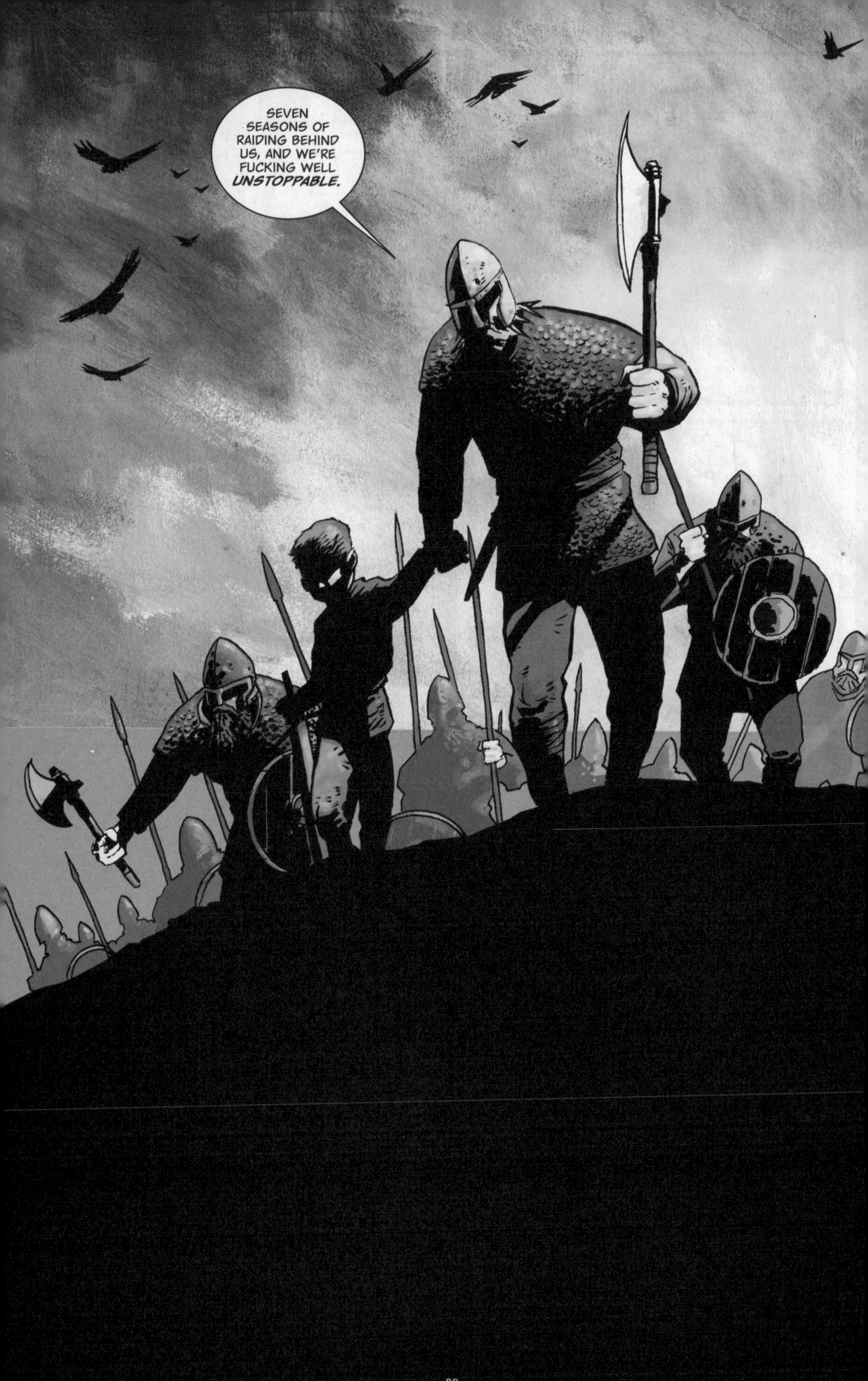
SEVEN SEASONS OF RAIDING BEHIND US, AND WE'RE FUCKING WELL *UNSTOPPABLE.*

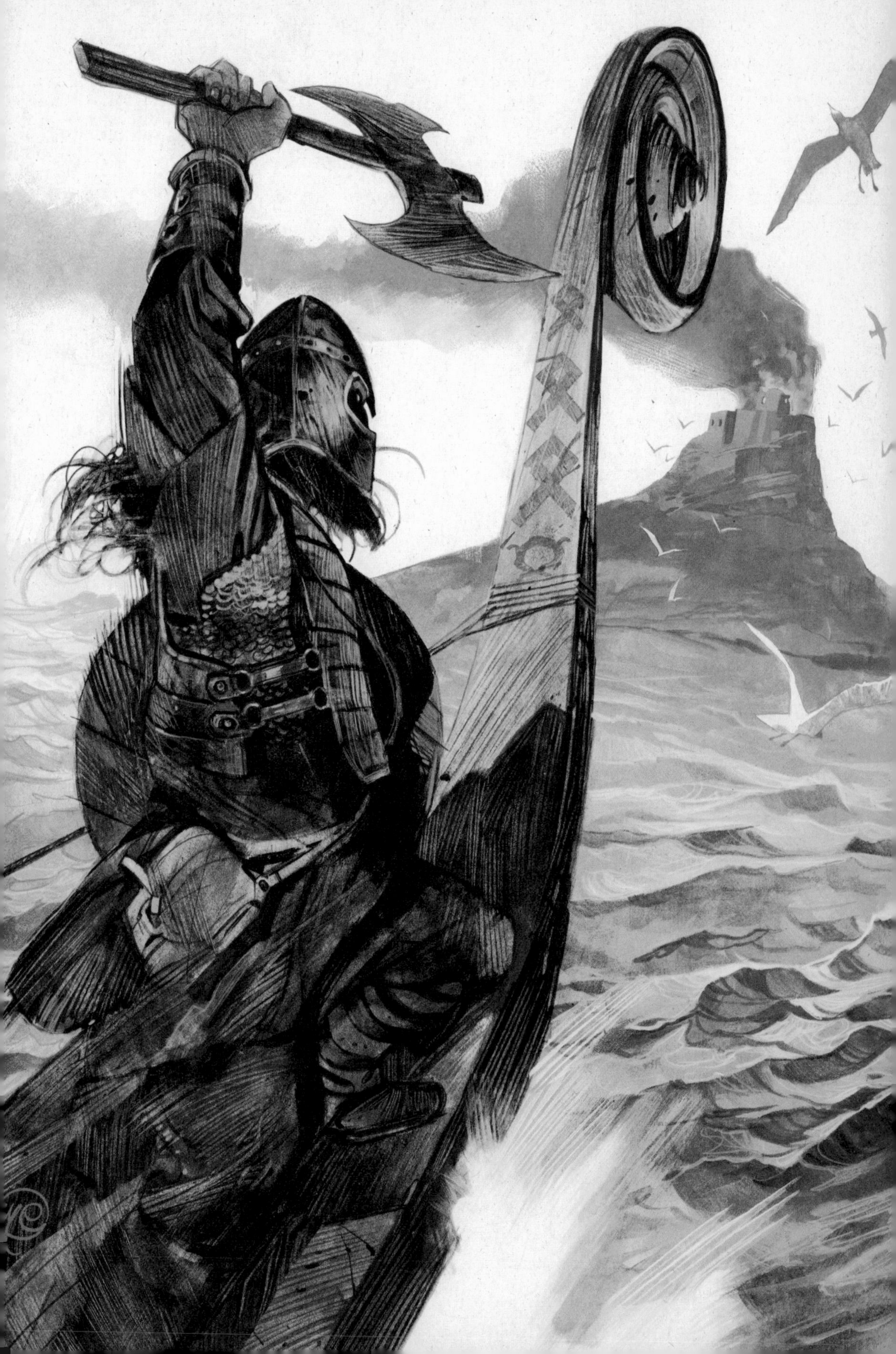

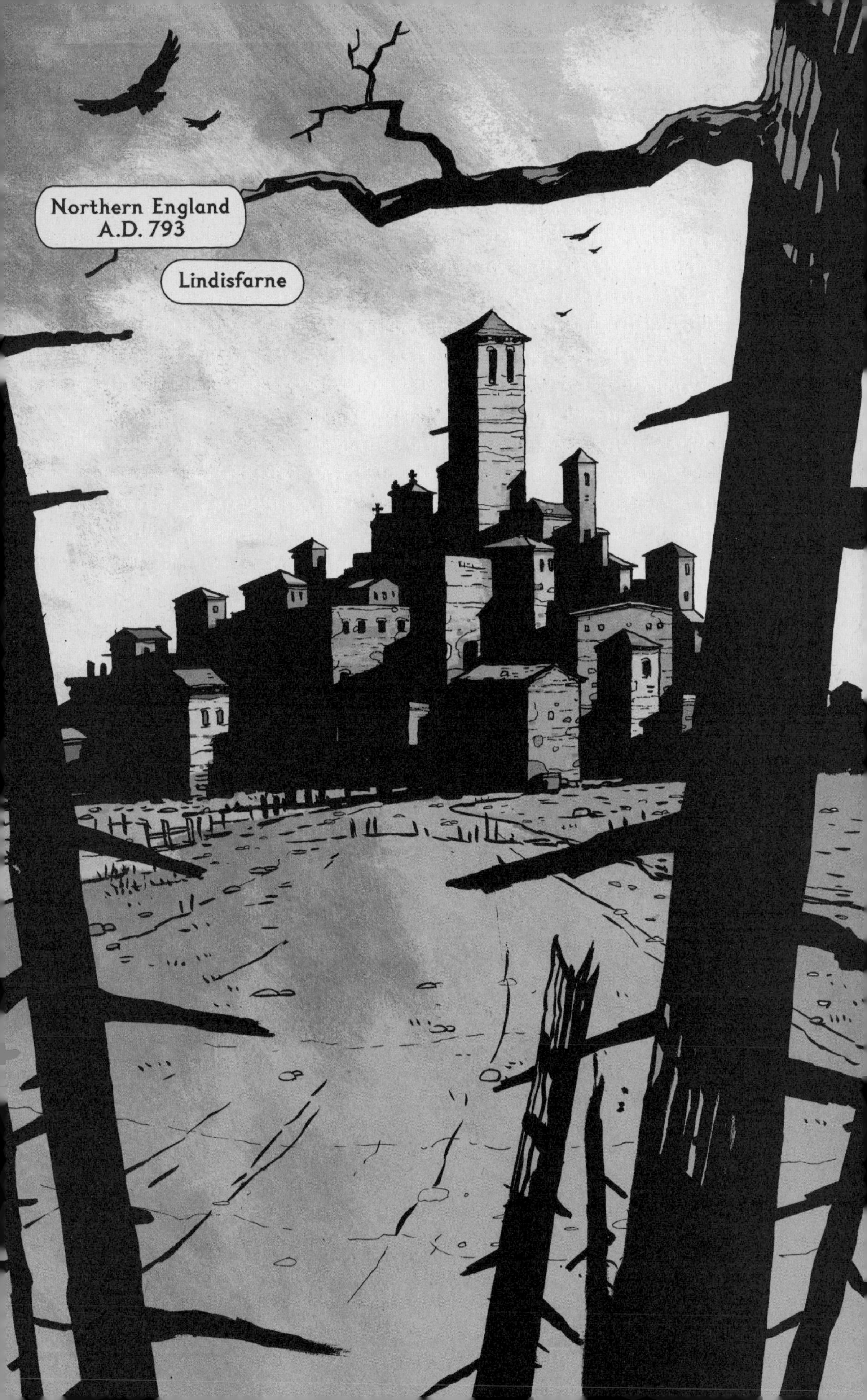
Northern England A.D. 793
Lindisfarne

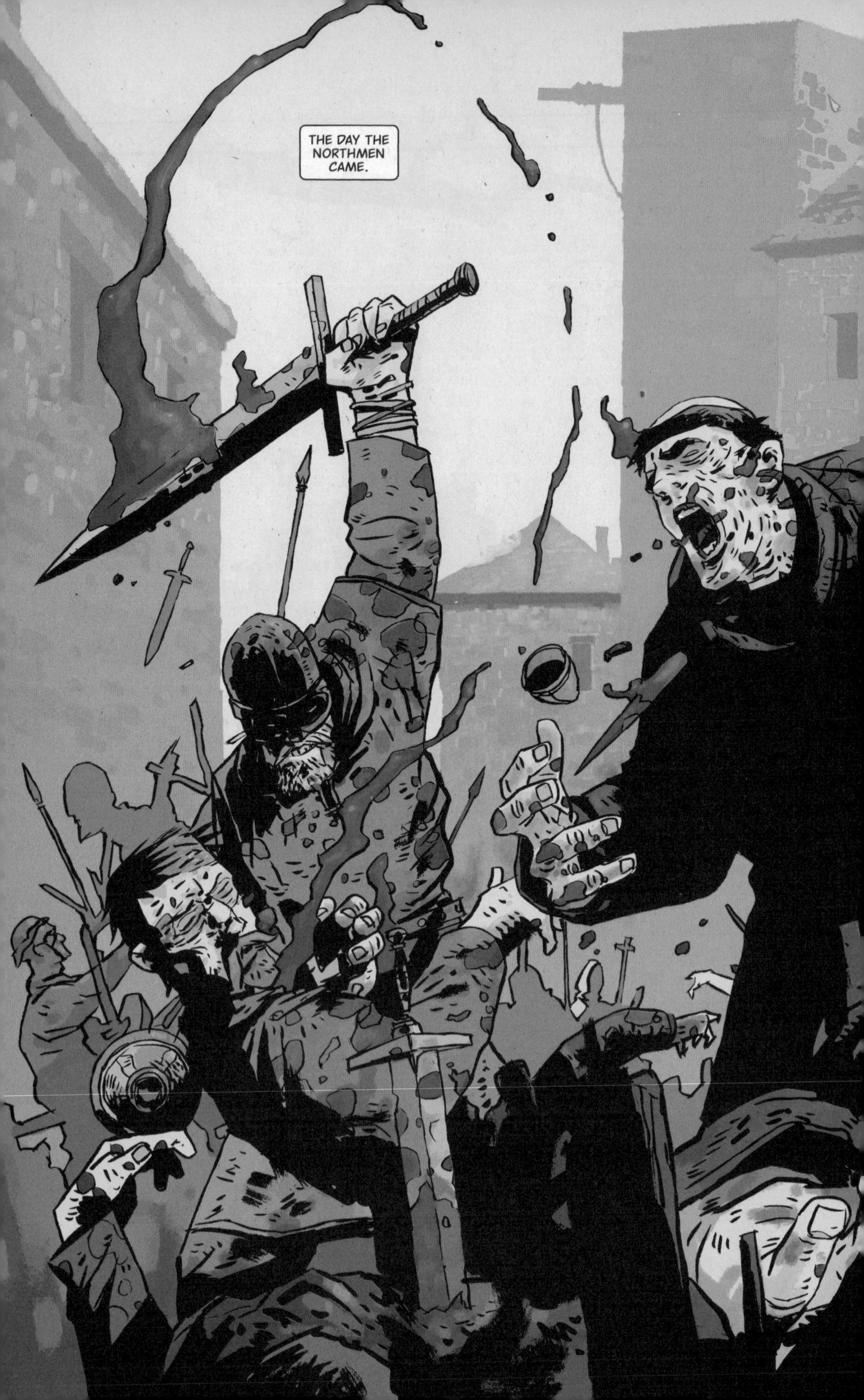
THE DAY THE NORTHMEN CAME.

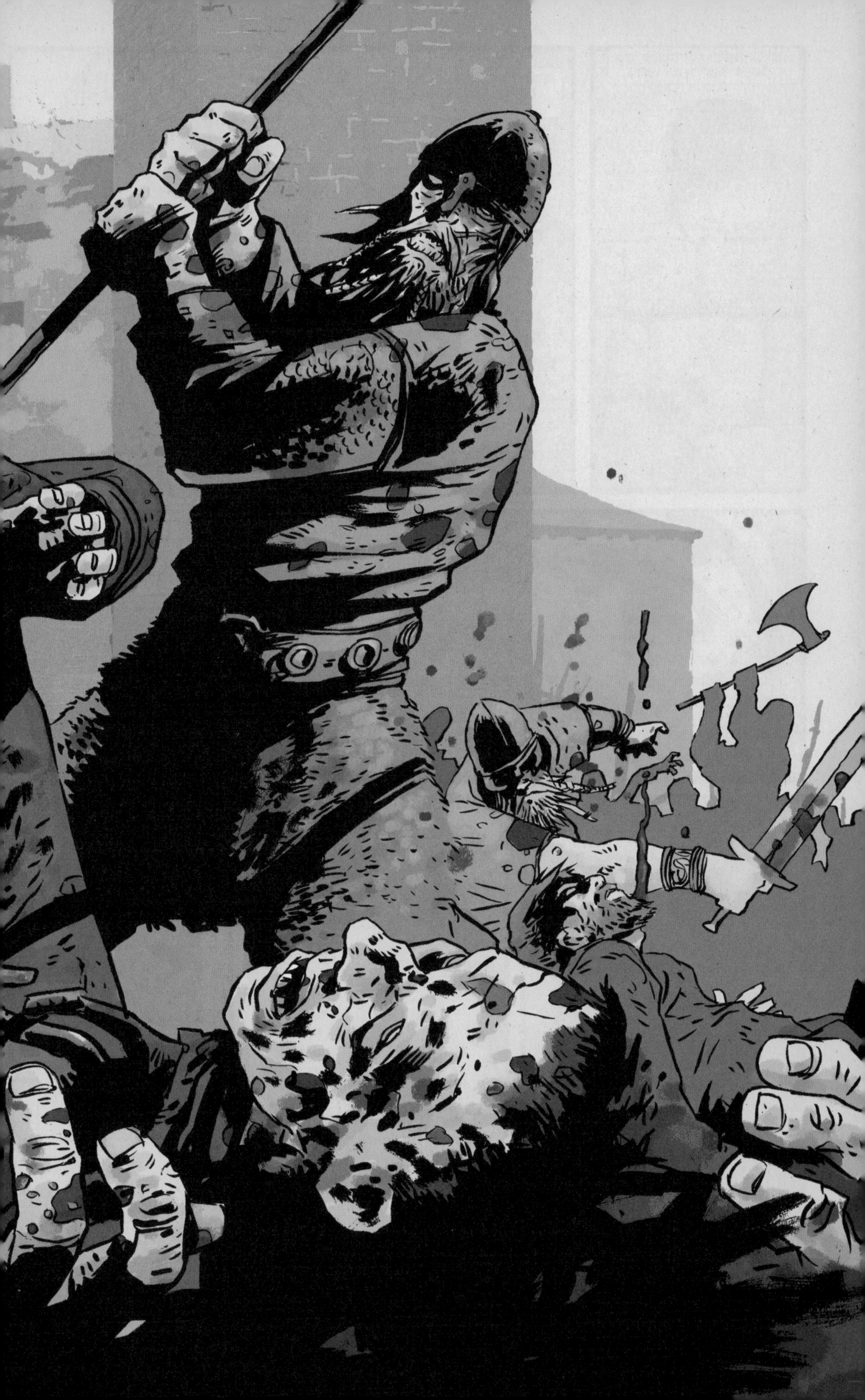

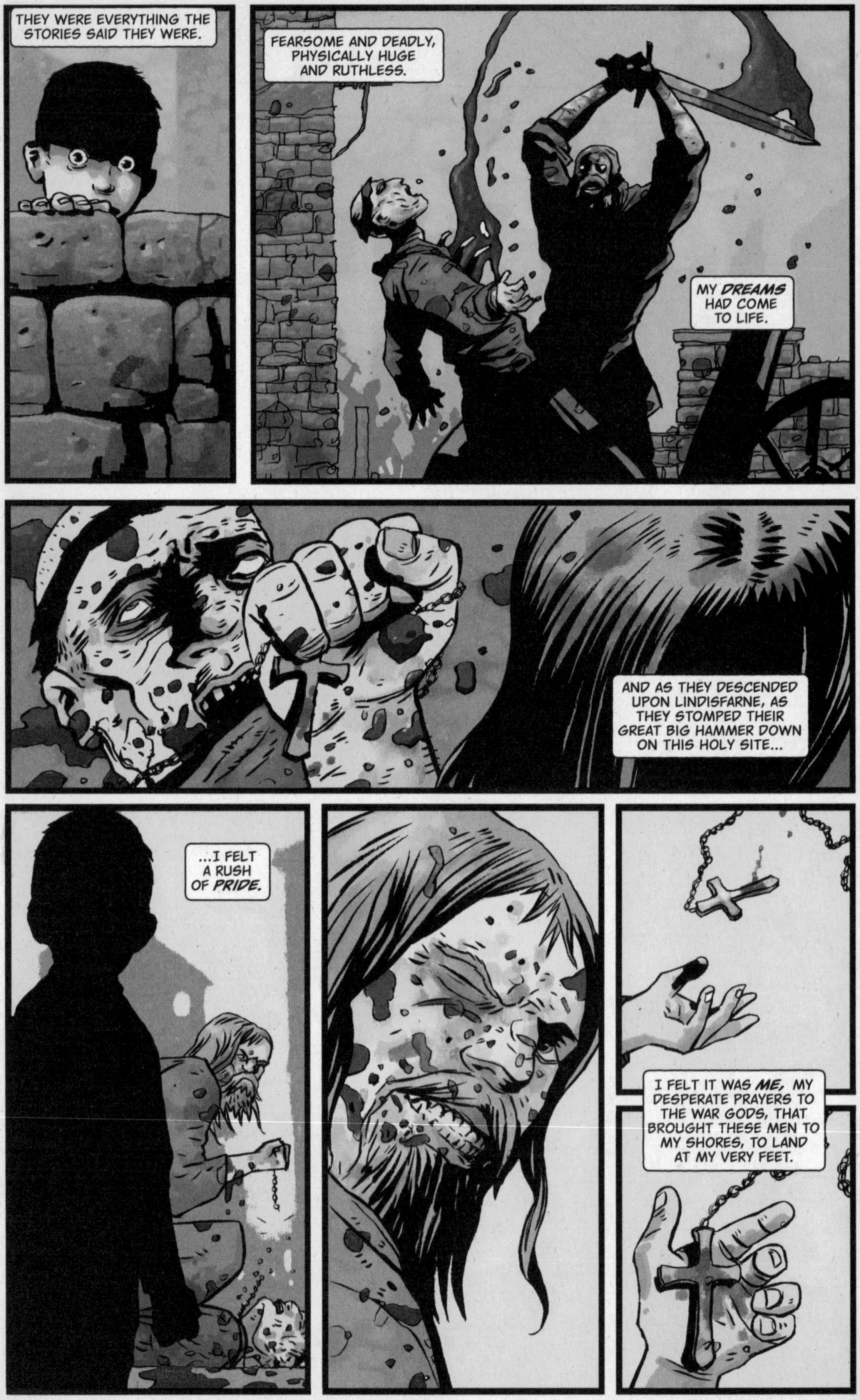
THEY WERE EVERYTHING THE STORIES SAID THEY WERE.
FEARSOME AND DEADLY, PHYSICALLY HUGE AND RUTHLESS.
MY DREAMS HAD COME TO LIFE.
AND AS THEY DESCENDED UPON LINDISFARNE, AS THEY STOMPED THEIR GREAT BIG HAMMER DOWN ON THIS HOLY SITE...
...I FELT A RUSH OF PRIDE.
I FELT IT WAS ME, MY DESPERATE PRAYERS TO THE WAR GODS, THAT BROUGHT THESE MEN TO MY SHORES, TO LAND AT MY VERY FEET.

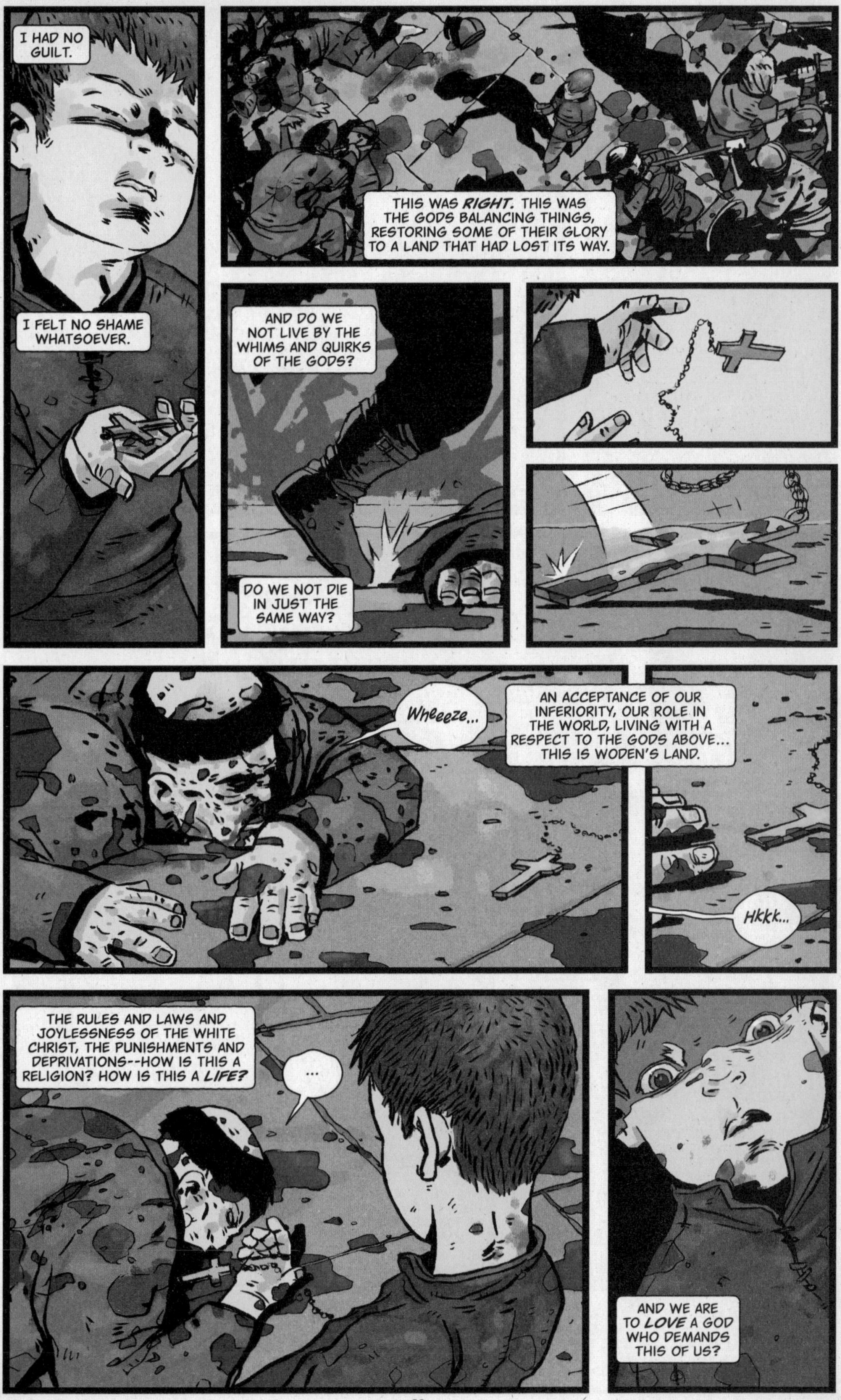
I HAD NO GUILT.
I FELT NO SHAME WHATSOEVER.
THIS WAS *RIGHT.* THIS WAS THE GODS BALANCING THINGS, RESTORING SOME OF THEIR GLORY TO A LAND THAT HAD LOST ITS WAY.
AND DO WE NOT LIVE BY THE WHIMS AND QUIRKS OF THE GODS?
DO WE NOT DIE IN JUST THE SAME WAY?
Wheeeze...
AN ACCEPTANCE OF OUR INFERIORITY, OUR ROLE IN THE WORLD, LIVING WITH A RESPECT TO THE GODS ABOVE... THIS IS WODEN'S LAND.
Hkkk...
THE RULES AND LAWS AND JOYLESSNESS OF THE WHITE CHRIST, THE PUNISHMENTS AND DEPRIVATIONS--HOW IS THIS A RELIGION? HOW IS THIS A *LIFE?*
...
AND WE ARE TO *LOVE* A GOD WHO DEMANDS THIS OF US?

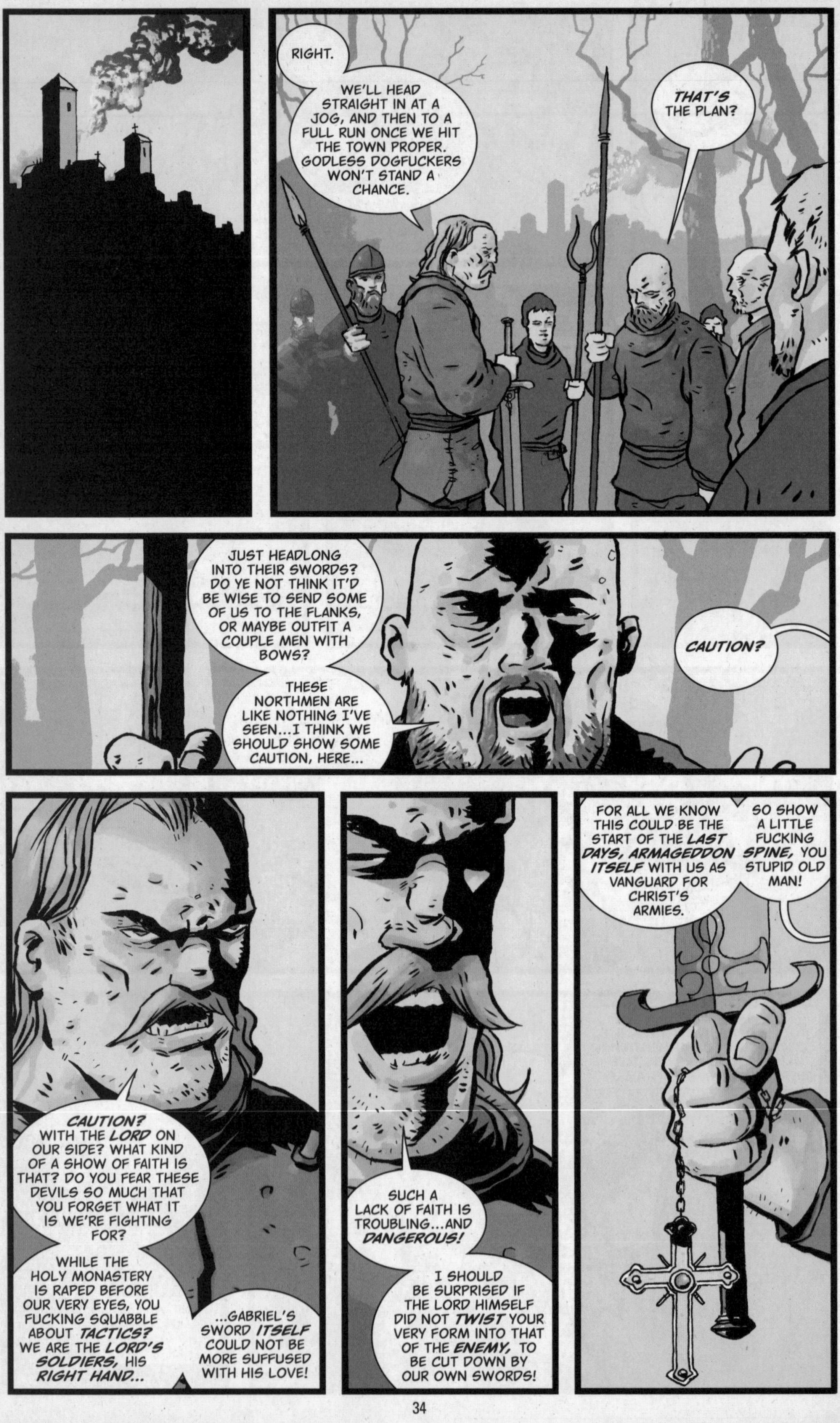
RIGHT.
WE'LL HEAD STRAIGHT IN AT A JOG, AND THEN TO A FULL RUN ONCE WE HIT THE TOWN PROPER. GODLESS DOGFUCKERS WON'T STAND A CHANCE.
THAT'S THE PLAN?
JUST HEADLONG INTO THEIR SWORDS? DO YE NOT THINK IT'D BE WISE TO SEND SOME OF US TO THE FLANKS, OR MAYBE OUTFIT A COUPLE MEN WITH BOWS?
THESE NORTHMEN ARE LIKE NOTHING I'VE SEEN...I THINK WE SHOULD SHOW SOME CAUTION, HERE...
CAUTION?
CAUTION? WITH THE LORD ON OUR SIDE? WHAT KIND OF A SHOW OF FAITH IS THAT? DO YOU FEAR THESE DEVILS SO MUCH THAT YOU FORGET WHAT IT IS WE'RE FIGHTING FOR?
WHILE THE HOLY MONASTERY IS RAPED BEFORE OUR VERY EYES, YOU FUCKING SQUABBLE ABOUT TACTICS? WE ARE THE LORD'S SOLDIERS, HIS RIGHT HAND...
...GABRIEL'S SWORD ITSELF COULD NOT BE MORE SUFFUSED WITH HIS LOVE!
SUCH A LACK OF FAITH IS TROUBLING...AND DANGEROUS!
I SHOULD BE SURPRISED IF THE LORD HIMSELF DID NOT TWIST YOUR VERY FORM INTO THAT OF THE ENEMY, TO BE CUT DOWN BY OUR OWN SWORDS!
FOR ALL WE KNOW THIS COULD BE THE START OF THE LAST DAYS, ARMAGEDDON ITSELF WITH US AS VANGUARD FOR CHRIST'S ARMIES.
SO SHOW A LITTLE FUCKING SPINE, YOU STUPID OLD MAN!

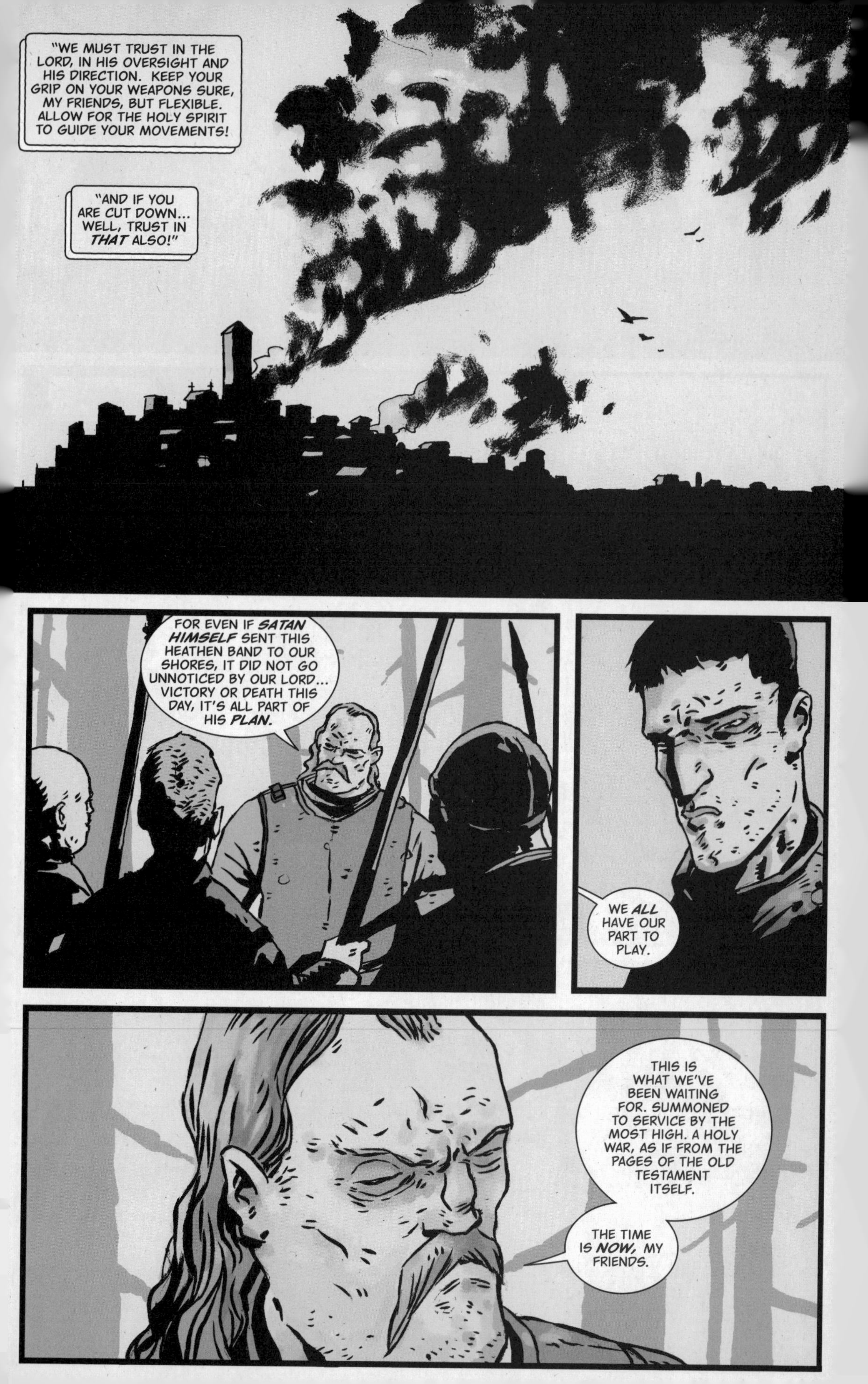
"WE MUST TRUST IN THE LORD, IN HIS OVERSIGHT AND HIS DIRECTION. KEEP YOUR GRIP ON YOUR WEAPONS SURE, MY FRIENDS, BUT FLEXIBLE. ALLOW FOR THE HOLY SPIRIT TO GUIDE YOUR MOVEMENTS!
"AND IF YOU ARE CUT DOWN... WELL, TRUST IN *THAT* ALSO!"
FOR EVEN IF *SATAN HIMSELF* SENT THIS HEATHEN BAND TO OUR SHORES, IT DID NOT GO UNNOTICED BY OUR LORD... VICTORY OR DEATH THIS DAY, IT'S ALL PART OF HIS *PLAN.*
WE *ALL* HAVE OUR PART TO PLAY.
THIS IS WHAT WE'VE BEEN WAITING FOR. SUMMONED TO SERVICE BY THE MOST HIGH. A HOLY WAR, AS IF FROM THE PAGES OF THE OLD TESTAMENT ITSELF.
THE TIME IS *NOW,* MY FRIENDS.

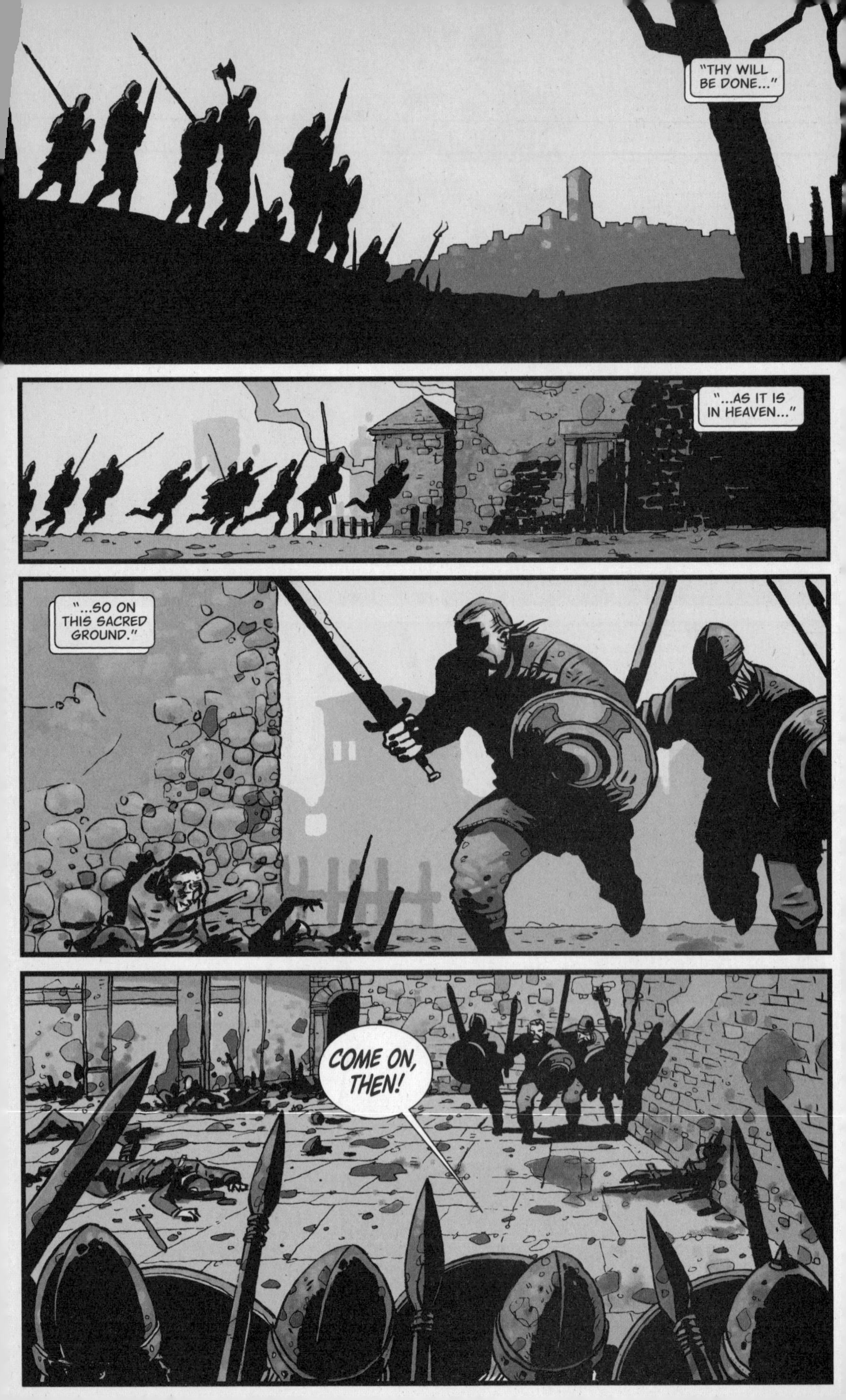
"THY WILL BE DONE..."
"...AS IT IS IN HEAVEN..."
"...SO ON THIS SACRED GROUND."
COME ON, THEN!

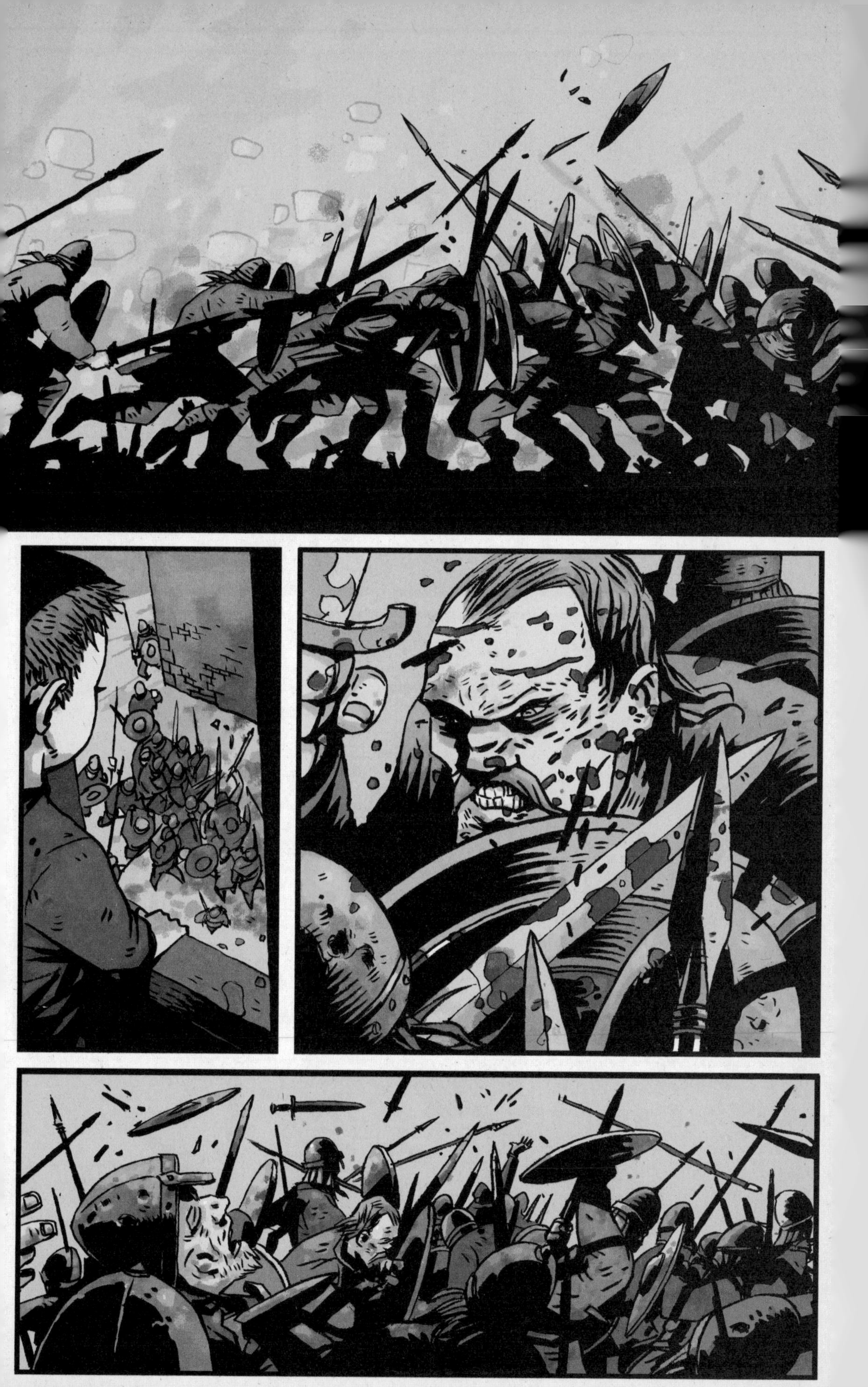

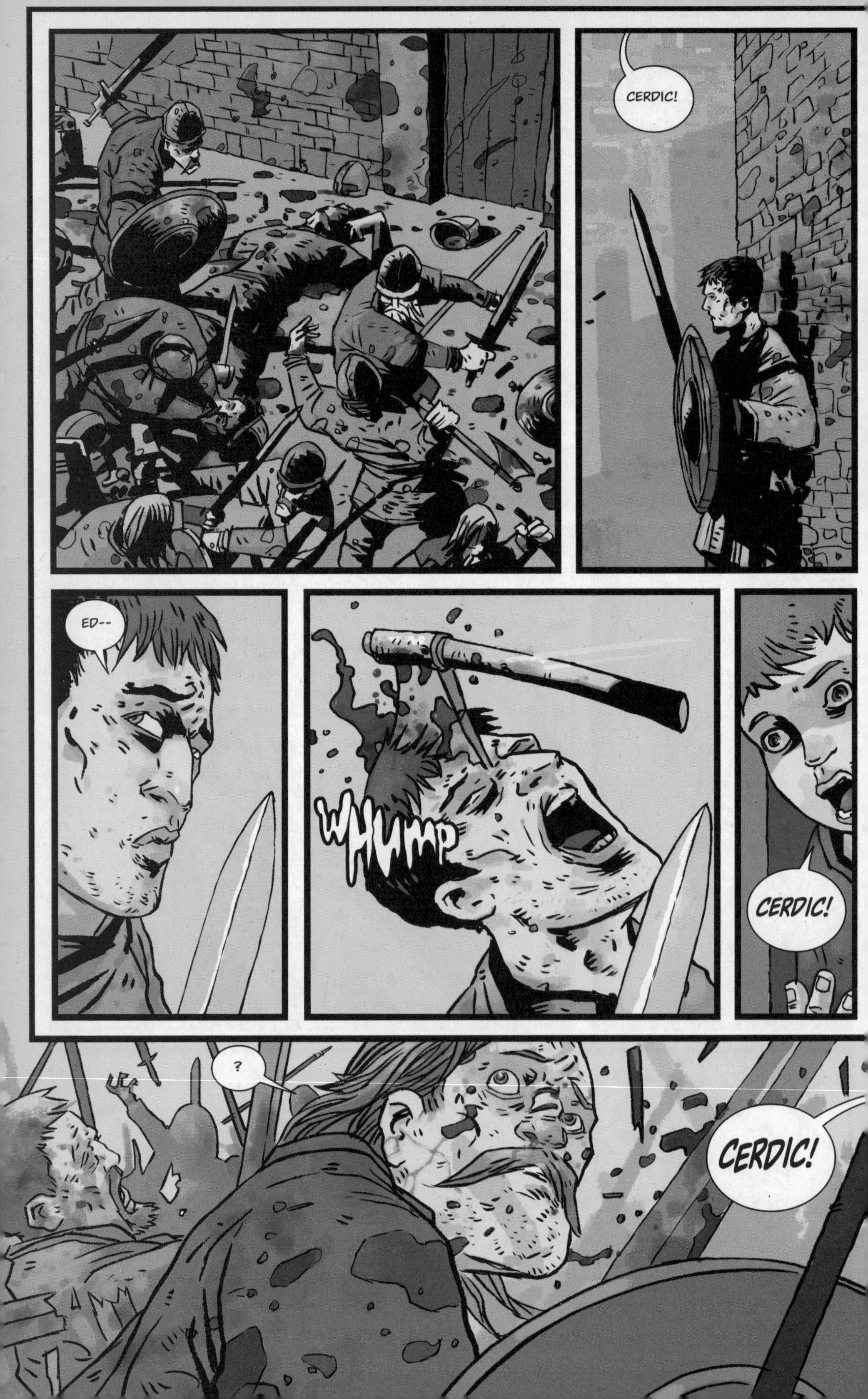
CERDIC!
ED--
WHUMP
CERDIC!
?
CERDIC!

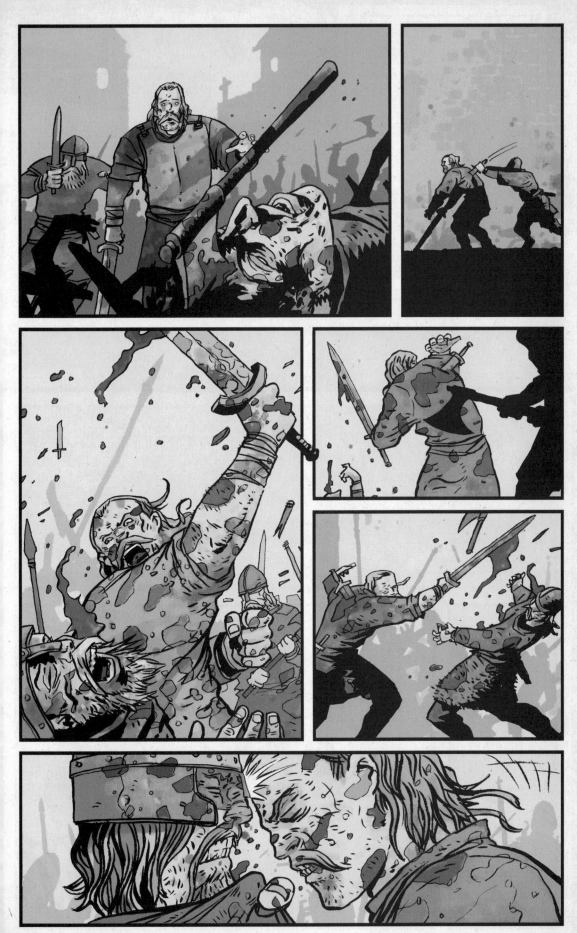

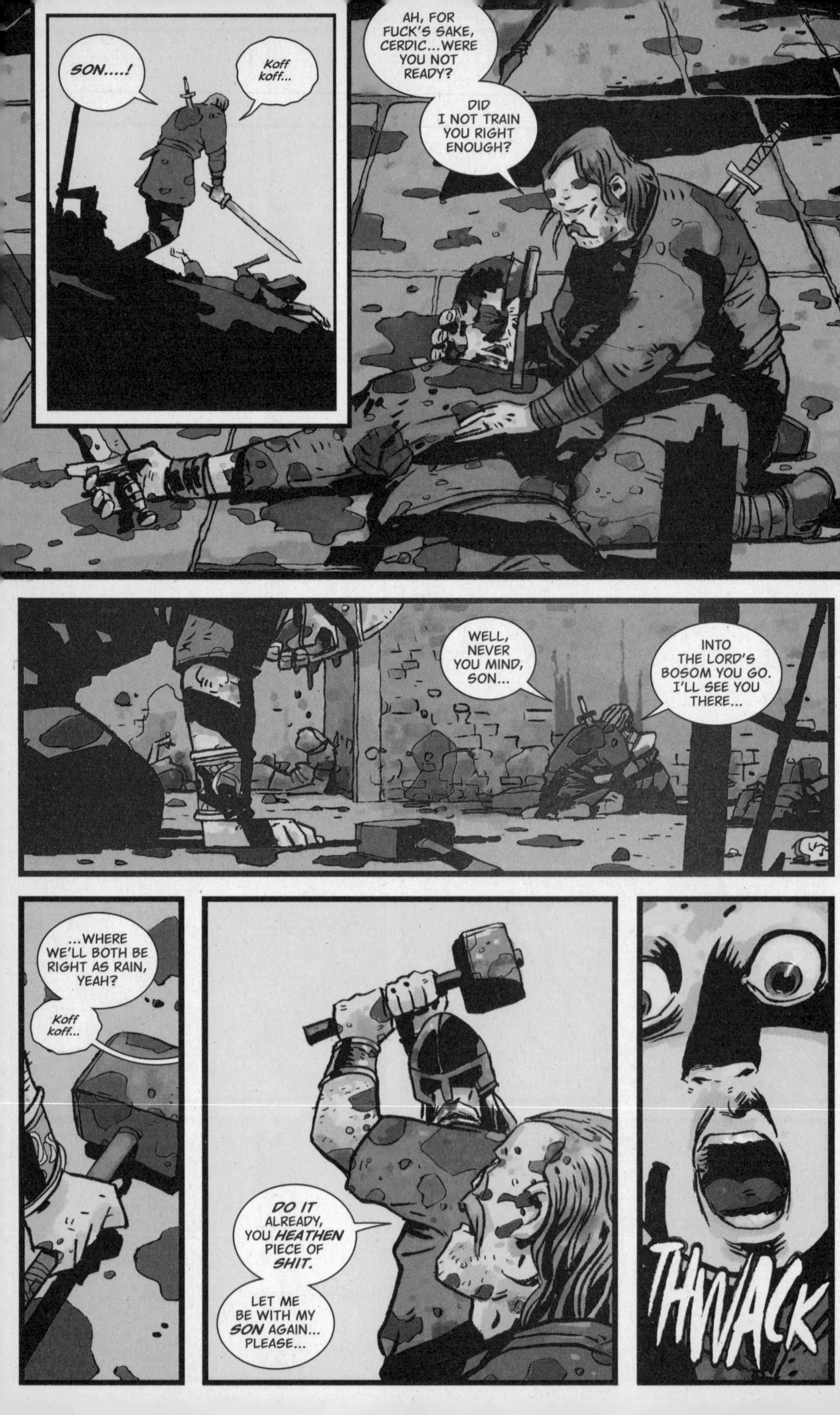
SON....!
Koff koff...
AH, FOR FUCK'S SAKE, CERDIC...WERE YOU NOT READY?
DID I NOT TRAIN YOU RIGHT ENOUGH?
WELL, NEVER YOU MIND, SON...
INTO THE LORD'S BOSOM YOU GO. I'LL SEE YOU THERE...
...WHERE WE'LL BOTH BE RIGHT AS RAIN, YEAH?
Koff koff...
DO IT ALREADY, YOU HEATHEN PIECE OF SHIT.
LET ME BE WITH MY SON AGAIN... PLEASE...
THWACK

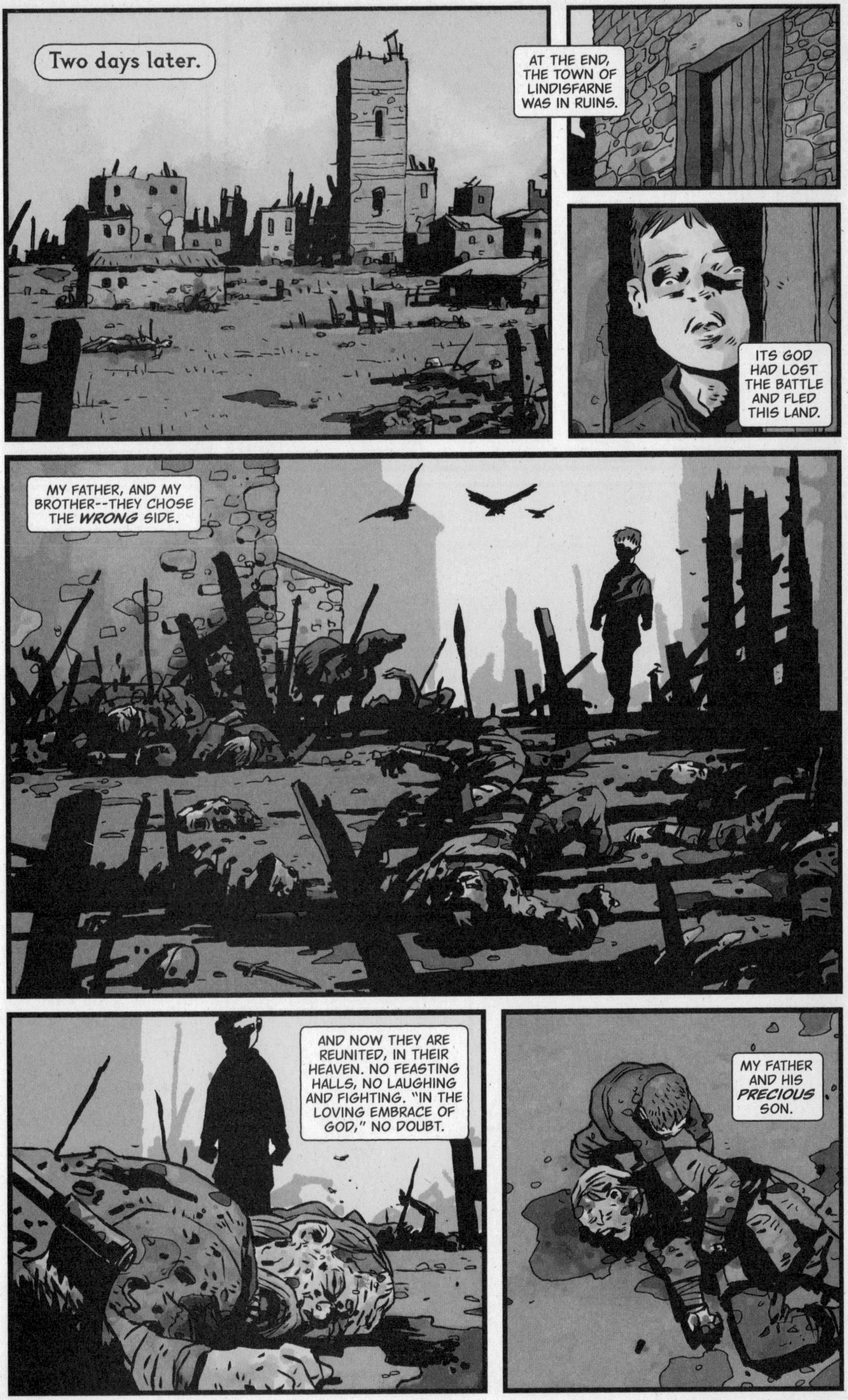

Two days later.
AT THE END, THE TOWN OF LINDISFARNE WAS IN RUINS.
ITS GOD HAD LOST THE BATTLE AND FLED THIS LAND.
MY FATHER, AND MY BROTHER--THEY CHOSE THE WRONG SIDE.
AND NOW THEY ARE REUNITED, IN THEIR HEAVEN. NO FEASTING HALLS, NO LAUGHING AND FIGHTING. "IN THE LOVING EMBRACE OF GOD," NO DOUBT.
MY FATHER AND HIS PRECIOUS SON.

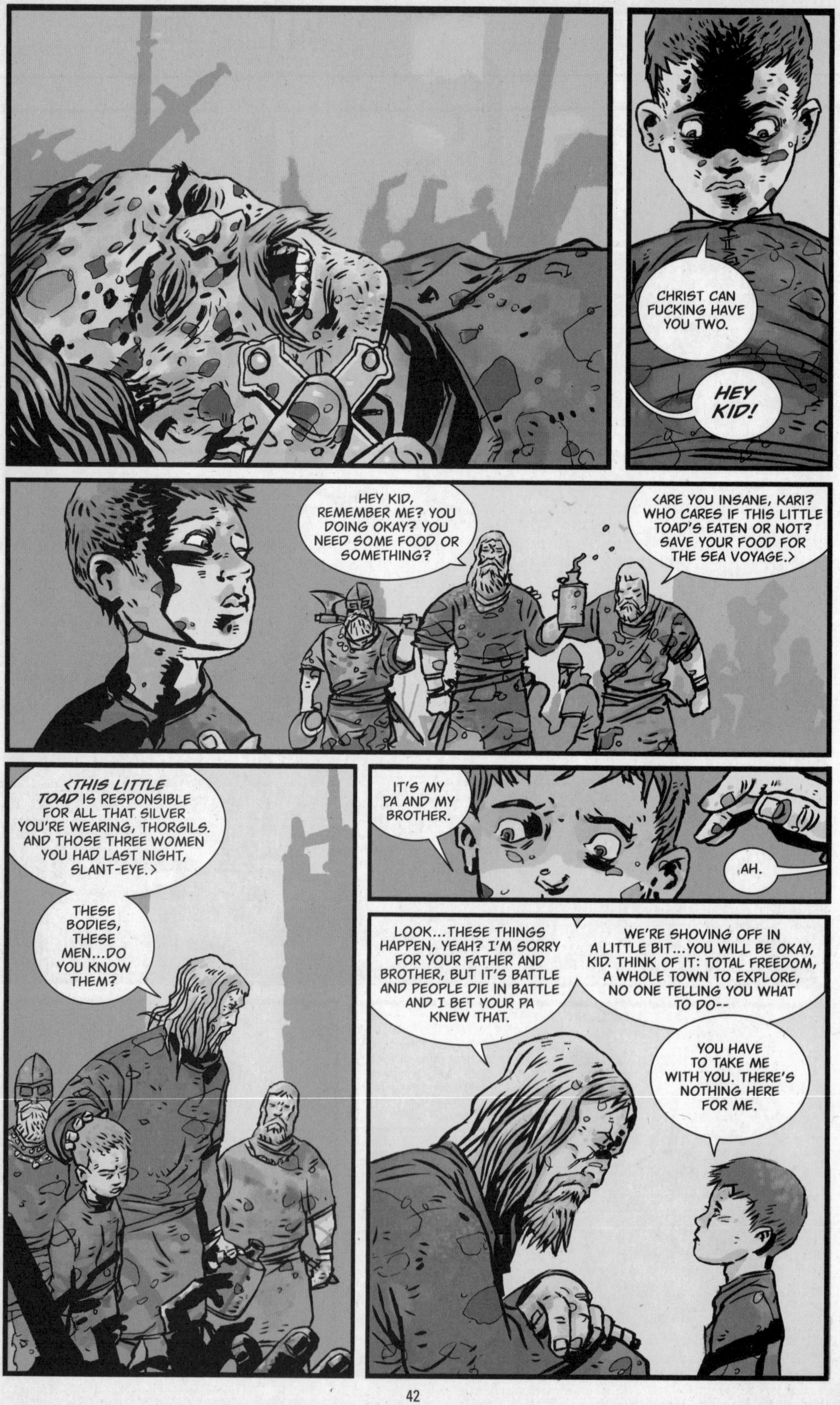
CHRIST CAN FUCKING HAVE YOU TWO.
HEY KID!
HEY KID, REMEMBER ME? YOU DOING OKAY? YOU NEED SOME FOOD OR SOMETHING?
<ARE YOU INSANE, KARI? WHO CARES IF THIS LITTLE TOAD'S EATEN OR NOT? SAVE YOUR FOOD FOR THE SEA VOYAGE.>
<THIS LITTLE TOAD IS RESPONSIBLE FOR ALL THAT SILVER YOU'RE WEARING, THORGILS. AND THOSE THREE WOMEN YOU HAD LAST NIGHT, SLANT-EYE.>
THESE BODIES, THESE MEN...DO YOU KNOW THEM?
IT'S MY PA AND MY BROTHER.
AH.
LOOK...THESE THINGS HAPPEN, YEAH? I'M SORRY FOR YOUR FATHER AND BROTHER, BUT IT'S BATTLE AND PEOPLE DIE IN BATTLE AND I BET YOUR PA KNEW THAT.
WE'RE SHOVING OFF IN A LITTLE BIT...YOU WILL BE OKAY, KID. THINK OF IT: TOTAL FREEDOM, A WHOLE TOWN TO EXPLORE, NO ONE TELLING YOU WHAT TO DO--
YOU HAVE TO TAKE ME WITH YOU. THERE'S NOTHING HERE FOR ME.

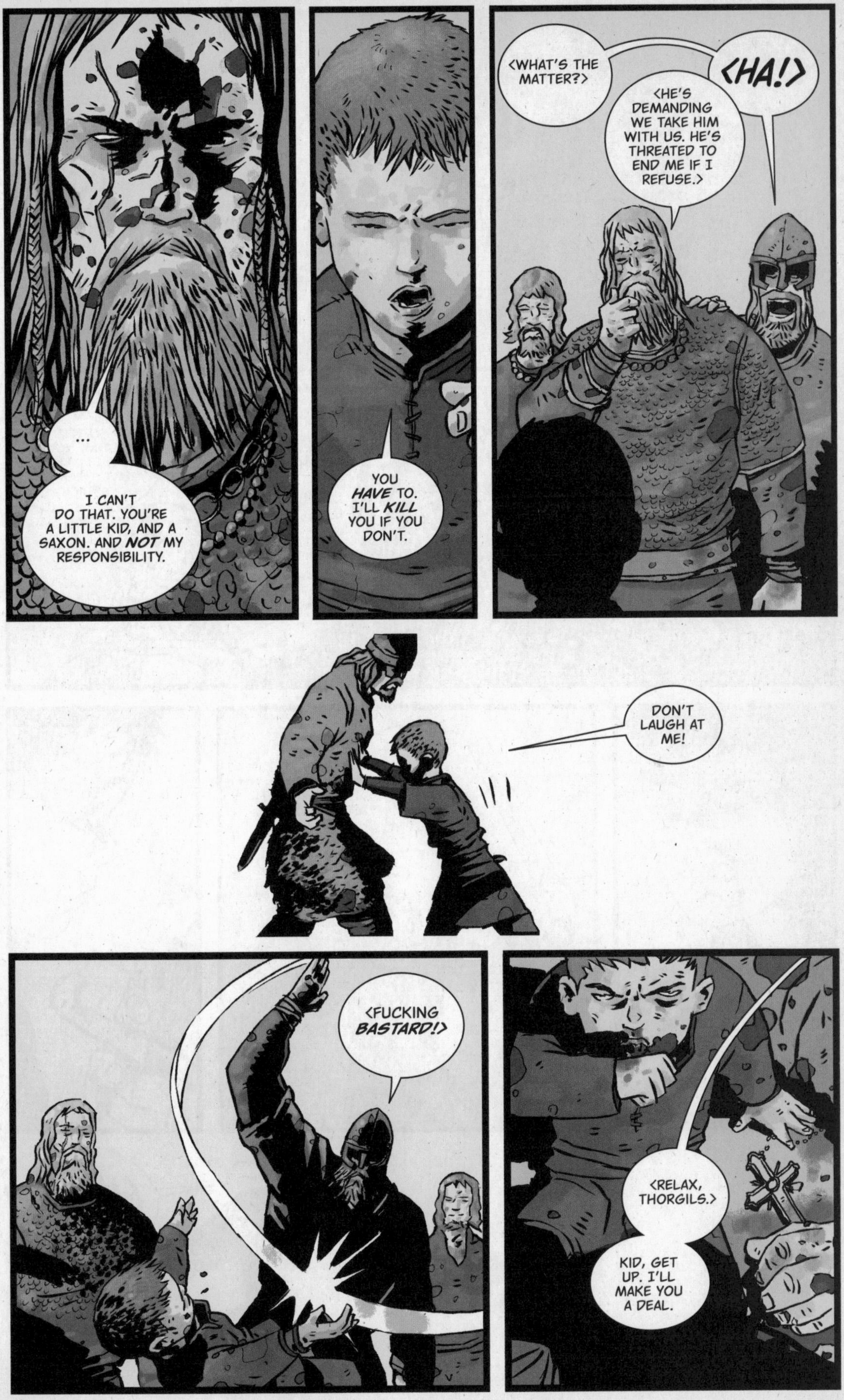
...
I CAN'T DO THAT. YOU'RE A LITTLE KID, AND A SAXON. AND NOT MY RESPONSIBILITY.
YOU HAVE TO. I'LL KILL YOU IF YOU DON'T.
<WHAT'S THE MATTER?>
<HE'S DEMANDING WE TAKE HIM WITH US. HE'S THREATED TO END ME IF I REFUSE.>
<HA!>
DON'T LAUGH AT ME!
<FUCKING BASTARD!>
<RELAX, THORGILS.>
KID, GET UP. I'LL MAKE YOU A DEAL.

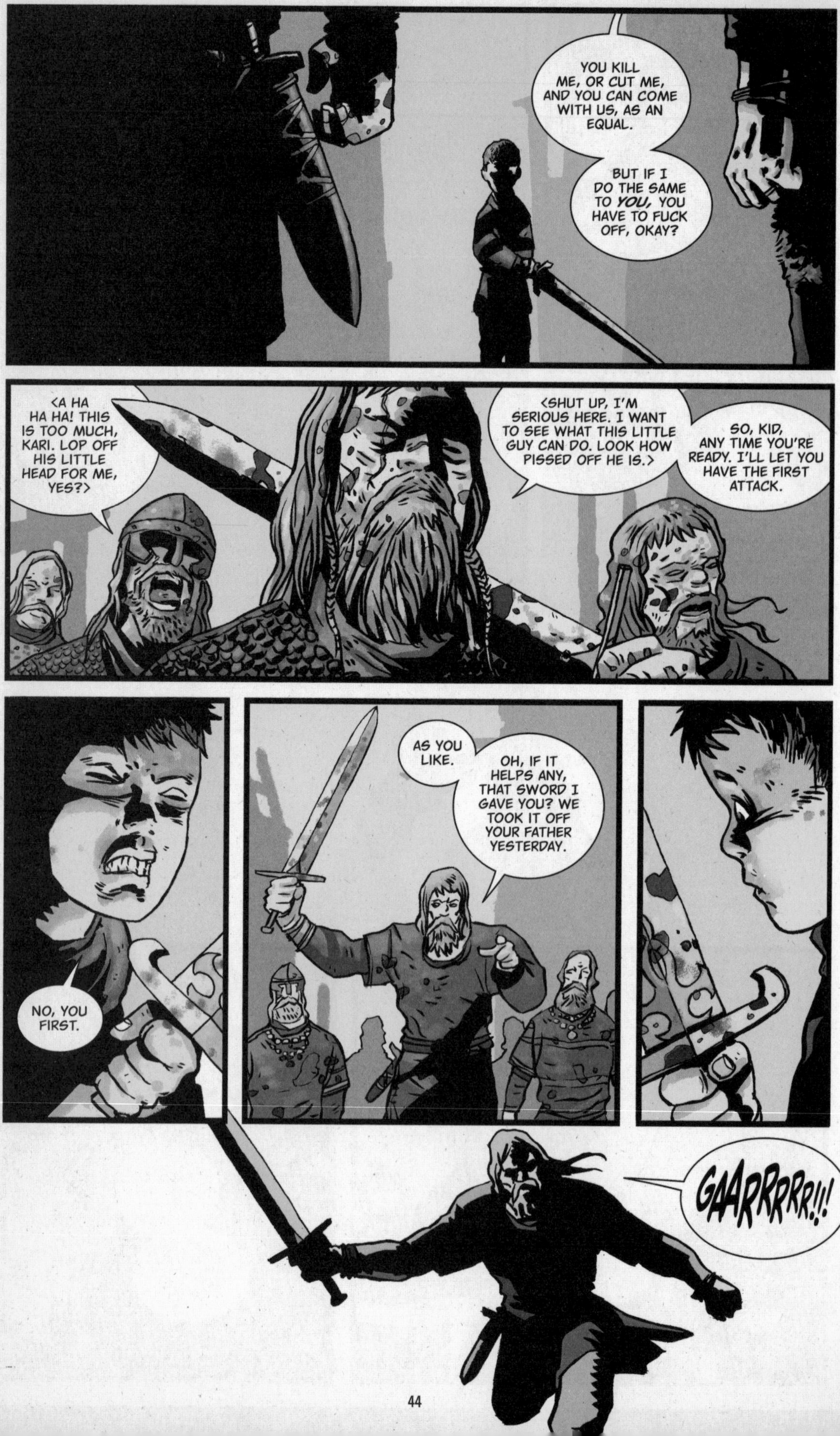
YOU KILL ME, OR CUT ME, AND YOU CAN COME WITH US, AS AN EQUAL.
BUT IF I DO THE SAME TO *YOU,* YOU HAVE TO FUCK OFF, OKAY?
<A HA HA HA! THIS IS TOO MUCH, KARI. LOP OFF HIS LITTLE HEAD FOR ME, YES?>
<SHUT UP, I'M SERIOUS HERE. I WANT TO SEE WHAT THIS LITTLE GUY CAN DO. LOOK HOW PISSED OFF HE IS.>
SO, KID, ANY TIME YOU'RE READY. I'LL LET YOU HAVE THE FIRST ATTACK.
NO, YOU FIRST.
AS YOU LIKE.
OH, IF IT HELPS ANY, THAT SWORD I GAVE YOU? WE TOOK IT OFF YOUR FATHER YESTERDAY.
GAARRRRR!!!

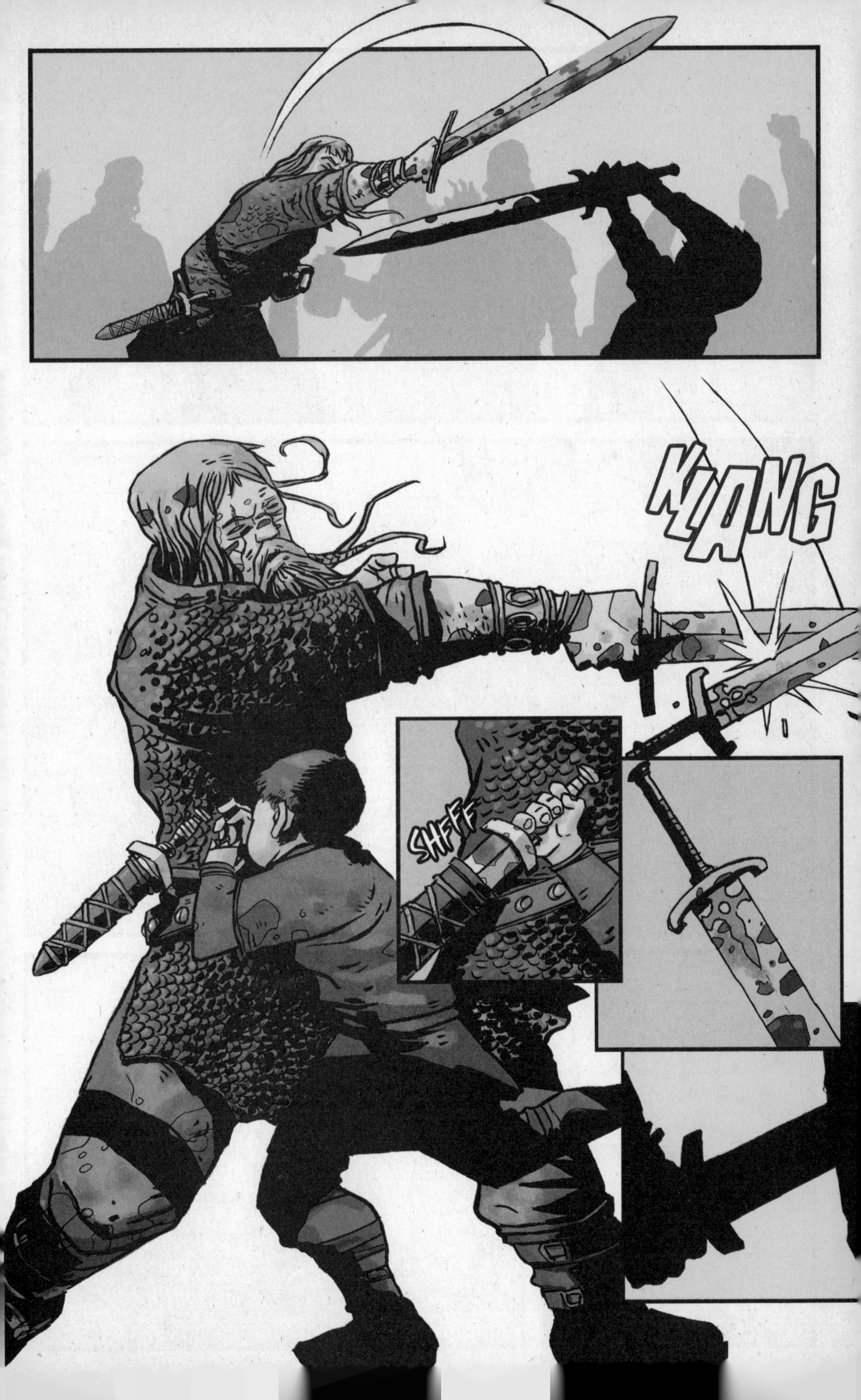
KLANG
SHFFF

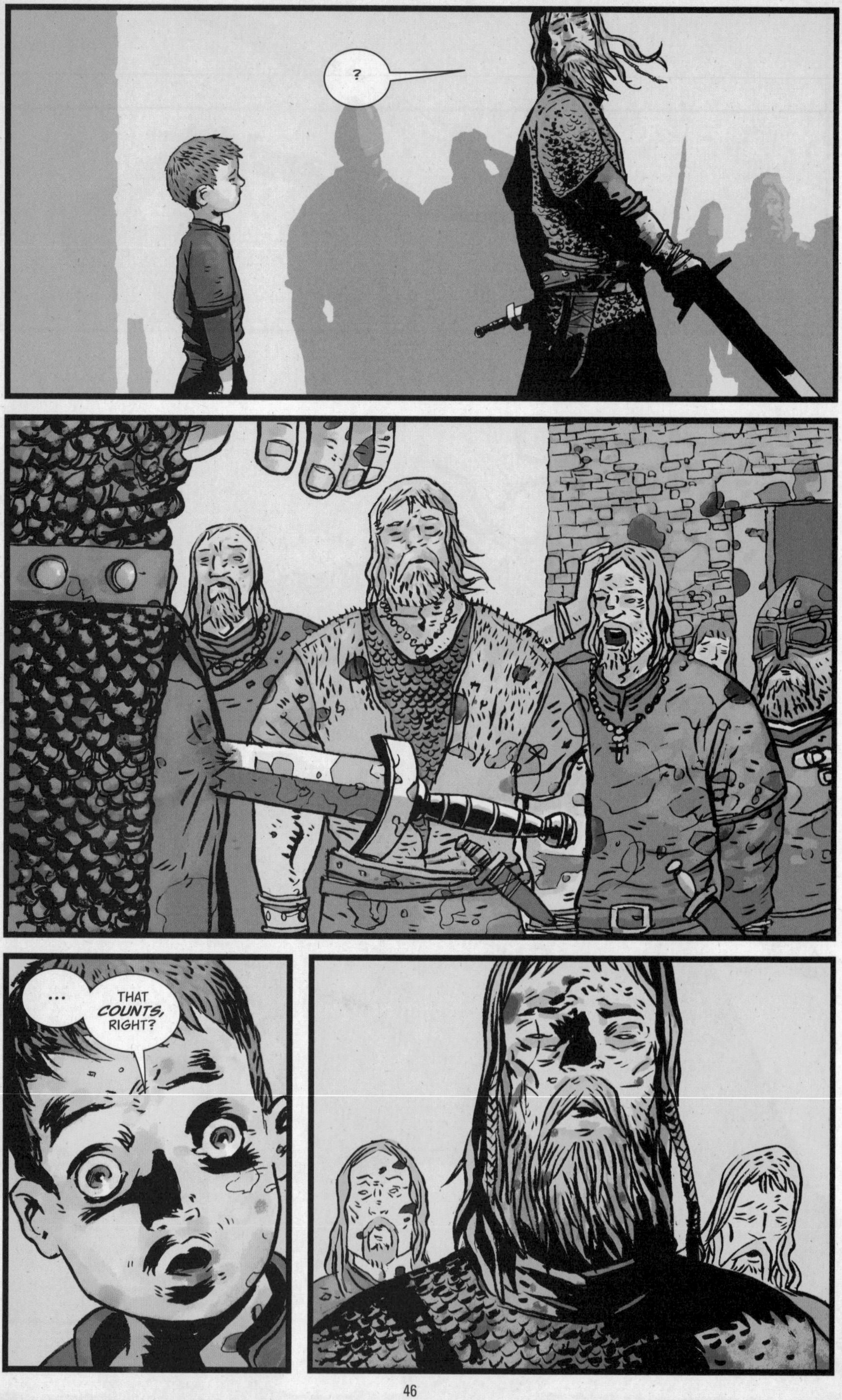
?
...
THAT COUNTS, RIGHT?

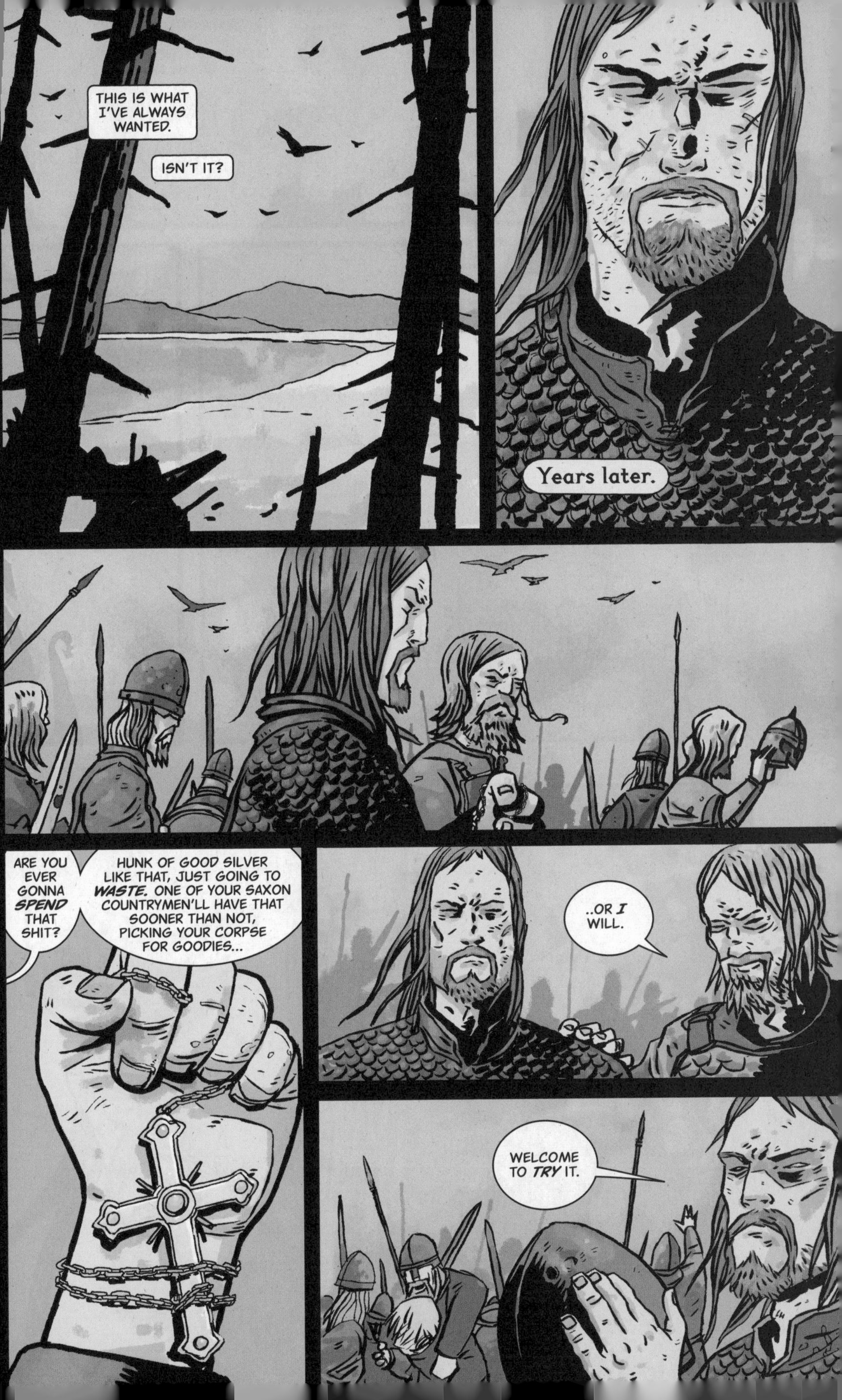
THIS IS WHAT I'VE ALWAYS WANTED.
ISN'T IT?
Years later.
ARE YOU EVER GONNA SPEND THAT SHIT?
HUNK OF GOOD SILVER LIKE THAT, JUST GOING TO WASTE. ONE OF YOUR SAXON COUNTRYMEN'LL HAVE THAT SOONER THAN NOT, PICKING YOUR CORPSE FOR GOODIES...
..OR I WILL.
WELCOME TO TRY IT.

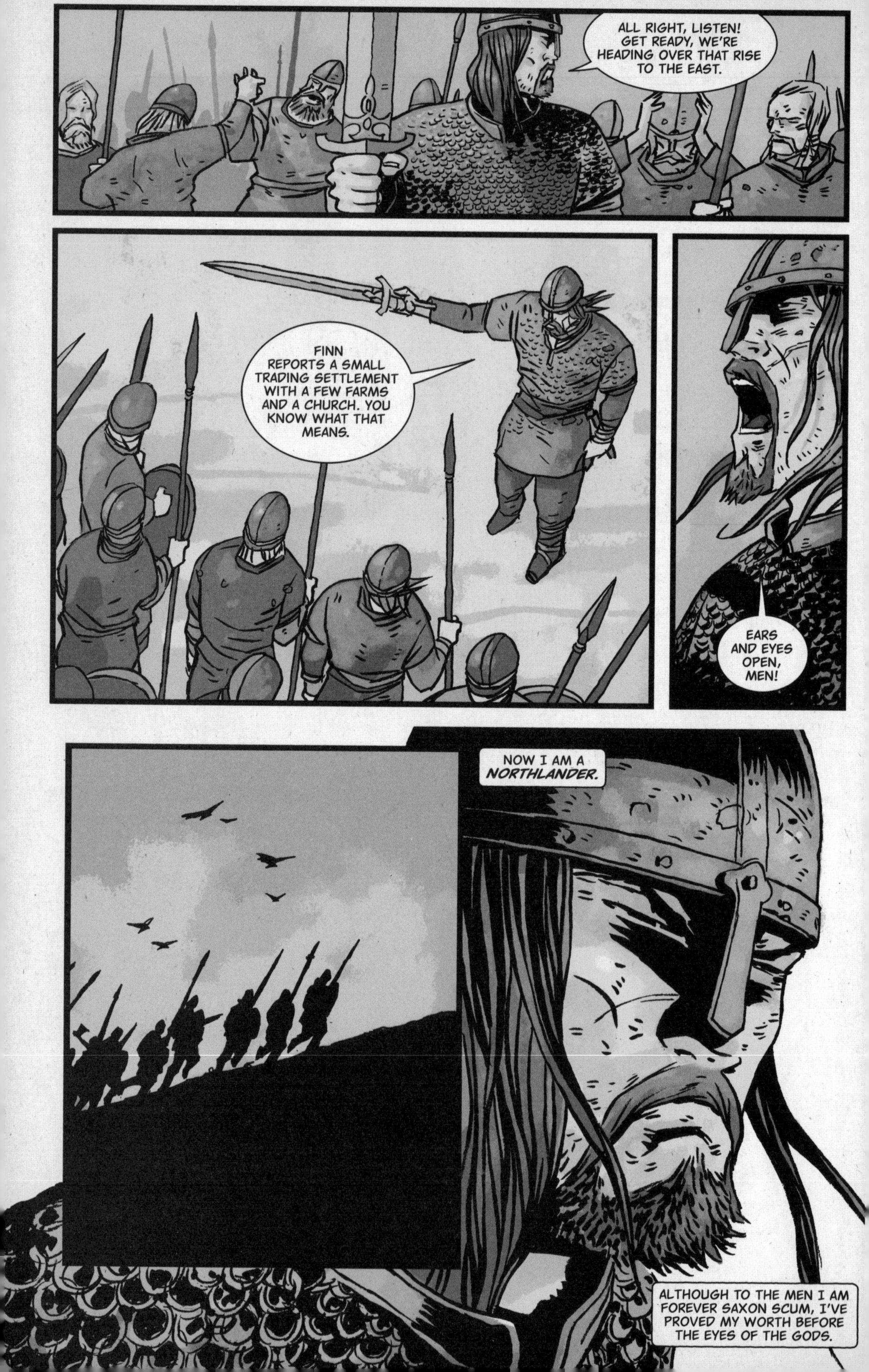
ALL RIGHT, LISTEN! GET READY, WE'RE HEADING OVER THAT RISE TO THE EAST.
FINN REPORTS A SMALL TRADING SETTLEMENT WITH A FEW FARMS AND A CHURCH. YOU KNOW WHAT THAT MEANS.
EARS AND EYES OPEN, MEN!
NOW I AM A *NORTHLANDER.*
ALTHOUGH TO THE MEN I AM FOREVER SAXON SCUM, I'VE PROVED MY WORTH BEFORE THE EYES OF THE GODS.

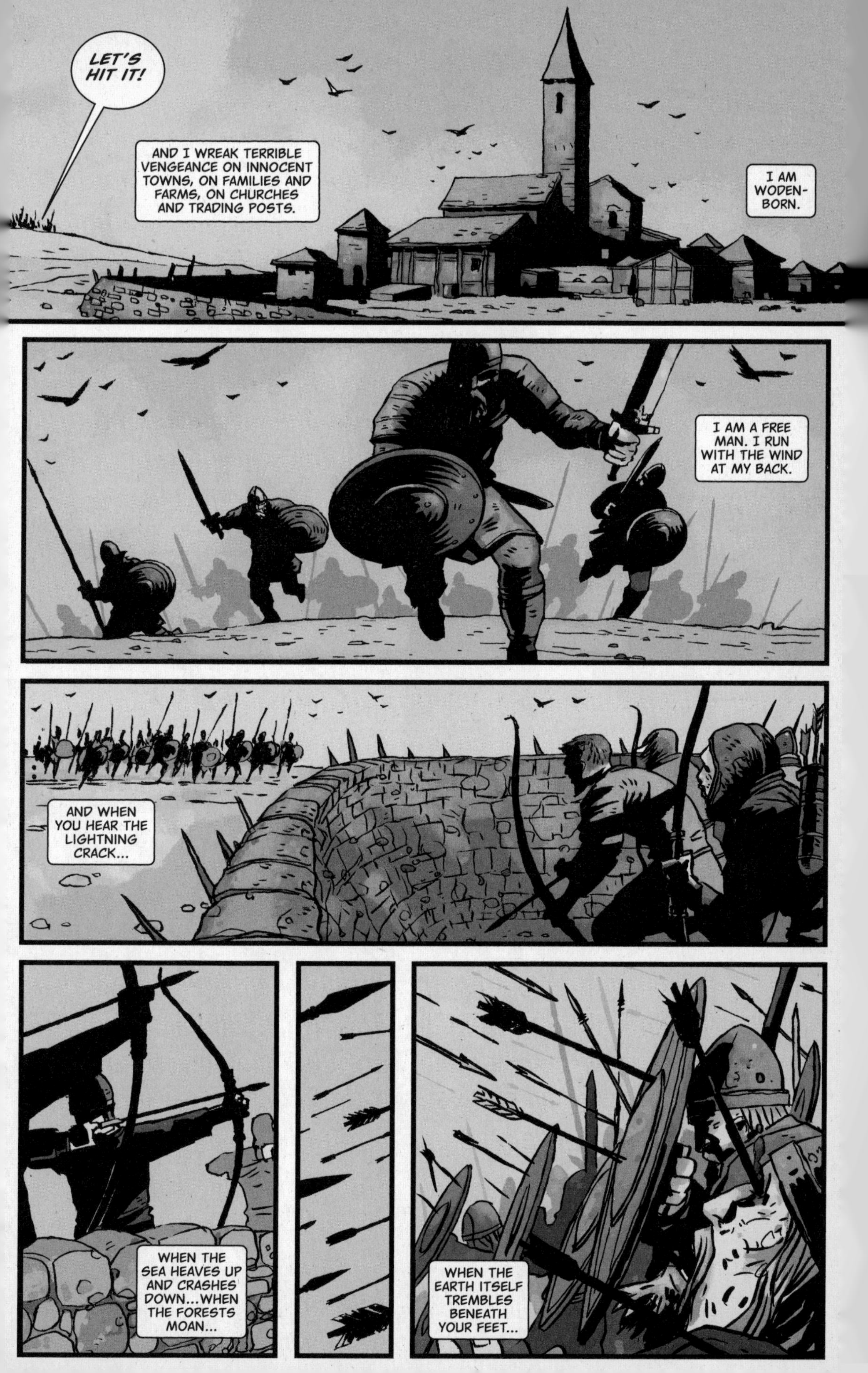
LET'S HIT IT!
AND I WREAK TERRIBLE VENGEANCE ON INNOCENT TOWNS, ON FAMILIES AND FARMS, ON CHURCHES AND TRADING POSTS.
I AM WODEN-BORN.
I AM A FREE MAN. I RUN WITH THE WIND AT MY BACK.
AND WHEN YOU HEAR THE LIGHTNING CRACK...
WHEN THE SEA HEAVES UP AND CRASHES DOWN...WHEN THE FORESTS MOAN...
WHEN THE EARTH ITSELF TREMBLES BENEATH YOUR FEET...

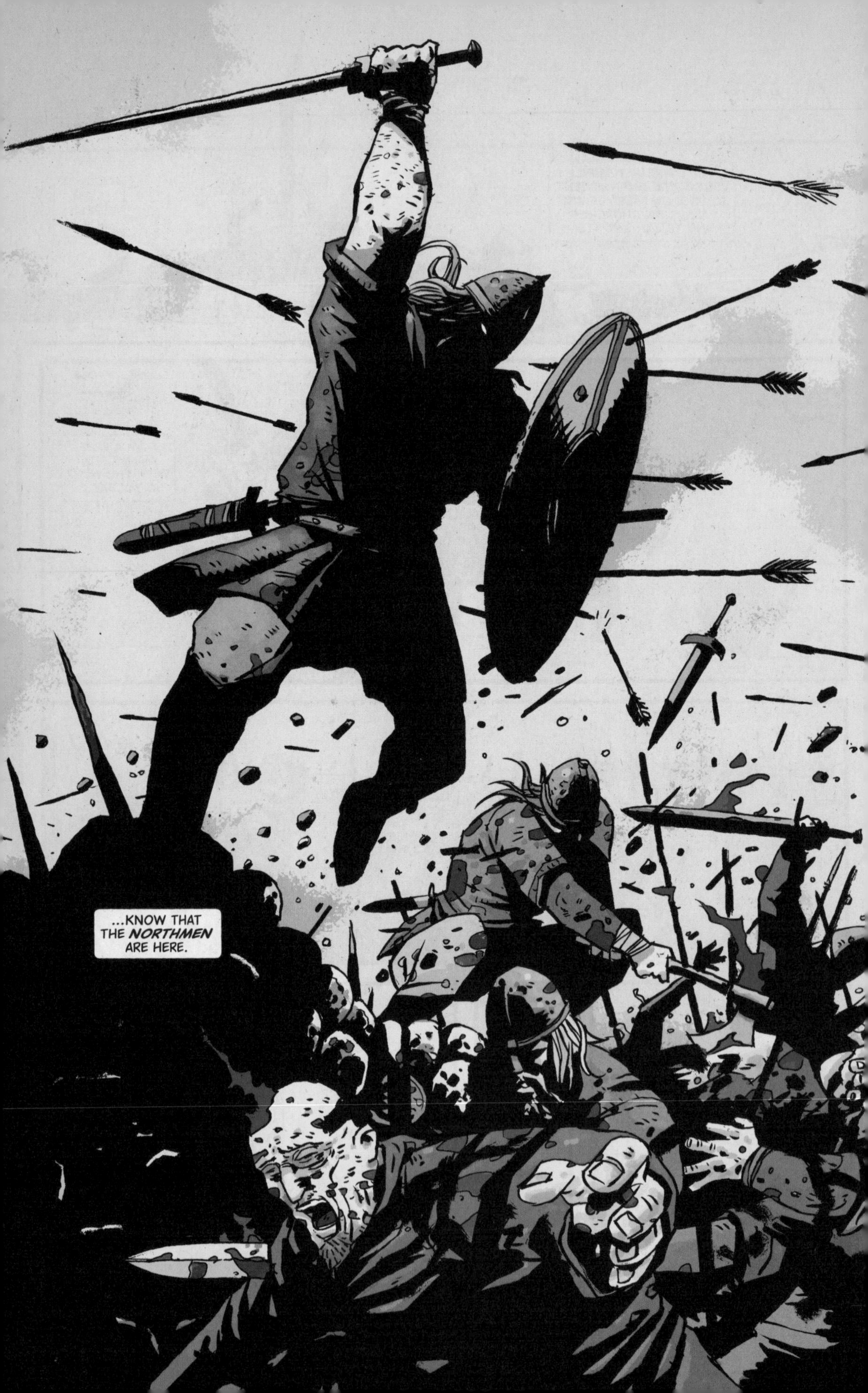
...KNOW THAT THE *NORTHMEN* ARE HERE.

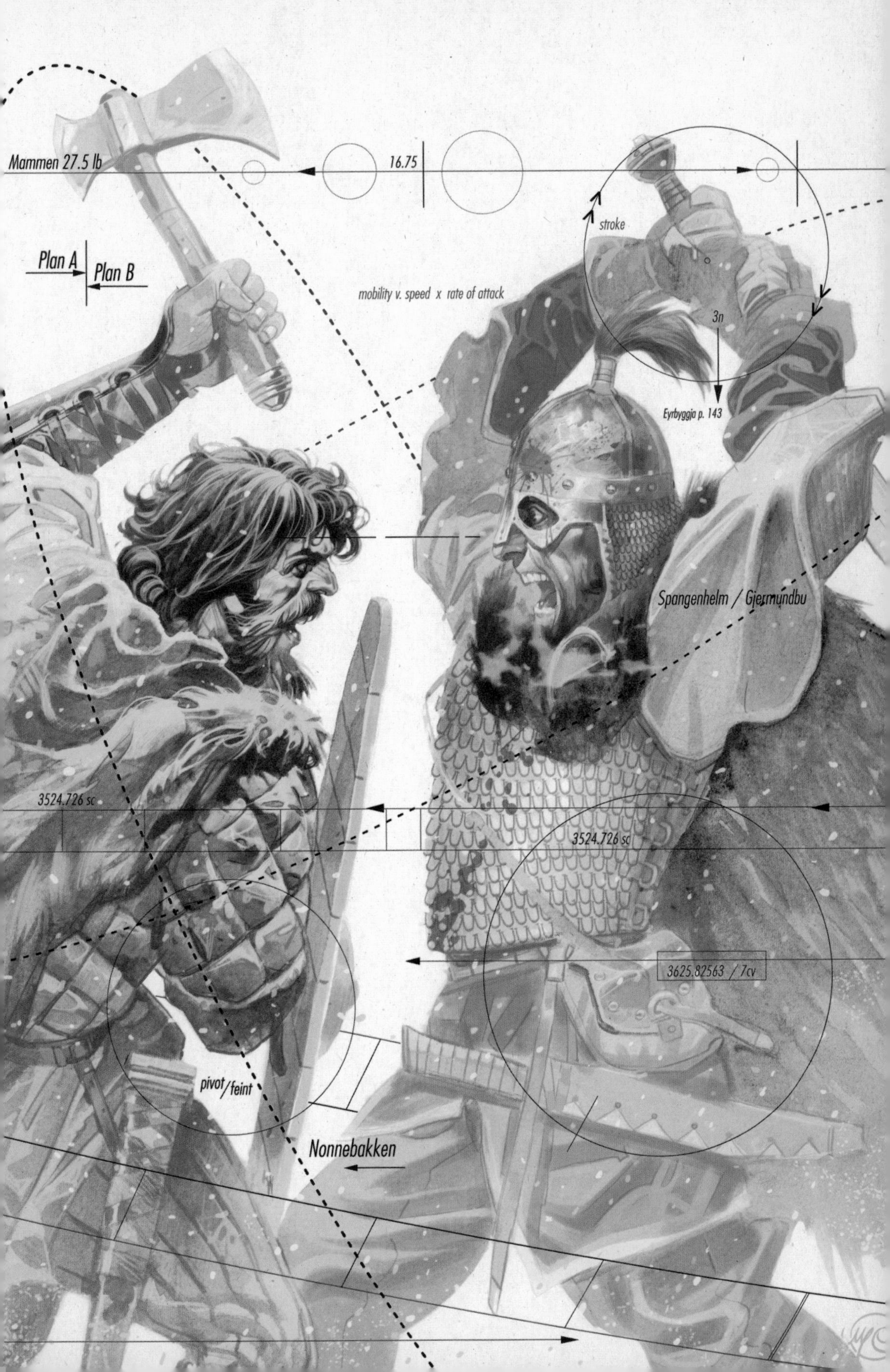
Mammen 27.5 lb
16.75
stroke
Plan A
Plan B
mobility v. speed x rate of attack
3n
Eyrbyggja p. 143
Spangenhelm / Gjermundbu
3524.726 sc
3524.726 sc
3625.82563 / 7cv
pivot/feint
Nonnebakken

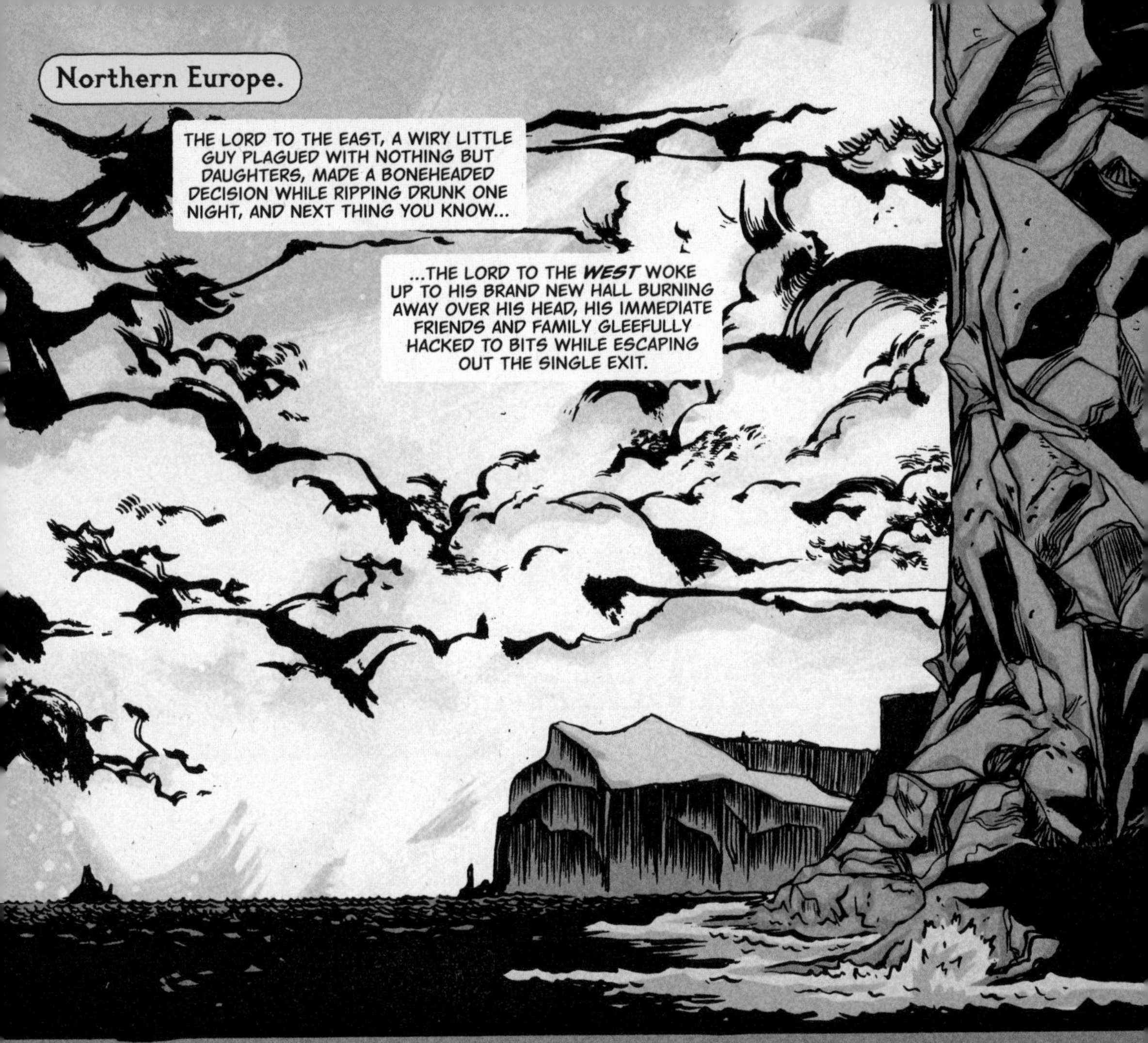
Northern Europe.
THE LORD TO THE EAST, A WIRY LITTLE GUY PLAGUED WITH NOTHING BUT DAUGHTERS, MADE A BONEHEADED DECISION WHILE RIPPING DRUNK ONE NIGHT, AND NEXT THING YOU KNOW...
...THE LORD TO THE WEST WOKE UP TO HIS BRAND NEW HALL BURNING AWAY OVER HIS HEAD, HIS IMMEDIATE FRIENDS AND FAMILY GLEEFULLY HACKED TO BITS WHILE ESCAPING OUT THE SINGLE EXIT.

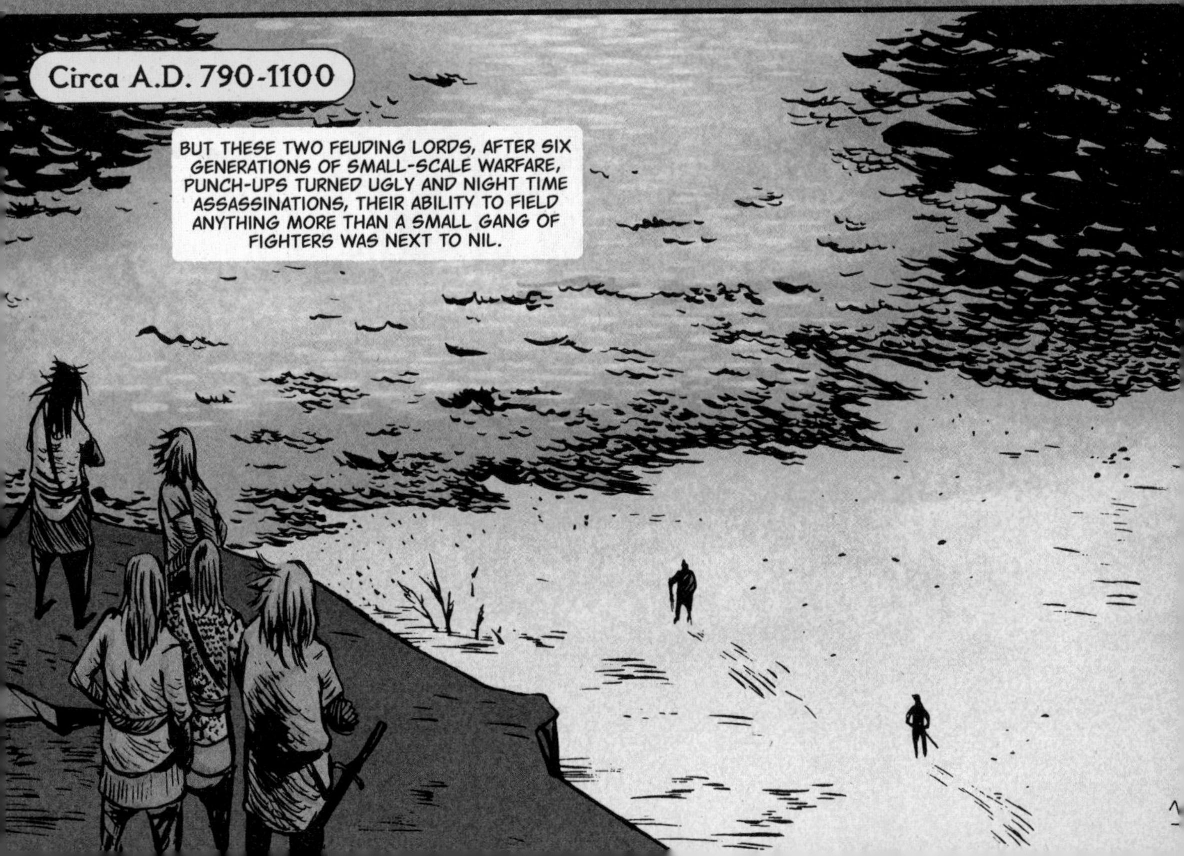
Circa A.D. 790-1100
BUT THESE TWO FEUDING LORDS, AFTER SIX GENERATIONS OF SMALL-SCALE WARFARE, PUNCH-UPS TURNED UGLY AND NIGHT TIME ASSASSINATIONS, THEIR ABILITY TO FIELD ANYTHING MORE THAN A SMALL GANG OF FIGHTERS WAS NEXT TO NIL.

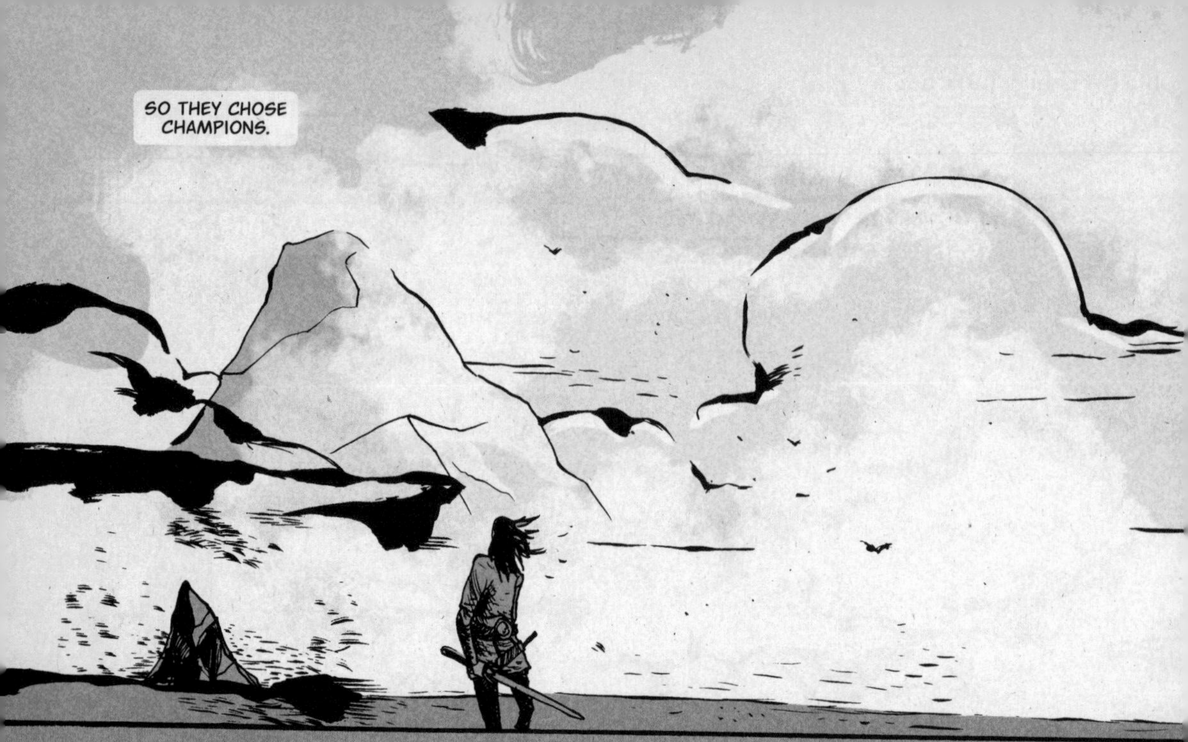
SO THEY CHOSE CHAMPIONS.

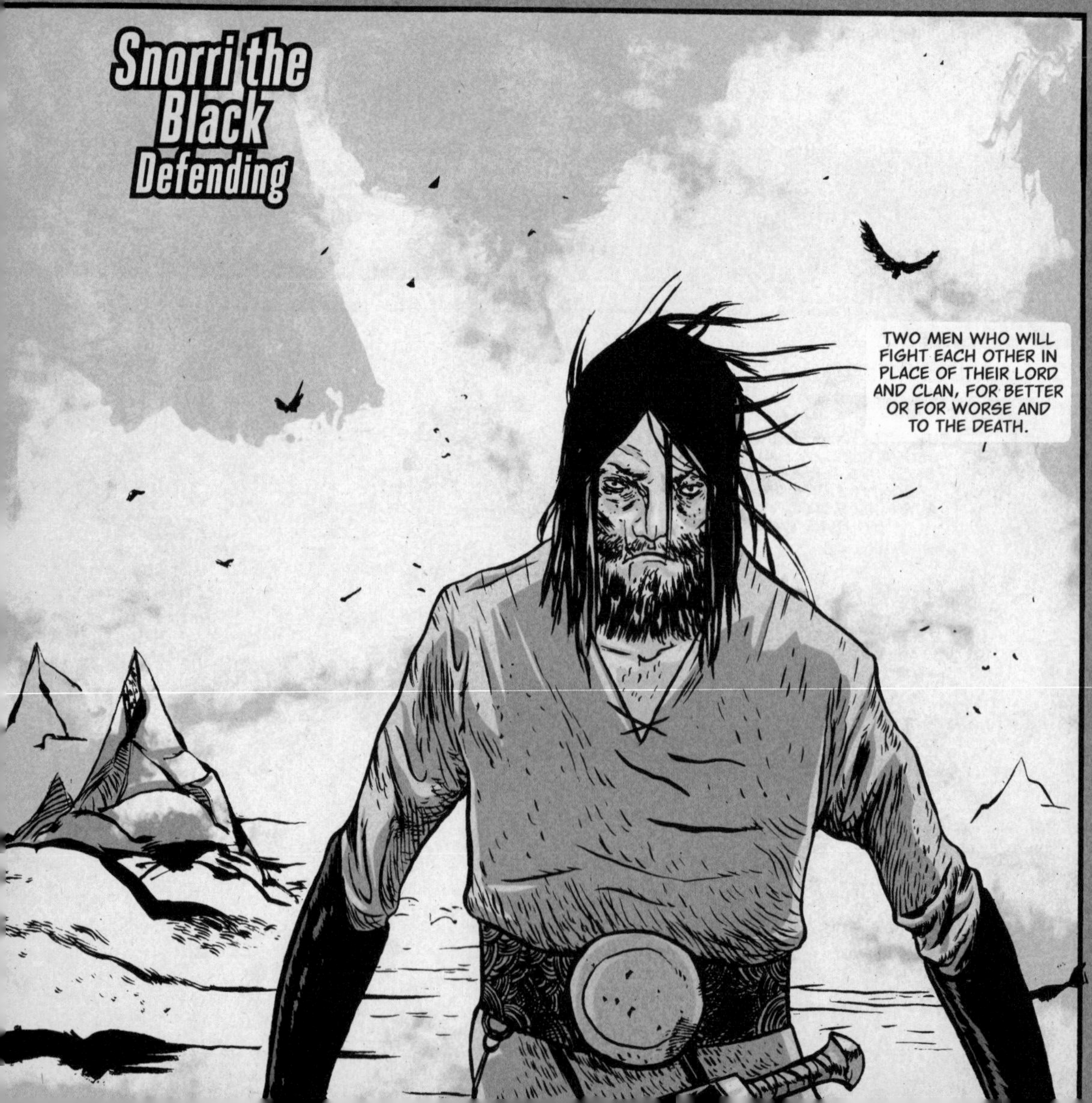
Snorri the Black Defending
TWO MEN WHO WILL FIGHT EACH OTHER IN PLACE OF THEIR LORD AND CLAN, FOR BETTER OR FOR WORSE AND TO THE DEATH.

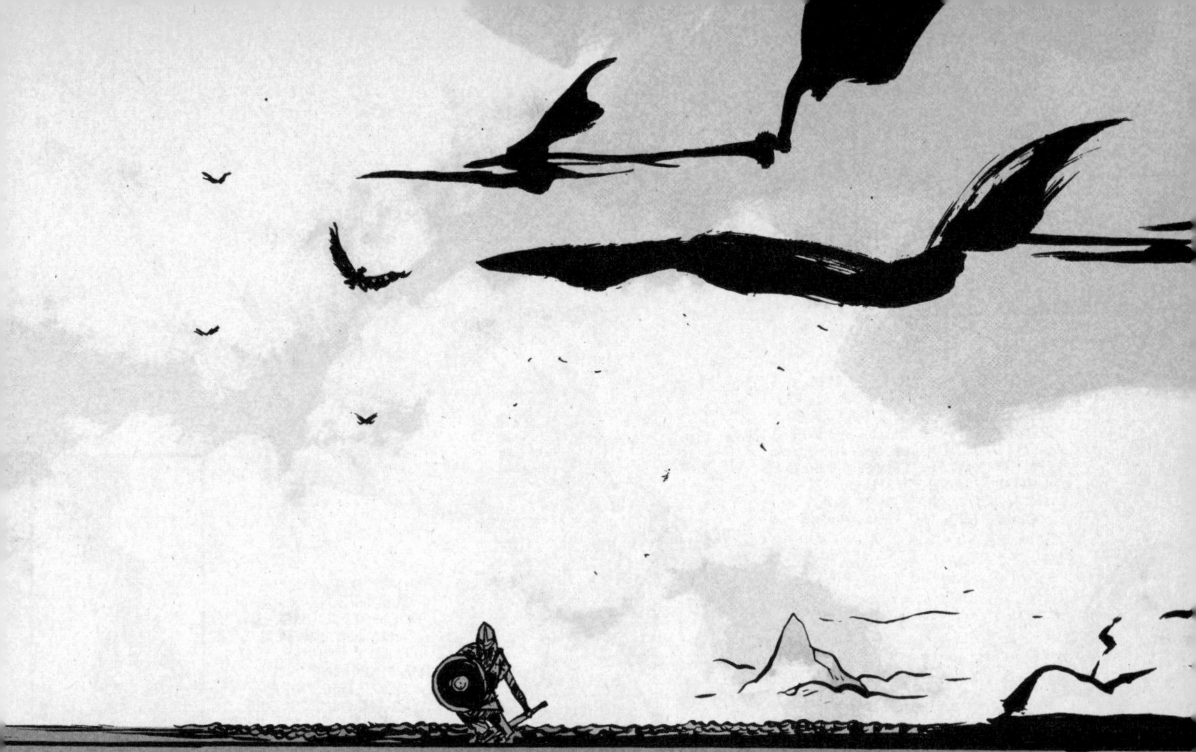

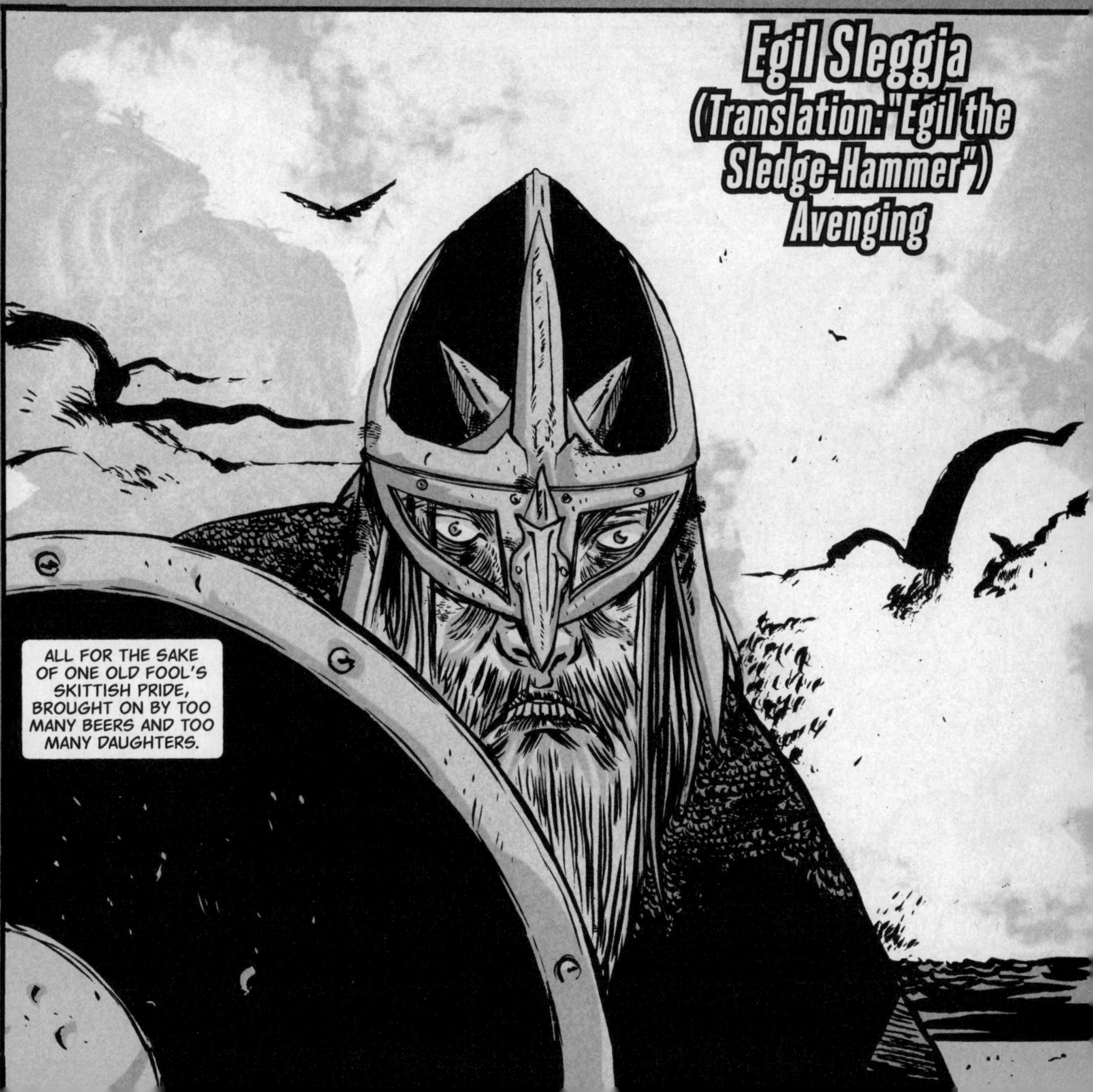
Egil Sleggja
(Translation: "Egil the Sledge-Hammer")
Avenging
ALL FOR THE SAKE OF ONE OLD FOOL'S SKITTISH PRIDE, BROUGHT ON BY TOO MANY BEERS AND TOO MANY DAUGHTERS.

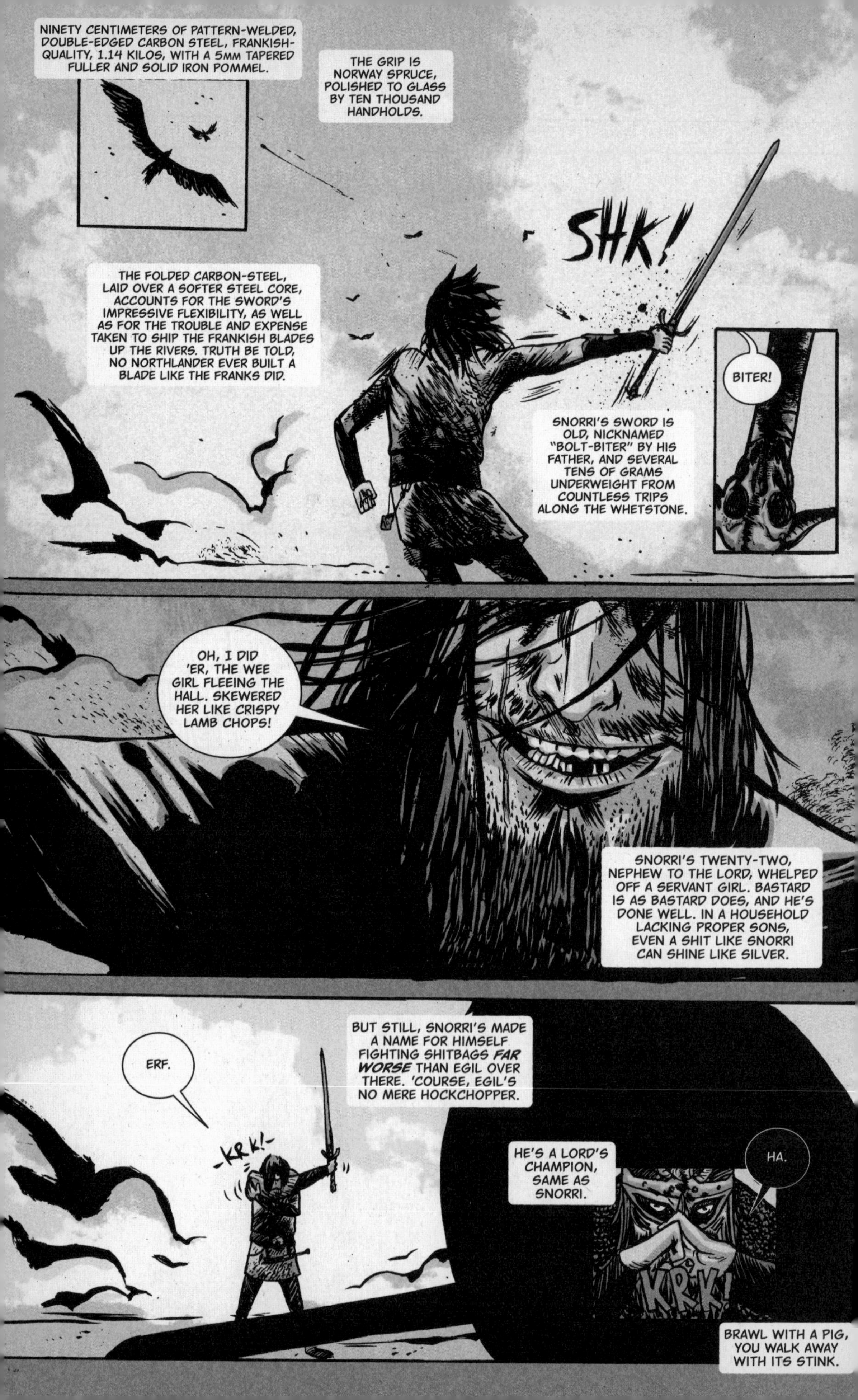
NINETY CENTIMETERS OF PATTERN-WELDED, DOUBLE-EDGED CARBON STEEL, FRANKISH-QUALITY, 1.14 KILOS, WITH A 5MM TAPERED FULLER AND SOLID IRON POMMEL.
THE GRIP IS NORWAY SPRUCE, POLISHED TO GLASS BY TEN THOUSAND HANDHOLDS.
SHK!
THE FOLDED CARBON-STEEL, LAID OVER A SOFTER STEEL CORE, ACCOUNTS FOR THE SWORD'S IMPRESSIVE FLEXIBILITY, AS WELL AS FOR THE TROUBLE AND EXPENSE TAKEN TO SHIP THE FRANKISH BLADES UP THE RIVERS. TRUTH BE TOLD, NO NORTHLANDER EVER BUILT A BLADE LIKE THE FRANKS DID.
SNORRI'S SWORD IS OLD, NICKNAMED "BOLT-BITER" BY HIS FATHER, AND SEVERAL TENS OF GRAMS UNDERWEIGHT FROM COUNTLESS TRIPS ALONG THE WHETSTONE.
BITER!
OH, I DID 'ER, THE WEE GIRL FLEEING THE HALL. SKEWERED HER LIKE CRISPY LAMB CHOPS!
SNORRI'S TWENTY-TWO, NEPHEW TO THE LORD, WHELPED OFF A SERVANT GIRL. BASTARD IS AS BASTARD DOES, AND HE'S DONE WELL. IN A HOUSEHOLD LACKING PROPER SONS, EVEN A SHIT LIKE SNORRI CAN SHINE LIKE SILVER.
ERF.
BUT STILL, SNORRI'S MADE A NAME FOR HIMSELF FIGHTING SHITBAGS *FAR WORSE* THAN EGIL OVER THERE. 'COURSE, EGIL'S NO MERE HOCKCHOPPER.
KRK!
HE'S A LORD'S CHAMPION, SAME AS SNORRI.
HA.
KRK!
BRAWL WITH A PIG, YOU WALK AWAY WITH ITS STINK.

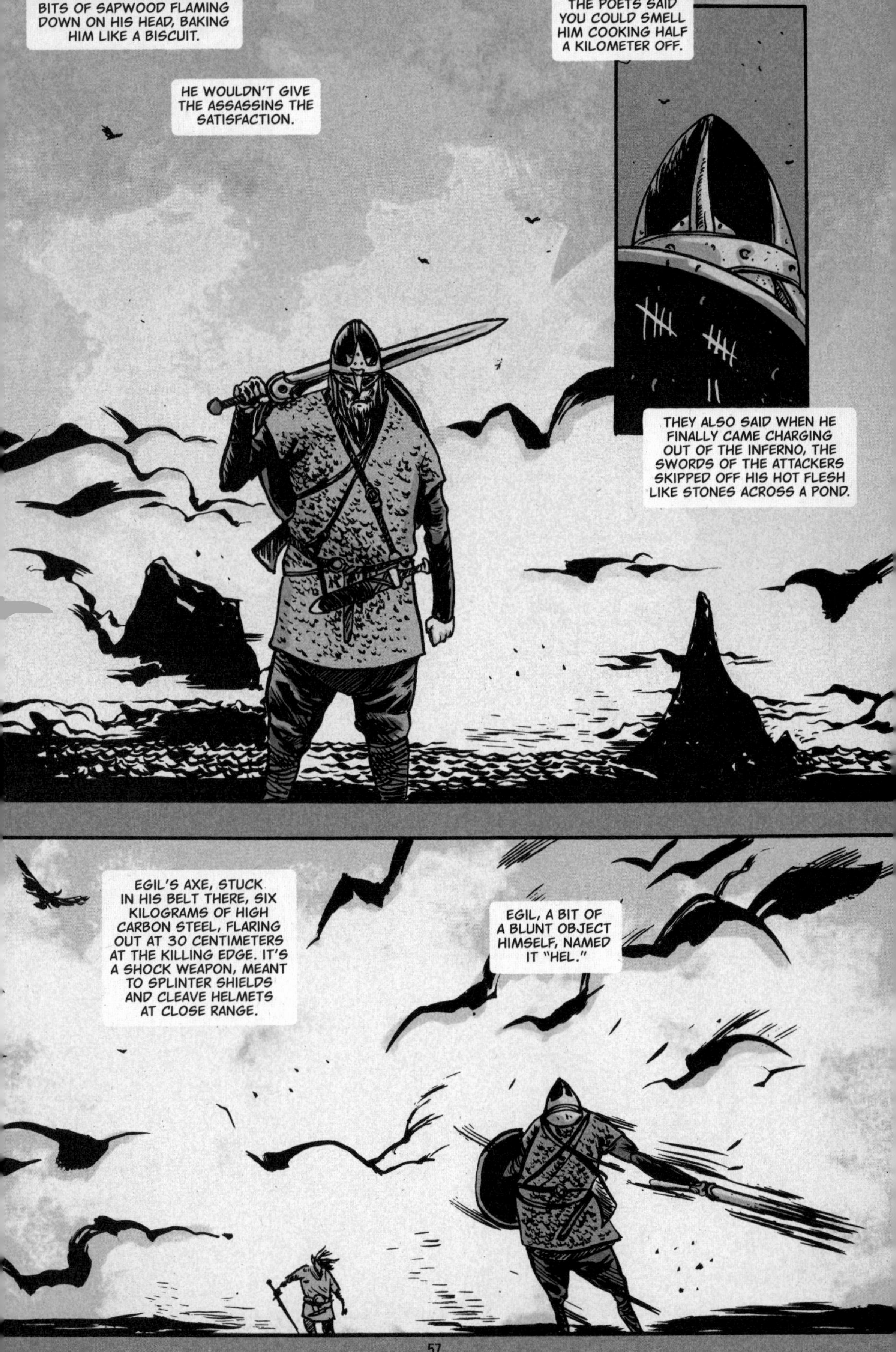
EGIL STOOD IN THAT BURNING HALL LONGER THAN ANYONE; BITS OF SAPWOOD FLAMING DOWN ON HIS HEAD, BAKING HIM LIKE A BISCUIT.
HE WOULDN'T GIVE THE ASSASSINS THE SATISFACTION.
THE POETS SAID YOU COULD SMELL HIM COOKING HALF A KILOMETER OFF.
THEY ALSO SAID WHEN HE FINALLY CAME CHARGING OUT OF THE INFERNO, THE SWORDS OF THE ATTACKERS SKIPPED OFF HIS HOT FLESH LIKE STONES ACROSS A POND.
EGIL'S AXE, STUCK IN HIS BELT THERE, SIX KILOGRAMS OF HIGH CARBON STEEL, FLARING OUT AT 30 CENTIMETERS AT THE KILLING EDGE. IT'S A SHOCK WEAPON, MEANT TO SPLINTER SHIELDS AND CLEAVE HELMETS AT CLOSE RANGE.
EGIL, A BIT OF A BLUNT OBJECT HIMSELF, NAMED IT "HEL."

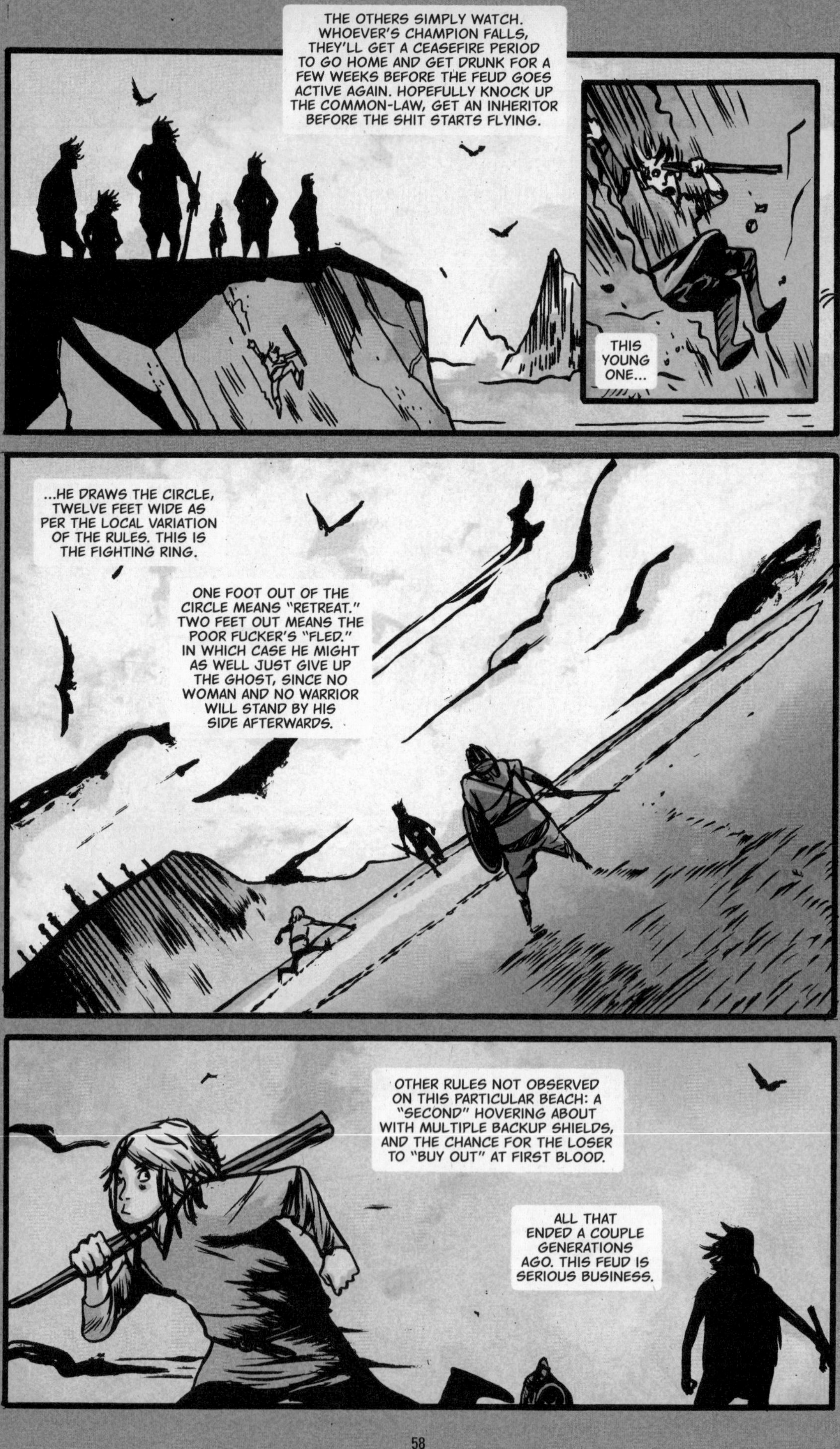
THE OTHERS SIMPLY WATCH. WHOEVER'S CHAMPION FALLS, THEY'LL GET A CEASEFIRE PERIOD TO GO HOME AND GET DRUNK FOR A FEW WEEKS BEFORE THE FEUD GOES ACTIVE AGAIN. HOPEFULLY KNOCK UP THE COMMON-LAW, GET AN INHERITOR BEFORE THE SHIT STARTS FLYING.
THIS YOUNG ONE...
...HE DRAWS THE CIRCLE, TWELVE FEET WIDE AS PER THE LOCAL VARIATION OF THE RULES. THIS IS THE FIGHTING RING.
ONE FOOT OUT OF THE CIRCLE MEANS "RETREAT." TWO FEET OUT MEANS THE POOR FUCKER'S "FLED." IN WHICH CASE HE MIGHT AS WELL JUST GIVE UP THE GHOST, SINCE NO WOMAN AND NO WARRIOR WILL STAND BY HIS SIDE AFTERWARDS.
OTHER RULES NOT OBSERVED ON THIS PARTICULAR BEACH: A "SECOND" HOVERING ABOUT WITH MULTIPLE BACKUP SHIELDS, AND THE CHANCE FOR THE LOSER TO "BUY OUT" AT FIRST BLOOD.
ALL THAT ENDED A COUPLE GENERATIONS AGO. THIS FEUD IS SERIOUS BUSINESS.

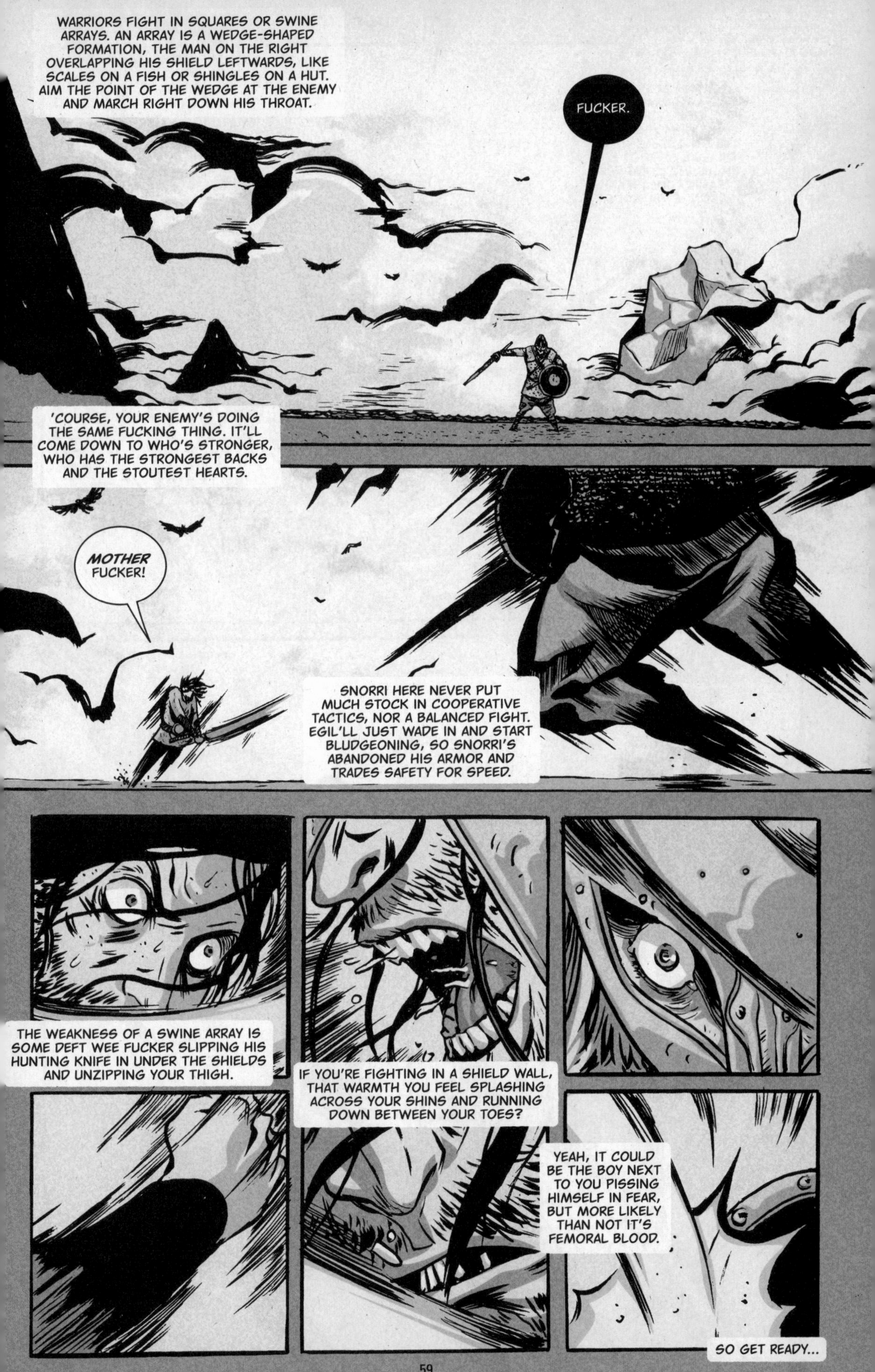

WARRIORS FIGHT IN SQUARES OR SWINE ARRAYS. AN ARRAY IS A WEDGE-SHAPED FORMATION, THE MAN ON THE RIGHT OVERLAPPING HIS SHIELD LEFTWARDS, LIKE SCALES ON A FISH OR SHINGLES ON A HUT. AIM THE POINT OF THE WEDGE AT THE ENEMY AND MARCH RIGHT DOWN HIS THROAT.
FUCKER.
'COURSE, YOUR ENEMY'S DOING THE SAME FUCKING THING. IT'LL COME DOWN TO WHO'S STRONGER, WHO HAS THE STRONGEST BACKS AND THE STOUTEST HEARTS.
MOTHER FUCKER!
SNORRI HERE NEVER PUT MUCH STOCK IN COOPERATIVE TACTICS, NOR A BALANCED FIGHT. EGIL'LL JUST WADE IN AND START BLUDGEONING, SO SNORRI'S ABANDONED HIS ARMOR AND TRADES SAFETY FOR SPEED.
THE WEAKNESS OF A SWINE ARRAY IS SOME DEFT WEE FUCKER SLIPPING HIS HUNTING KNIFE IN UNDER THE SHIELDS AND UNZIPPING YOUR THIGH.
IF YOU'RE FIGHTING IN A SHIELD WALL, THAT WARMTH YOU FEEL SPLASHING ACROSS YOUR SHINS AND RUNNING DOWN BETWEEN YOUR TOES?
YEAH, IT COULD BE THE BOY NEXT TO YOU PISSING HIMSELF IN FEAR, BUT MORE LIKELY THAN NOT IT'S FEMORAL BLOOD.
SO GET READY...

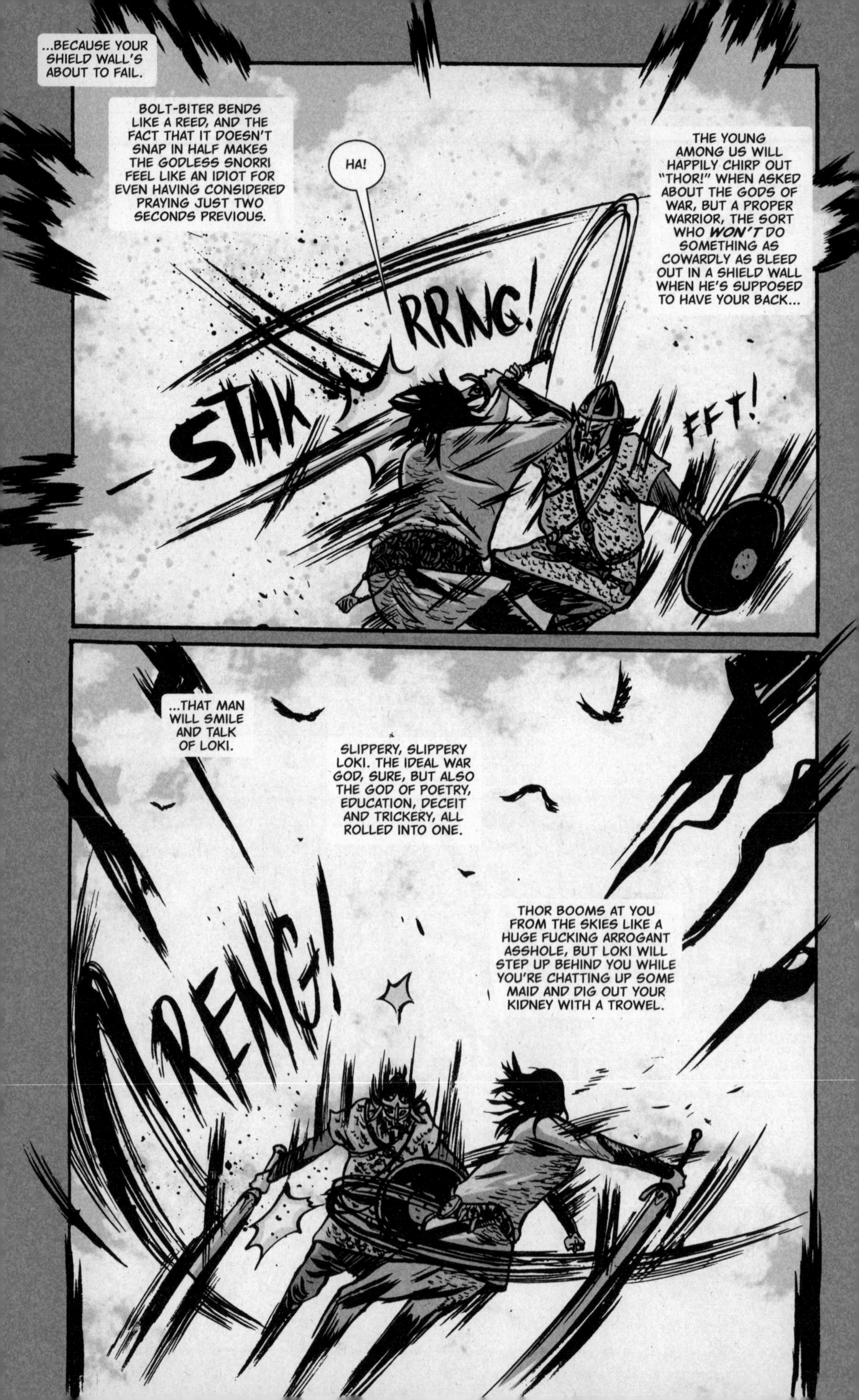
...BECAUSE YOUR SHIELD WALL'S ABOUT TO FAIL.
BOLT-BITER BENDS LIKE A REED, AND THE FACT THAT IT DOESN'T SNAP IN HALF MAKES THE GODLESS SNORRI FEEL LIKE AN IDIOT FOR EVEN HAVING CONSIDERED PRAYING JUST TWO SECONDS PREVIOUS.
HA!
THE YOUNG AMONG US WILL HAPPILY CHIRP OUT "THOR!" WHEN ASKED ABOUT THE GODS OF WAR, BUT A PROPER WARRIOR, THE SORT WHO WON'T DO SOMETHING AS COWARDLY AS BLEED OUT IN A SHIELD WALL WHEN HE'S SUPPOSED TO HAVE YOUR BACK...
RRNG!
STAK
FFT!
...THAT MAN WILL SMILE AND TALK OF LOKI.
SLIPPERY, SLIPPERY LOKI. THE IDEAL WAR GOD, SURE, BUT ALSO THE GOD OF POETRY, EDUCATION, DECEIT AND TRICKERY, ALL ROLLED INTO ONE.
THOR BOOMS AT YOU FROM THE SKIES LIKE A HUGE FUCKING ARROGANT ASSHOLE, BUT LOKI WILL STEP UP BEHIND YOU WHILE YOU'RE CHATTING UP SOME MAID AND DIG OUT YOUR KIDNEY WITH A TROWEL.
RENG!

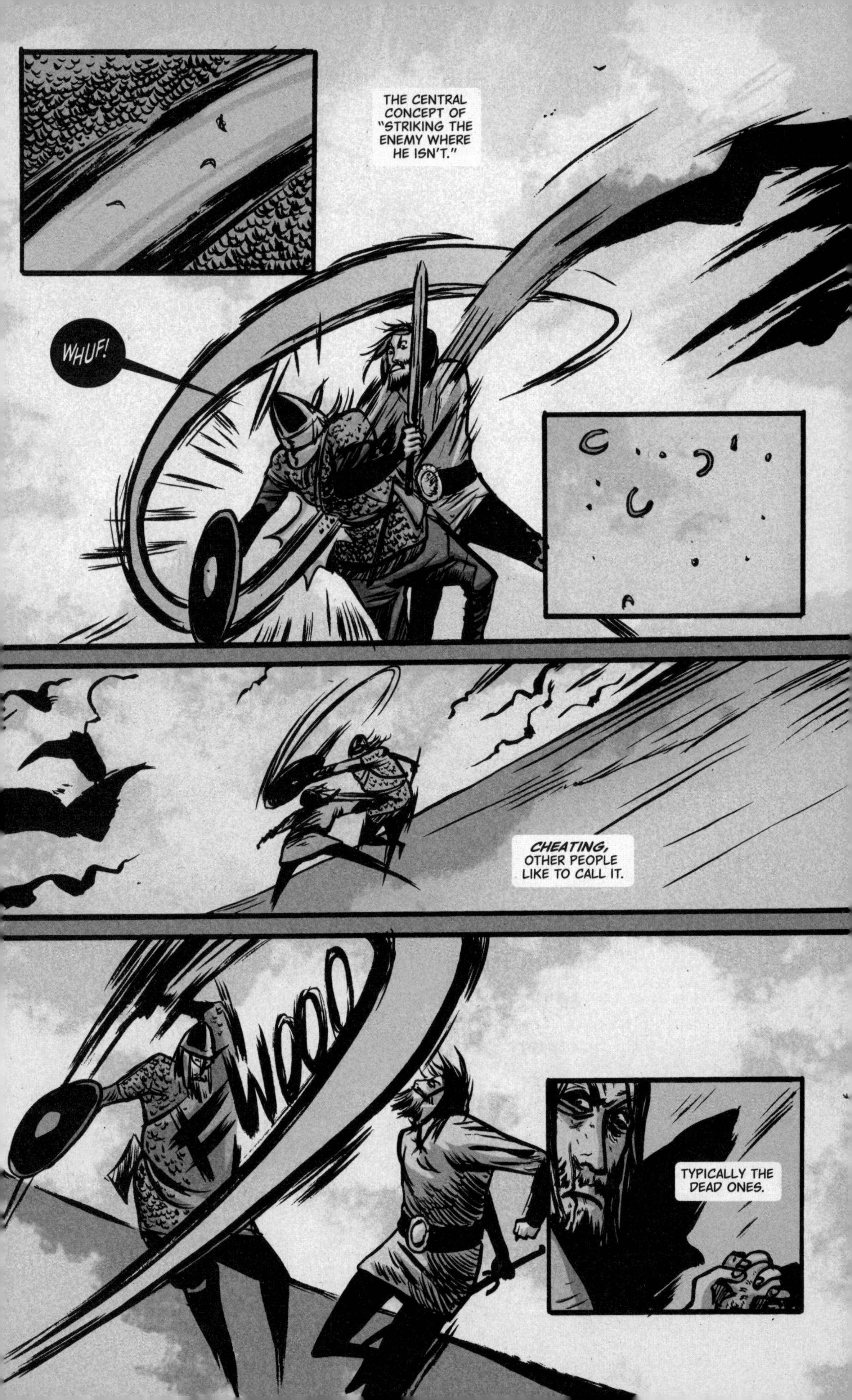

THE CENTRAL CONCEPT OF "STRIKING THE ENEMY WHERE HE ISN'T."
WHUF!
CHEATING, OTHER PEOPLE LIKE TO CALL IT.
FWAAA
TYPICALLY THE DEAD ONES.

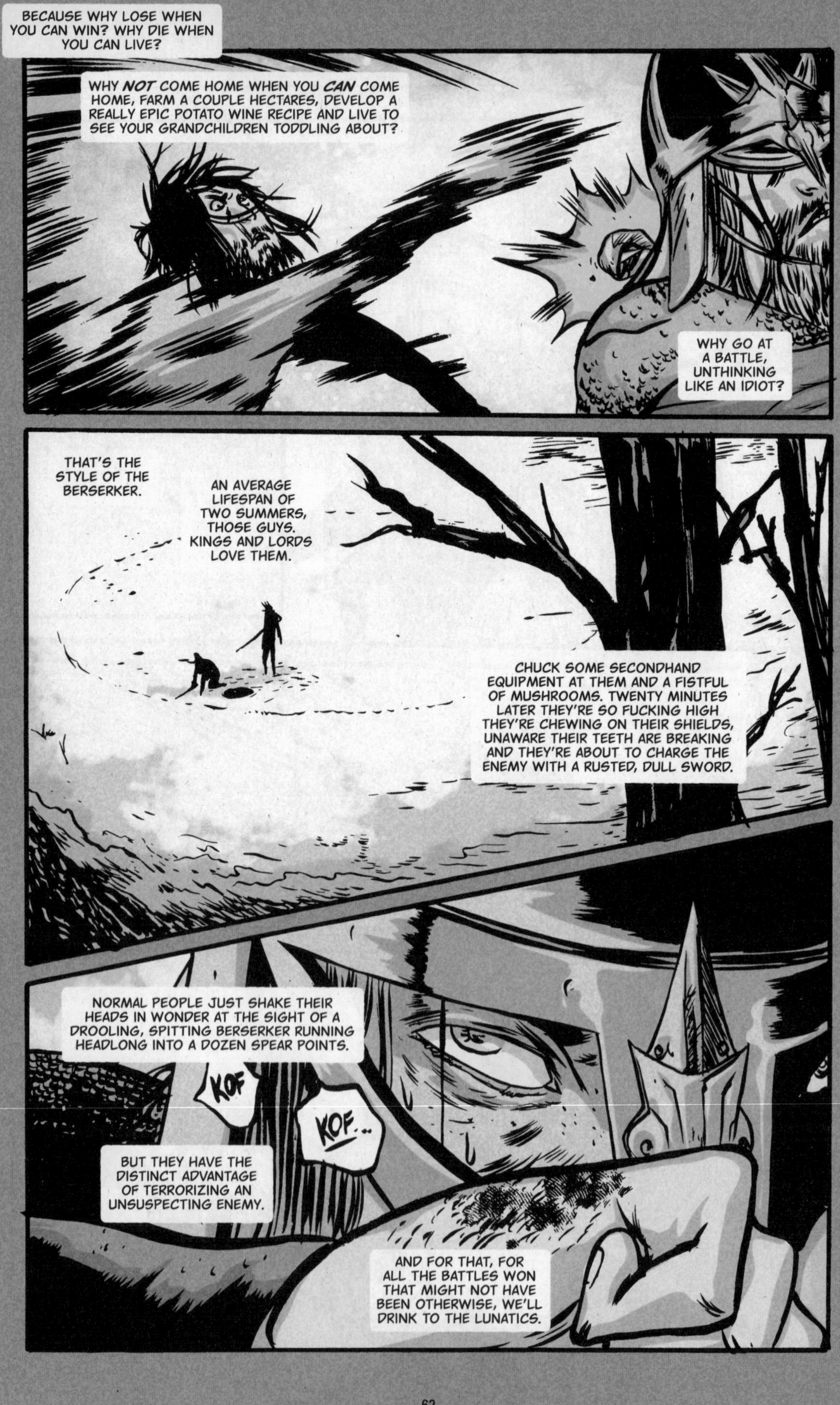
BECAUSE WHY LOSE WHEN YOU CAN WIN? WHY DIE WHEN YOU CAN LIVE?
WHY NOT COME HOME WHEN YOU CAN COME HOME, FARM A COUPLE HECTARES, DEVELOP A REALLY EPIC POTATO WINE RECIPE AND LIVE TO SEE YOUR GRANDCHILDREN TODDLING ABOUT?
WHY GO AT A BATTLE, UNTHINKING LIKE AN IDIOT?
THAT'S THE STYLE OF THE BERSERKER.
AN AVERAGE LIFESPAN OF TWO SUMMERS, THOSE GUYS. KINGS AND LORDS LOVE THEM.
CHUCK SOME SECONDHAND EQUIPMENT AT THEM AND A FISTFUL OF MUSHROOMS. TWENTY MINUTES LATER THEY'RE SO FUCKING HIGH THEY'RE CHEWING ON THEIR SHIELDS, UNAWARE THEIR TEETH ARE BREAKING AND THEY'RE ABOUT TO CHARGE THE ENEMY WITH A RUSTED, DULL SWORD.
NORMAL PEOPLE JUST SHAKE THEIR HEADS IN WONDER AT THE SIGHT OF A DROOLING, SPITTING BERSERKER RUNNING HEADLONG INTO A DOZEN SPEAR POINTS.
KOF
KOF...
BUT THEY HAVE THE DISTINCT ADVANTAGE OF TERRORIZING AN UNSUSPECTING ENEMY.
AND FOR THAT, FOR ALL THE BATTLES WON THAT MIGHT NOT HAVE BEEN OTHERWISE, WE'LL DRINK TO THE LUNATICS.

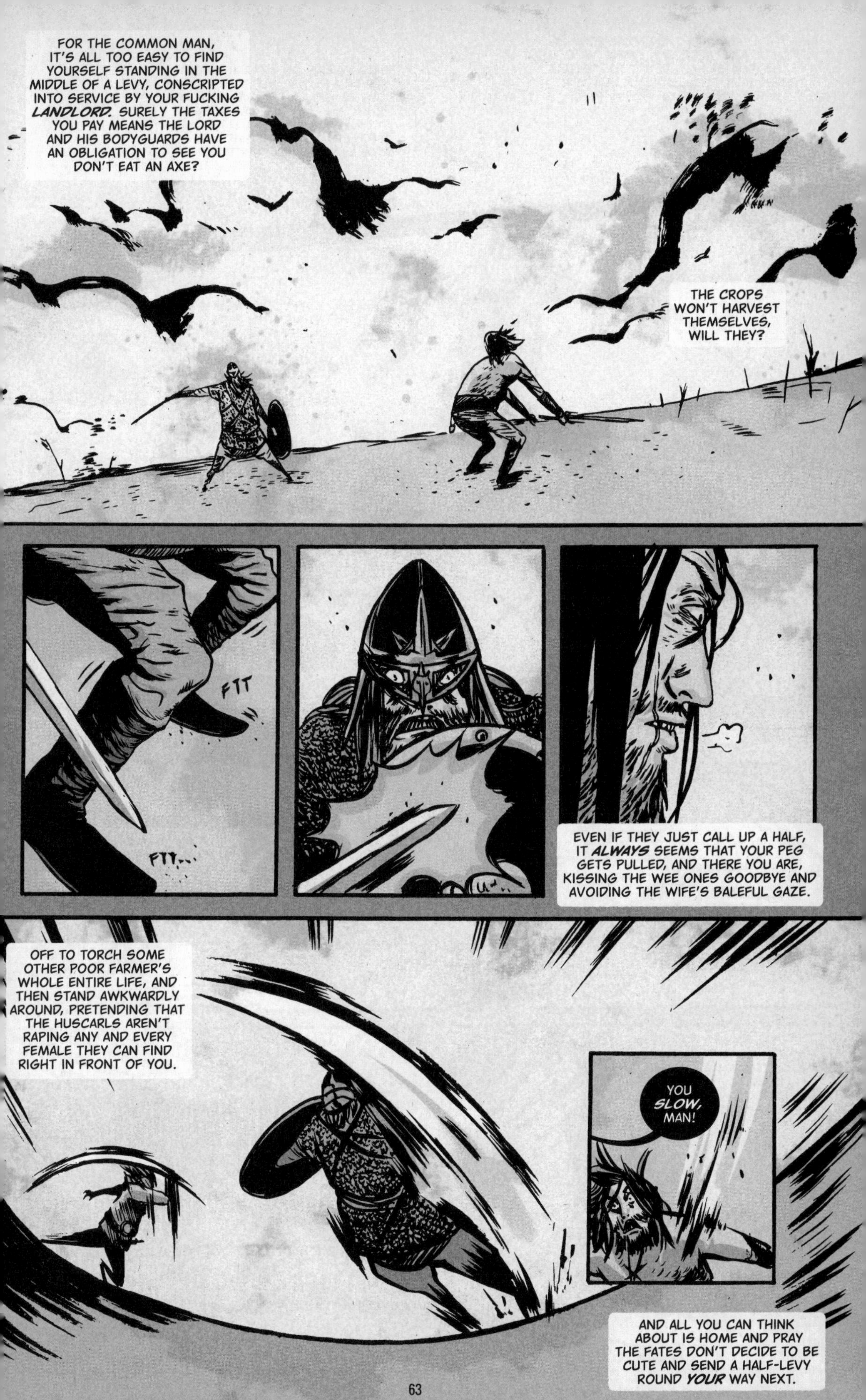
FOR THE COMMON MAN, IT'S ALL TOO EASY TO FIND YOURSELF STANDING IN THE MIDDLE OF A LEVY, CONSCRIPTED INTO SERVICE BY YOUR FUCKING LANDLORD. SURELY THE TAXES YOU PAY MEANS THE LORD AND HIS BODYGUARDS HAVE AN OBLIGATION TO SEE YOU DON'T EAT AN AXE?
THE CROPS WON'T HARVEST THEMSELVES, WILL THEY?
FTT
FTT...
EVEN IF THEY JUST CALL UP A HALF, IT ALWAYS SEEMS THAT YOUR PEG GETS PULLED, AND THERE YOU ARE, KISSING THE WEE ONES GOODBYE AND AVOIDING THE WIFE'S BALEFUL GAZE.
OFF TO TORCH SOME OTHER POOR FARMER'S WHOLE ENTIRE LIFE, AND THEN STAND AWKWARDLY AROUND, PRETENDING THAT THE HUSCARLS AREN'T RAPING ANY AND EVERY FEMALE THEY CAN FIND RIGHT IN FRONT OF YOU.
YOU SLOW, MAN!
AND ALL YOU CAN THINK ABOUT IS HOME AND PRAY THE FATES DON'T DECIDE TO BE CUTE AND SEND A HALF-LEVY ROUND YOUR WAY NEXT.

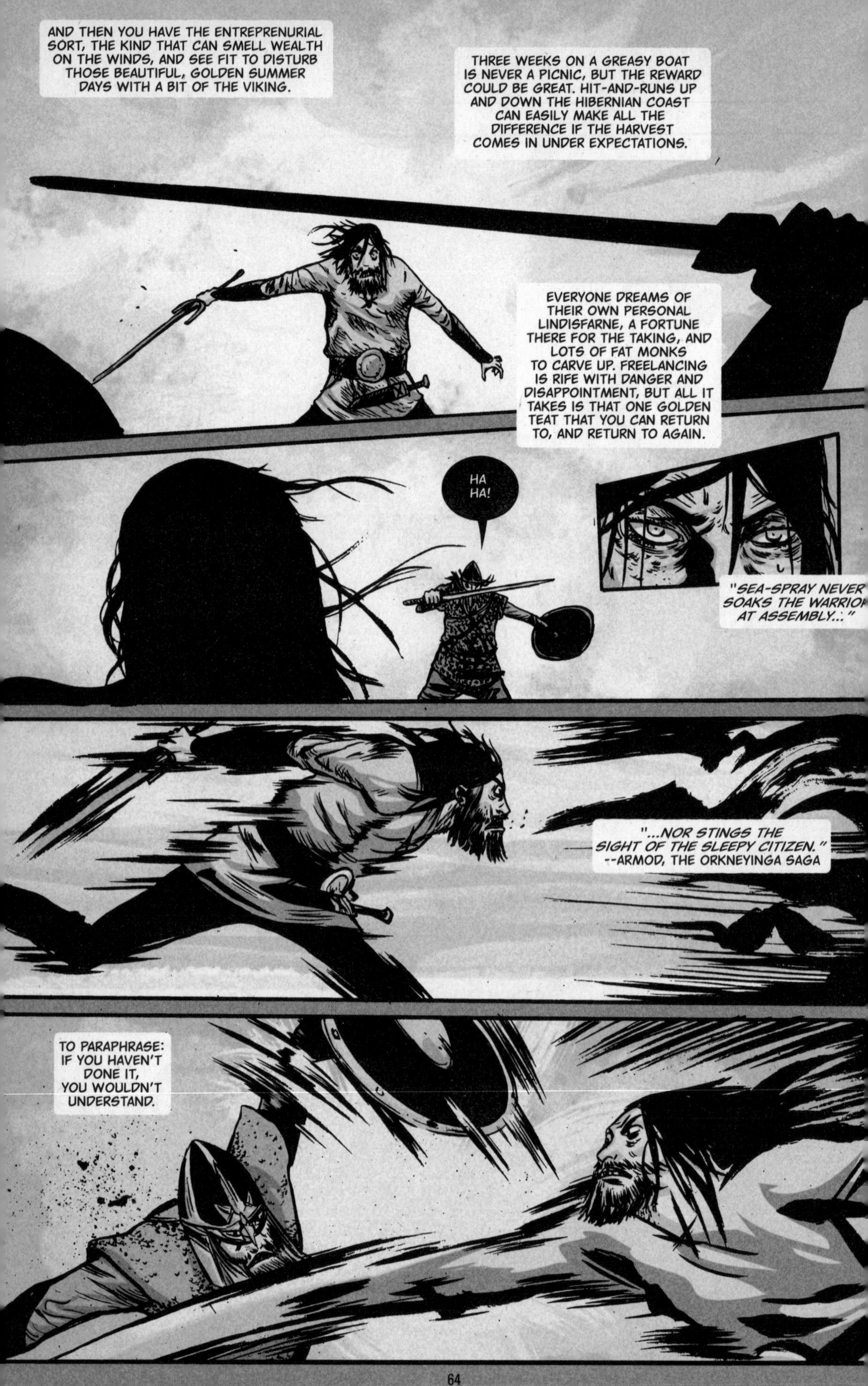
AND THEN YOU HAVE THE ENTREPRENURIAL SORT, THE KIND THAT CAN SMELL WEALTH ON THE WINDS, AND SEE FIT TO DISTURB THOSE BEAUTIFUL, GOLDEN SUMMER DAYS WITH A BIT OF THE VIKING.
THREE WEEKS ON A GREASY BOAT IS NEVER A PICNIC, BUT THE REWARD COULD BE GREAT. HIT-AND-RUNS UP AND DOWN THE HIBERNIAN COAST CAN EASILY MAKE ALL THE DIFFERENCE IF THE HARVEST COMES IN UNDER EXPECTATIONS.
EVERYONE DREAMS OF THEIR OWN PERSONAL LINDISFARNE, A FORTUNE THERE FOR THE TAKING, AND LOTS OF FAT MONKS TO CARVE UP. FREELANCING IS RIFE WITH DANGER AND DISAPPOINTMENT, BUT ALL IT TAKES IS THAT ONE GOLDEN TEAT THAT YOU CAN RETURN TO, AND RETURN TO AGAIN.
HA HA!
"SEA-SPRAY NEVER SOAKS THE WARRIOR AT ASSEMBLY..."
"...NOR STINGS THE SIGHT OF THE SLEEPY CITIZEN." --ARMOD, THE ORKNEYINGA SAGA
TO PARAPHRASE: IF YOU HAVEN'T DONE IT, YOU WOULDN'T UNDERSTAND.

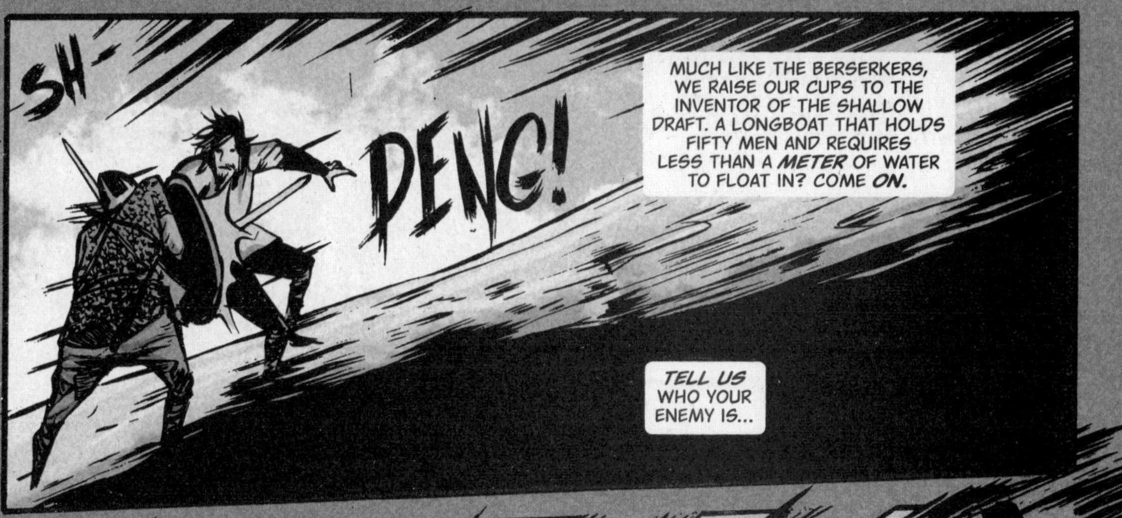
SH-
DENG!
MUCH LIKE THE BERSERKERS, WE RAISE OUR CUPS TO THE INVENTOR OF THE SHALLOW DRAFT. A LONGBOAT THAT HOLDS FIFTY MEN AND REQUIRES LESS THAN A METER OF WATER TO FLOAT IN? COME ON.
TELL US WHO YOUR ENEMY IS...

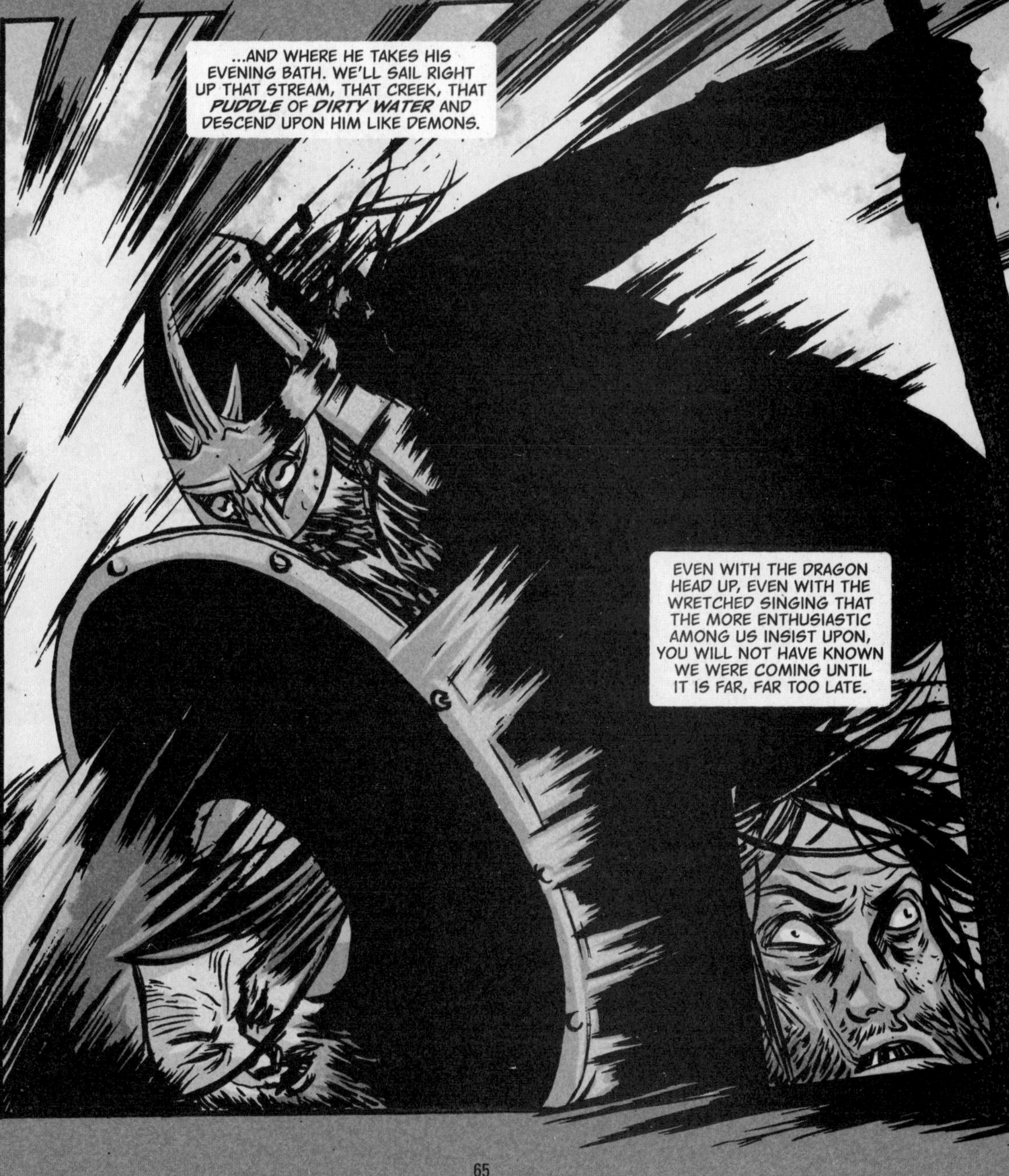
...AND WHERE HE TAKES HIS EVENING BATH. WE'LL SAIL RIGHT UP THAT STREAM, THAT CREEK, THAT PUDDLE OF DIRTY WATER AND DESCEND UPON HIM LIKE DEMONS.
EVEN WITH THE DRAGON HEAD UP, EVEN WITH THE WRETCHED SINGING THAT THE MORE ENTHUSIASTIC AMONG US INSIST UPON, YOU WILL NOT HAVE KNOWN WE WERE COMING UNTIL IT IS FAR, FAR TOO LATE.

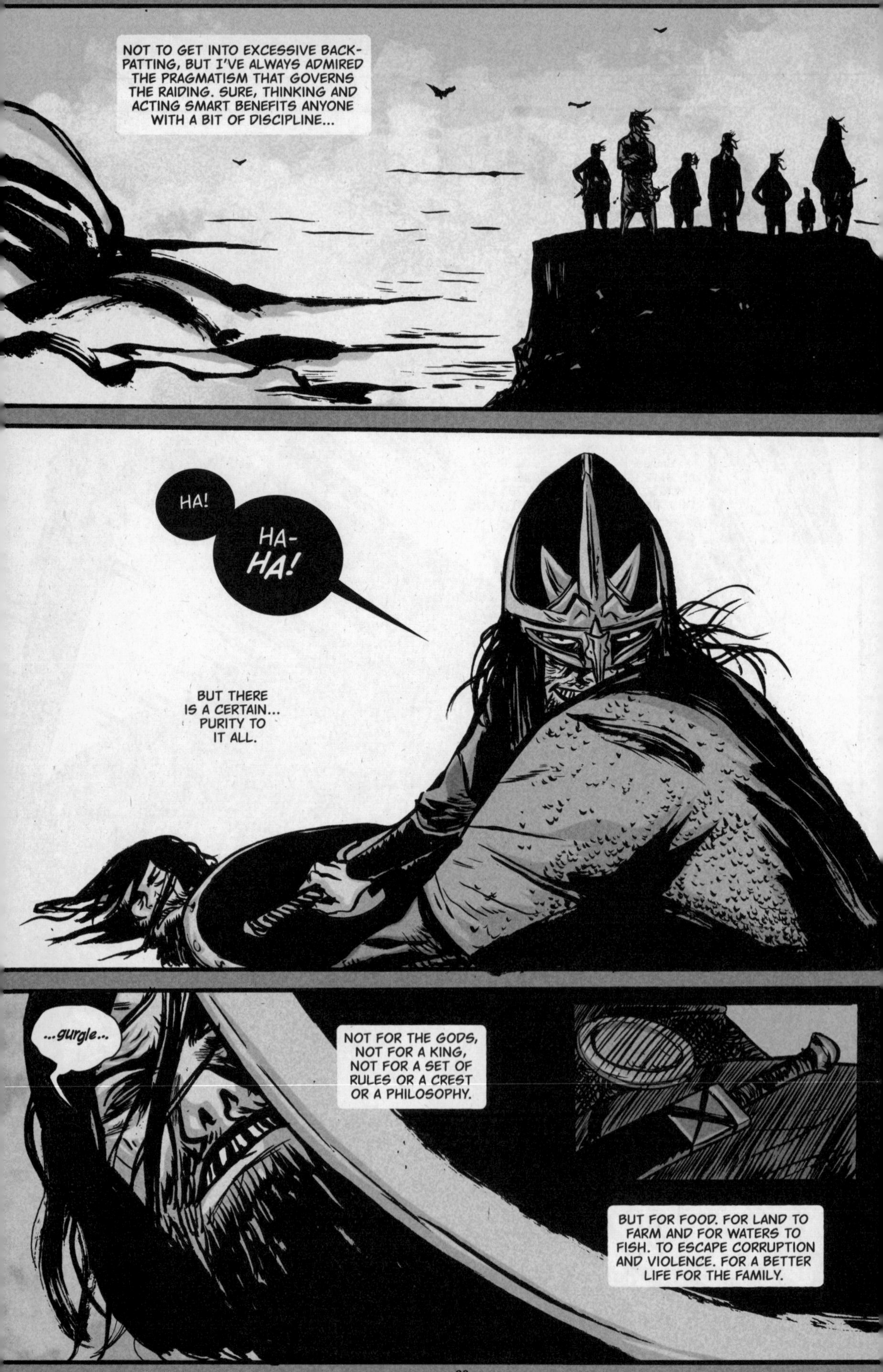
NOT TO GET INTO EXCESSIVE BACK-PATTING, BUT I'VE ALWAYS ADMIRED THE PRAGMATISM THAT GOVERNS THE RAIDING. SURE, THINKING AND ACTING SMART BENEFITS ANYONE WITH A BIT OF DISCIPLINE...
HA!
HA-HA!
BUT THERE IS A CERTAIN... PURITY TO IT ALL.
...gurgle...
NOT FOR THE GODS, NOT FOR A KING, NOT FOR A SET OF RULES OR A CREST OR A PHILOSOPHY.
BUT FOR FOOD. FOR LAND TO FARM AND FOR WATERS TO FISH. TO ESCAPE CORRUPTION AND VIOLENCE. FOR A BETTER LIFE FOR THE FAMILY.

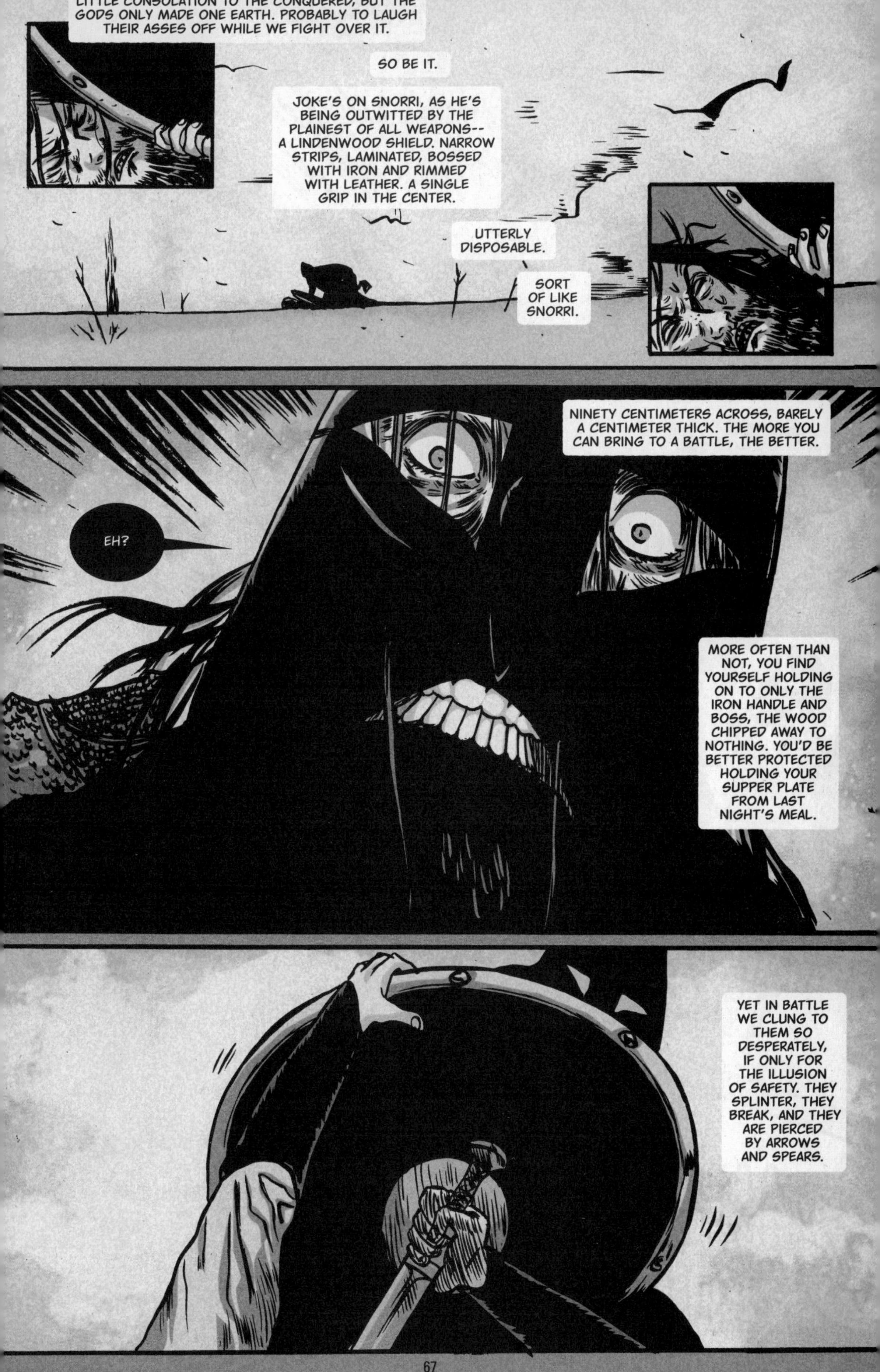
LITTLE CONSOLATION TO THE CONQUERED, BUT THE GODS ONLY MADE ONE EARTH. PROBABLY TO LAUGH THEIR ASSES OFF WHILE WE FIGHT OVER IT.
SO BE IT.
JOKE'S ON SNORRI, AS HE'S BEING OUTWITTED BY THE PLAINEST OF ALL WEAPONS-- A LINDENWOOD SHIELD. NARROW STRIPS, LAMINATED, BOSSED WITH IRON AND RIMMED WITH LEATHER. A SINGLE GRIP IN THE CENTER.
UTTERLY DISPOSABLE.
SORT OF LIKE SNORRI.
NINETY CENTIMETERS ACROSS, BARELY A CENTIMETER THICK. THE MORE YOU CAN BRING TO A BATTLE, THE BETTER.
EH?
MORE OFTEN THAN NOT, YOU FIND YOURSELF HOLDING ON TO ONLY THE IRON HANDLE AND BOSS, THE WOOD CHIPPED AWAY TO NOTHING. YOU'D BE BETTER PROTECTED HOLDING YOUR SUPPER PLATE FROM LAST NIGHT'S MEAL.
YET IN BATTLE WE CLUNG TO THEM SO DESPERATELY, IF ONLY FOR THE ILLUSION OF SAFETY. THEY SPLINTER, THEY BREAK, AND THEY ARE PIERCED BY ARROWS AND SPEARS.

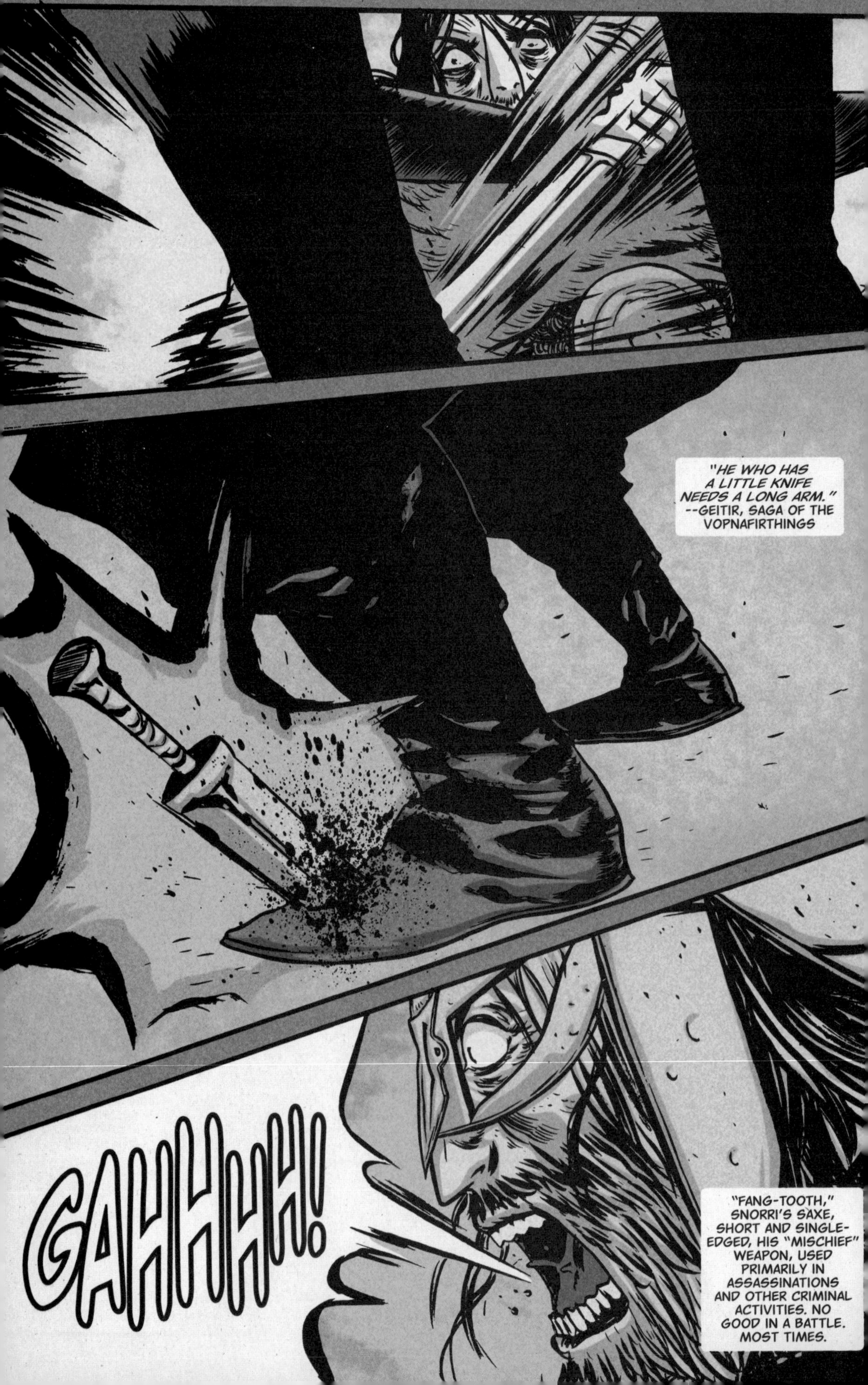
"HE WHO HAS A LITTLE KNIFE NEEDS A LONG ARM." --GEITIR, SAGA OF THE VOPNAFIRTHINGS
GAHHHH!
"FANG-TOOTH," SNORRI'S SAXE, SHORT AND SINGLE-EDGED, HIS "MISCHIEF" WEAPON, USED PRIMARILY IN ASSASSINATIONS AND OTHER CRIMINAL ACTIVITIES. NO GOOD IN A BATTLE. MOST TIMES.

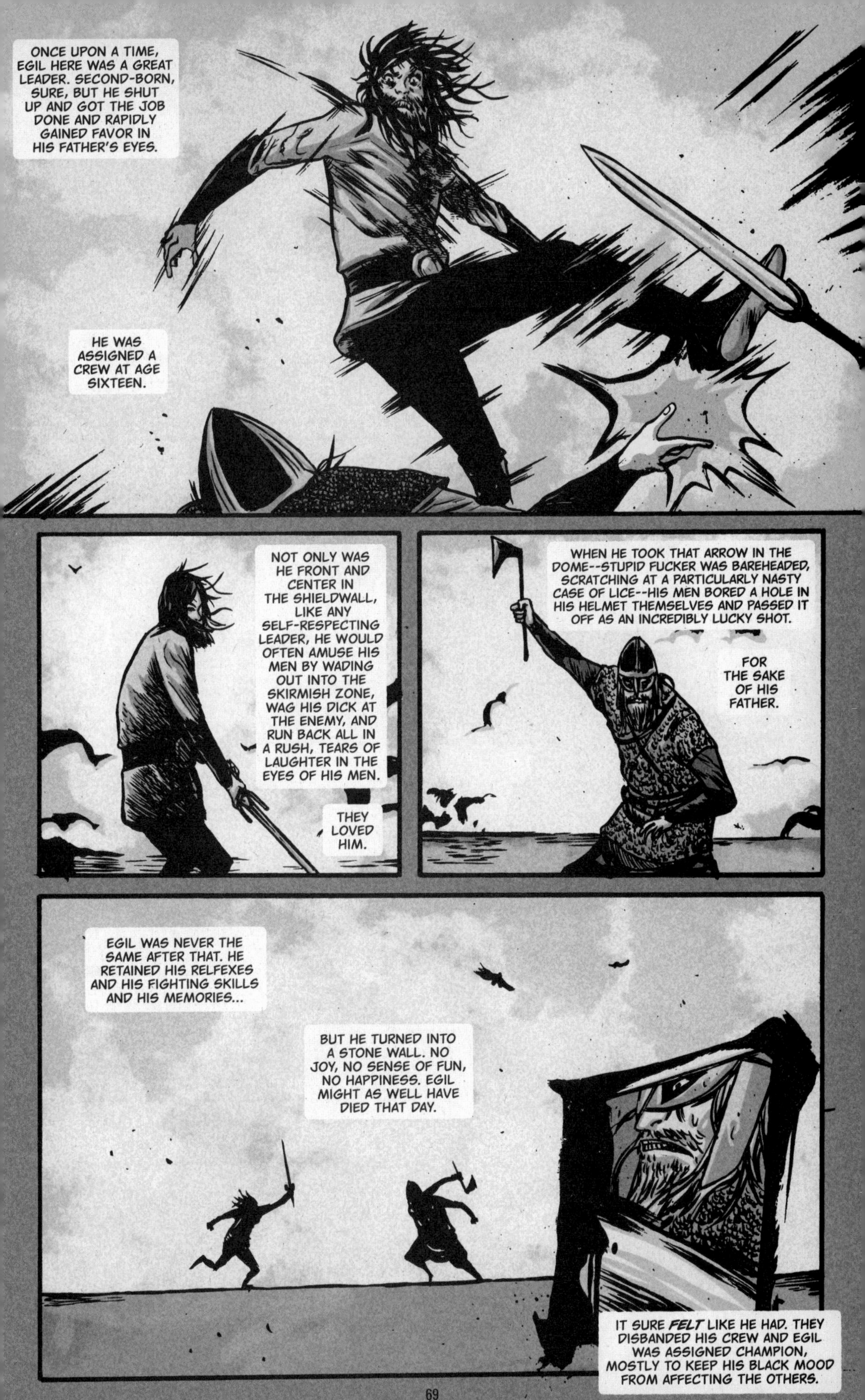
ONCE UPON A TIME, EGIL HERE WAS A GREAT LEADER. SECOND-BORN, SURE, BUT HE SHUT UP AND GOT THE JOB DONE AND RAPIDLY GAINED FAVOR IN HIS FATHER'S EYES.
HE WAS ASSIGNED A CREW AT AGE SIXTEEN.
NOT ONLY WAS HE FRONT AND CENTER IN THE SHIELDWALL, LIKE ANY SELF-RESPECTING LEADER, HE WOULD OFTEN AMUSE HIS MEN BY WADING OUT INTO THE SKIRMISH ZONE, WAG HIS DICK AT THE ENEMY, AND RUN BACK ALL IN A RUSH, TEARS OF LAUGHTER IN THE EYES OF HIS MEN.
THEY LOVED HIM.
WHEN HE TOOK THAT ARROW IN THE DOME--STUPID FUCKER WAS BAREHEADED, SCRATCHING AT A PARTICULARLY NASTY CASE OF LICE--HIS MEN BORED A HOLE IN HIS HELMET THEMSELVES AND PASSED IT OFF AS AN INCREDIBLY LUCKY SHOT.
FOR THE SAKE OF HIS FATHER.
EGIL WAS NEVER THE SAME AFTER THAT. HE RETAINED HIS RELFEXES AND HIS FIGHTING SKILLS AND HIS MEMORIES...
BUT HE TURNED INTO A STONE WALL. NO JOY, NO SENSE OF FUN, NO HAPPINESS. EGIL MIGHT AS WELL HAVE DIED THAT DAY.
IT SURE *FELT* LIKE HE HAD. THEY DISBANDED HIS CREW AND EGIL WAS ASSIGNED CHAMPION, MOSTLY TO KEEP HIS BLACK MOOD FROM AFFECTING THE OTHERS.

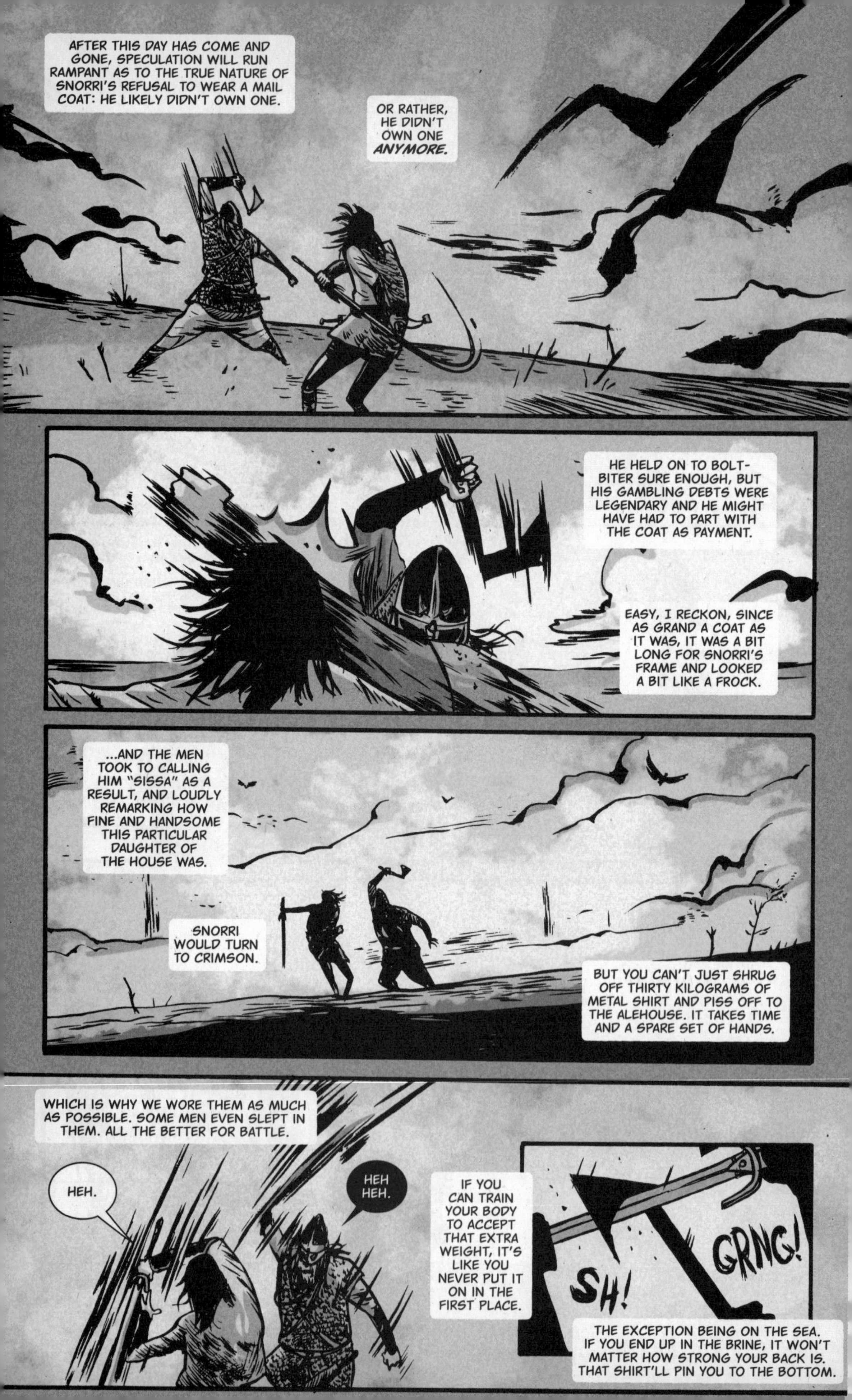
AFTER THIS DAY HAS COME AND GONE, SPECULATION WILL RUN RAMPANT AS TO THE TRUE NATURE OF SNORRI'S REFUSAL TO WEAR A MAIL COAT: HE LIKELY DIDN'T OWN ONE.
OR RATHER, HE DIDN'T OWN ONE *ANYMORE*.
HE HELD ON TO BOLT-BITER SURE ENOUGH, BUT HIS GAMBLING DEBTS WERE LEGENDARY AND HE MIGHT HAVE HAD TO PART WITH THE COAT AS PAYMENT.
EASY, I RECKON, SINCE AS GRAND A COAT AS IT WAS, IT WAS A BIT LONG FOR SNORRI'S FRAME AND LOOKED A BIT LIKE A FROCK.
...AND THE MEN TOOK TO CALLING HIM "SISSA" AS A RESULT, AND LOUDLY REMARKING HOW FINE AND HANDSOME THIS PARTICULAR DAUGHTER OF THE HOUSE WAS.
SNORRI WOULD TURN TO CRIMSON.
BUT YOU CAN'T JUST SHRUG OFF THIRTY KILOGRAMS OF METAL SHIRT AND PISS OFF TO THE ALEHOUSE. IT TAKES TIME AND A SPARE SET OF HANDS.
WHICH IS WHY WE WORE THEM AS MUCH AS POSSIBLE. SOME MEN EVEN SLEPT IN THEM. ALL THE BETTER FOR BATTLE.
HEH.
HEH HEH.
IF YOU CAN TRAIN YOUR BODY TO ACCEPT THAT EXTRA WEIGHT, IT'S LIKE YOU NEVER PUT IT ON IN THE FIRST PLACE.
SH!
GRNG!
THE EXCEPTION BEING ON THE SEA. IF YOU END UP IN THE BRINE, IT WON'T MATTER HOW STRONG YOUR BACK IS. THAT SHIRT'LL PIN YOU TO THE BOTTOM.

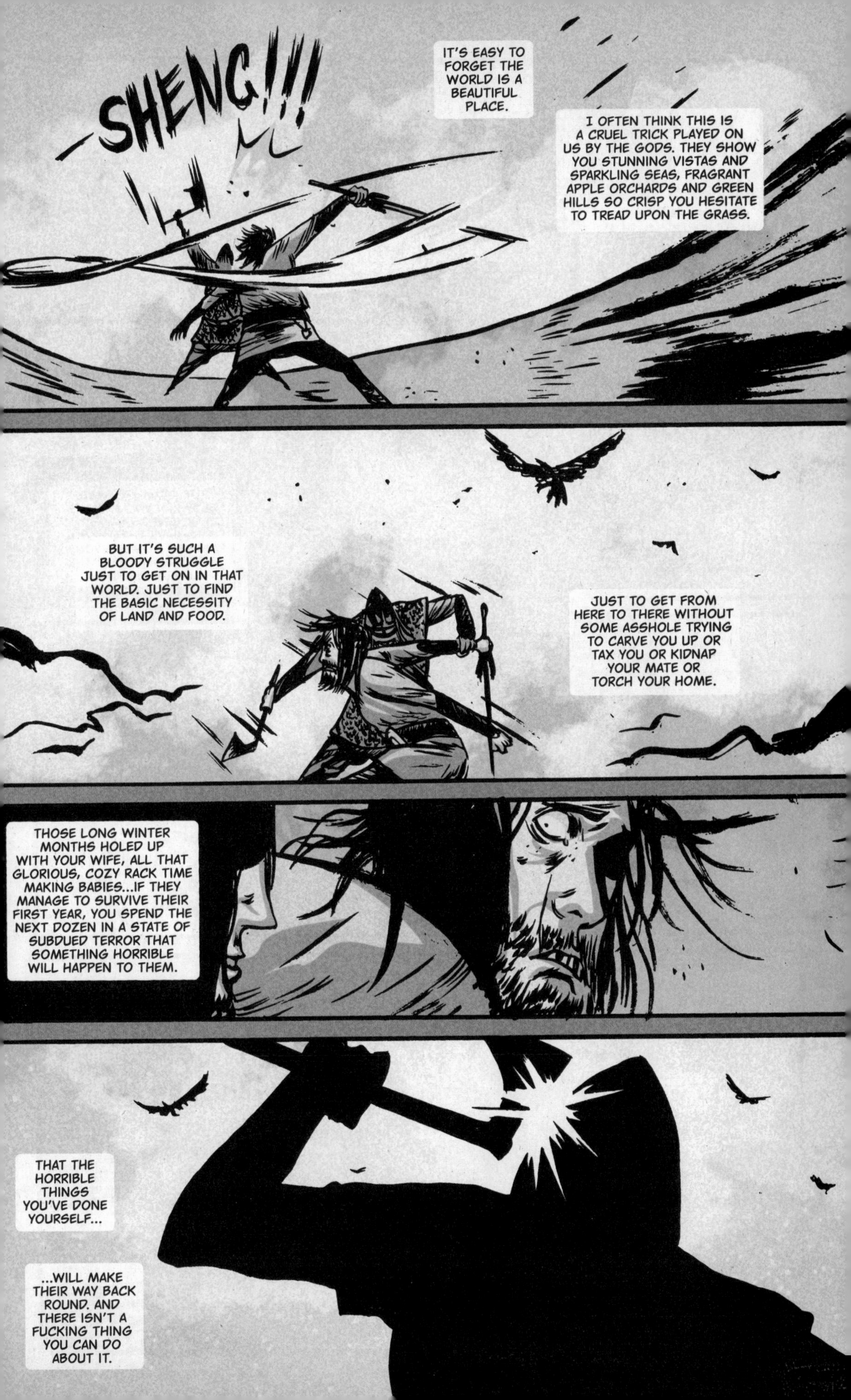
SHENG!!!
IT'S EASY TO FORGET THE WORLD IS A BEAUTIFUL PLACE.
I OFTEN THINK THIS IS A CRUEL TRICK PLAYED ON US BY THE GODS. THEY SHOW YOU STUNNING VISTAS AND SPARKLING SEAS, FRAGRANT APPLE ORCHARDS AND GREEN HILLS SO CRISP YOU HESITATE TO TREAD UPON THE GRASS.
BUT IT'S SUCH A BLOODY STRUGGLE JUST TO GET ON IN THAT WORLD. JUST TO FIND THE BASIC NECESSITY OF LAND AND FOOD.
JUST TO GET FROM HERE TO THERE WITHOUT SOME ASSHOLE TRYING TO CARVE YOU UP OR TAX YOU OR KIDNAP YOUR MATE OR TORCH YOUR HOME.
THOSE LONG WINTER MONTHS HOLED UP WITH YOUR WIFE, ALL THAT GLORIOUS, COZY RACK TIME MAKING BABIES...IF THEY MANAGE TO SURVIVE THEIR FIRST YEAR, YOU SPEND THE NEXT DOZEN IN A STATE OF SUBDUED TERROR THAT SOMETHING HORRIBLE WILL HAPPEN TO THEM.
THAT THE HORRIBLE THINGS YOU'VE DONE YOURSELF...
...WILL MAKE THEIR WAY BACK ROUND. AND THERE ISN'T A FUCKING THING YOU CAN DO ABOUT IT.

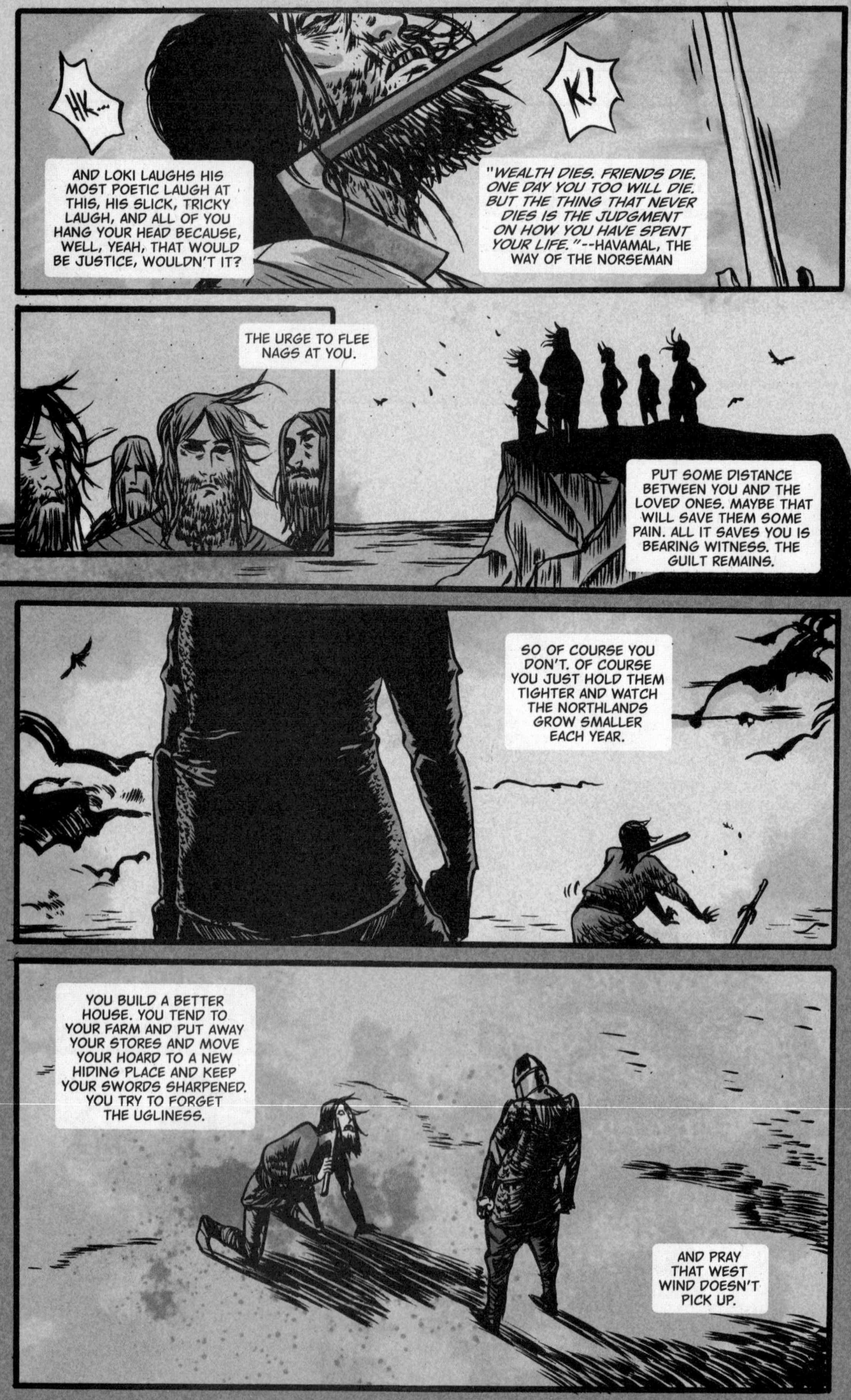
HK...
K!
AND LOKI LAUGHS HIS MOST POETIC LAUGH AT THIS, HIS SLICK, TRICKY LAUGH, AND ALL OF YOU HANG YOUR HEAD BECAUSE, WELL, YEAH, THAT WOULD BE JUSTICE, WOULDN'T IT?
"WEALTH DIES. FRIENDS DIE. ONE DAY YOU TOO WILL DIE. BUT THE THING THAT NEVER DIES IS THE JUDGMENT ON HOW YOU HAVE SPENT YOUR LIFE." --HAVAMAL, THE WAY OF THE NORSEMAN
THE URGE TO FLEE NAGS AT YOU.
PUT SOME DISTANCE BETWEEN YOU AND THE LOVED ONES. MAYBE THAT WILL SAVE THEM SOME PAIN. ALL IT SAVES YOU IS BEARING WITNESS. THE GUILT REMAINS.
SO OF COURSE YOU DON'T. OF COURSE YOU JUST HOLD THEM TIGHTER AND WATCH THE NORTHLANDS GROW SMALLER EACH YEAR.
YOU BUILD A BETTER HOUSE. YOU TEND TO YOUR FARM AND PUT AWAY YOUR STORES AND MOVE YOUR HOARD TO A NEW HIDING PLACE AND KEEP YOUR SWORDS SHARPENED. YOU TRY TO FORGET THE UGLINESS.
AND PRAY THAT WEST WIND DOESN'T PICK UP.

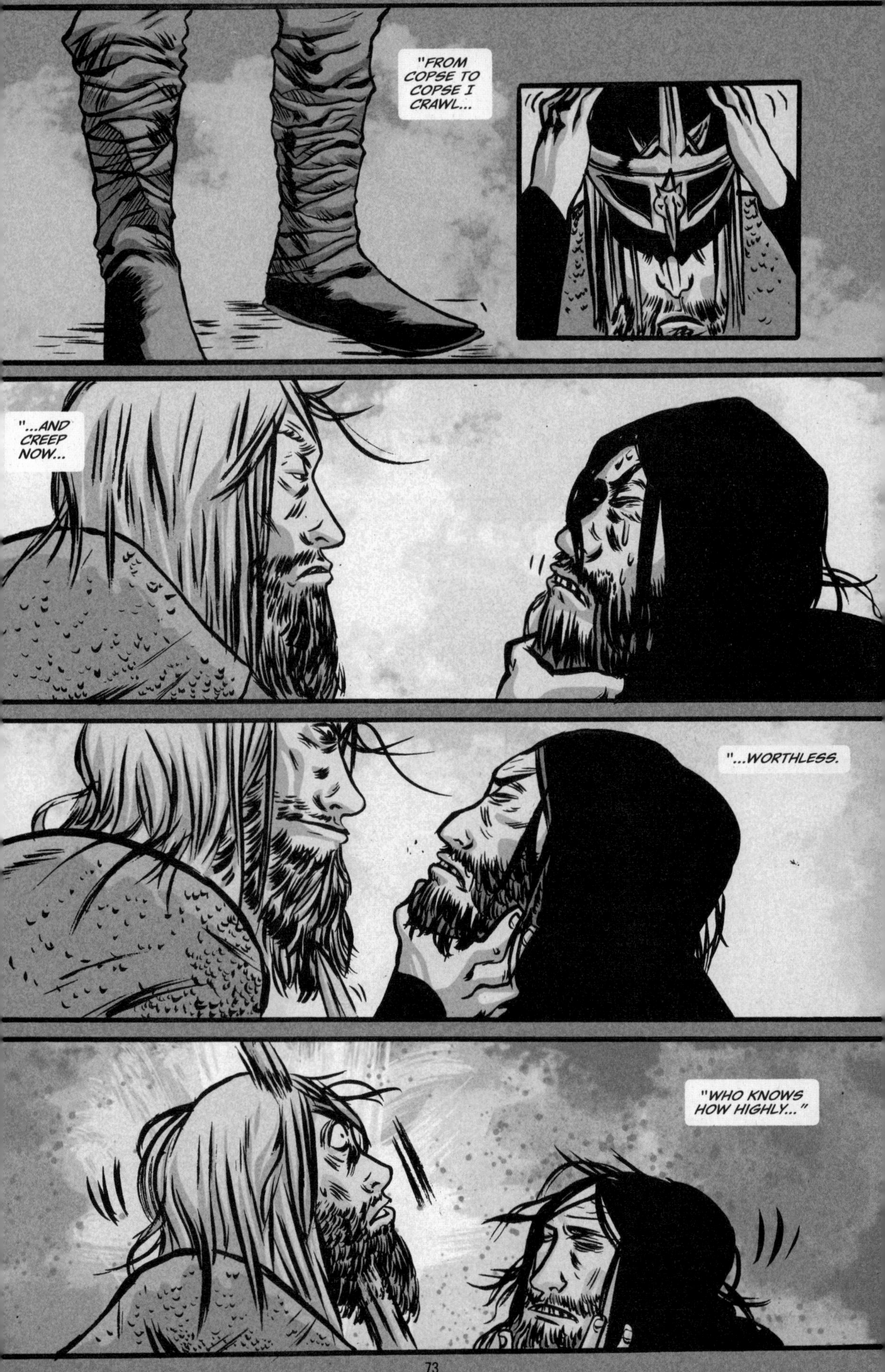
"FROM COPSE TO COPSE I CRAWL...
"...AND CREEP NOW...
"...WORTHLESS.
"WHO KNOWS HOW HIGHLY..."

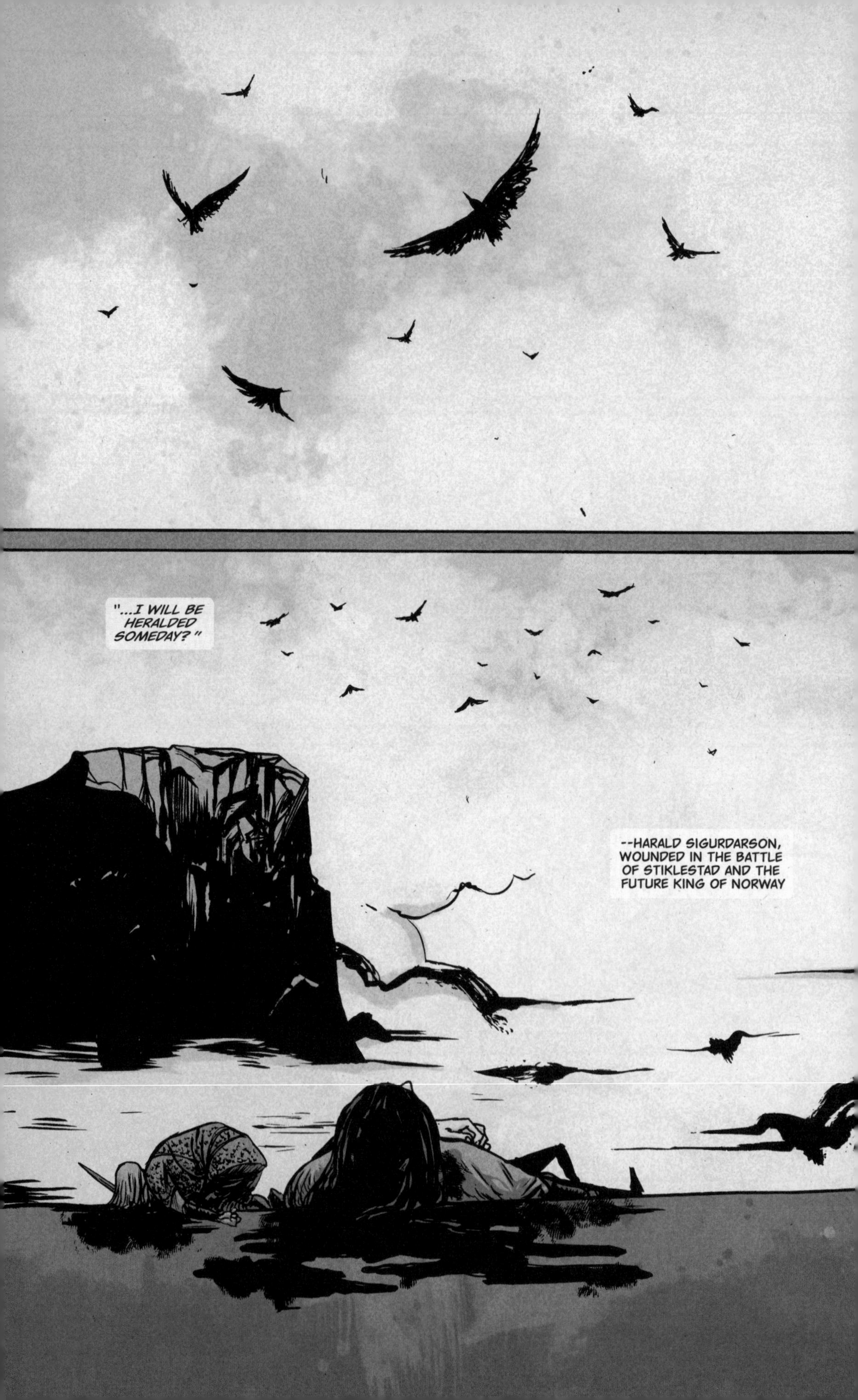
"...I WILL BE HERALDED SOMEDAY?"
--HARALD SIGURDARSON, WOUNDED IN THE BATTLE OF STIKLESTAD AND THE FUTURE KING OF NORWAY

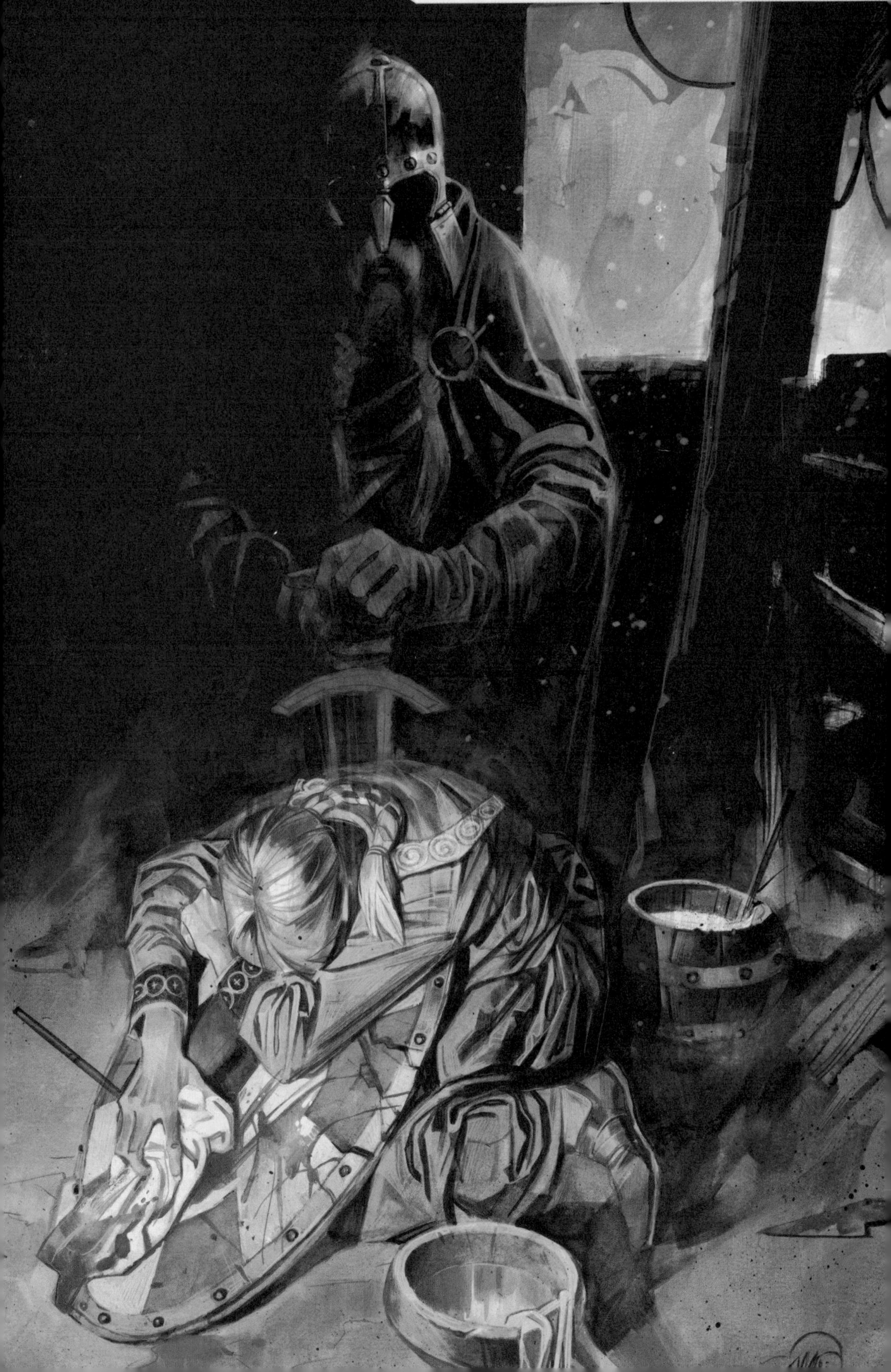

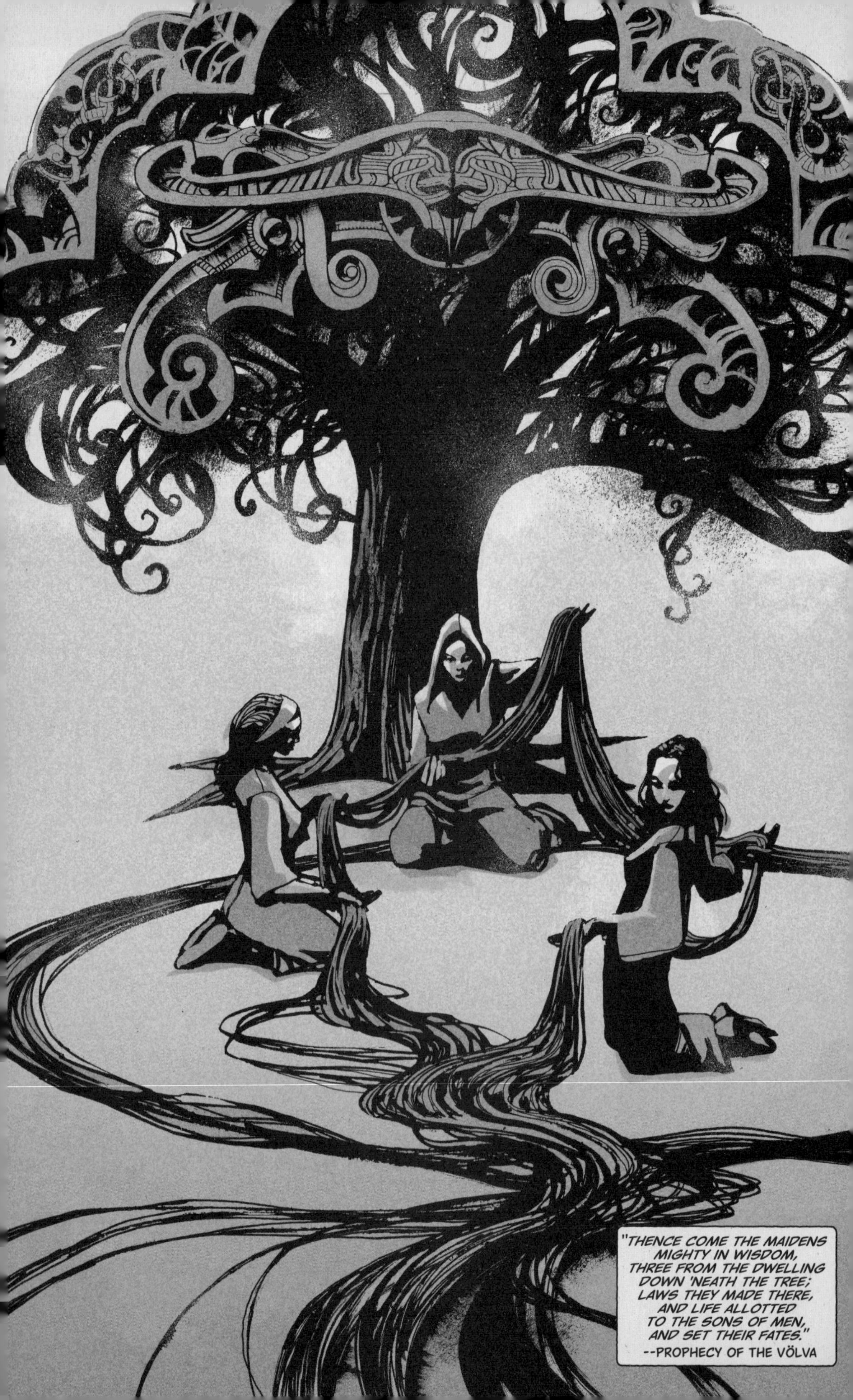
"THENCE COME THE MAIDENS MIGHTY IN WISDOM, THREE FROM THE DWELLING DOWN 'NEATH THE TREE; LAWS THEY MADE THERE, AND LIFE ALLOTTED TO THE SONS OF MEN, AND SET THEIR FATES."
--PROPHECY OF THE VÖLVA

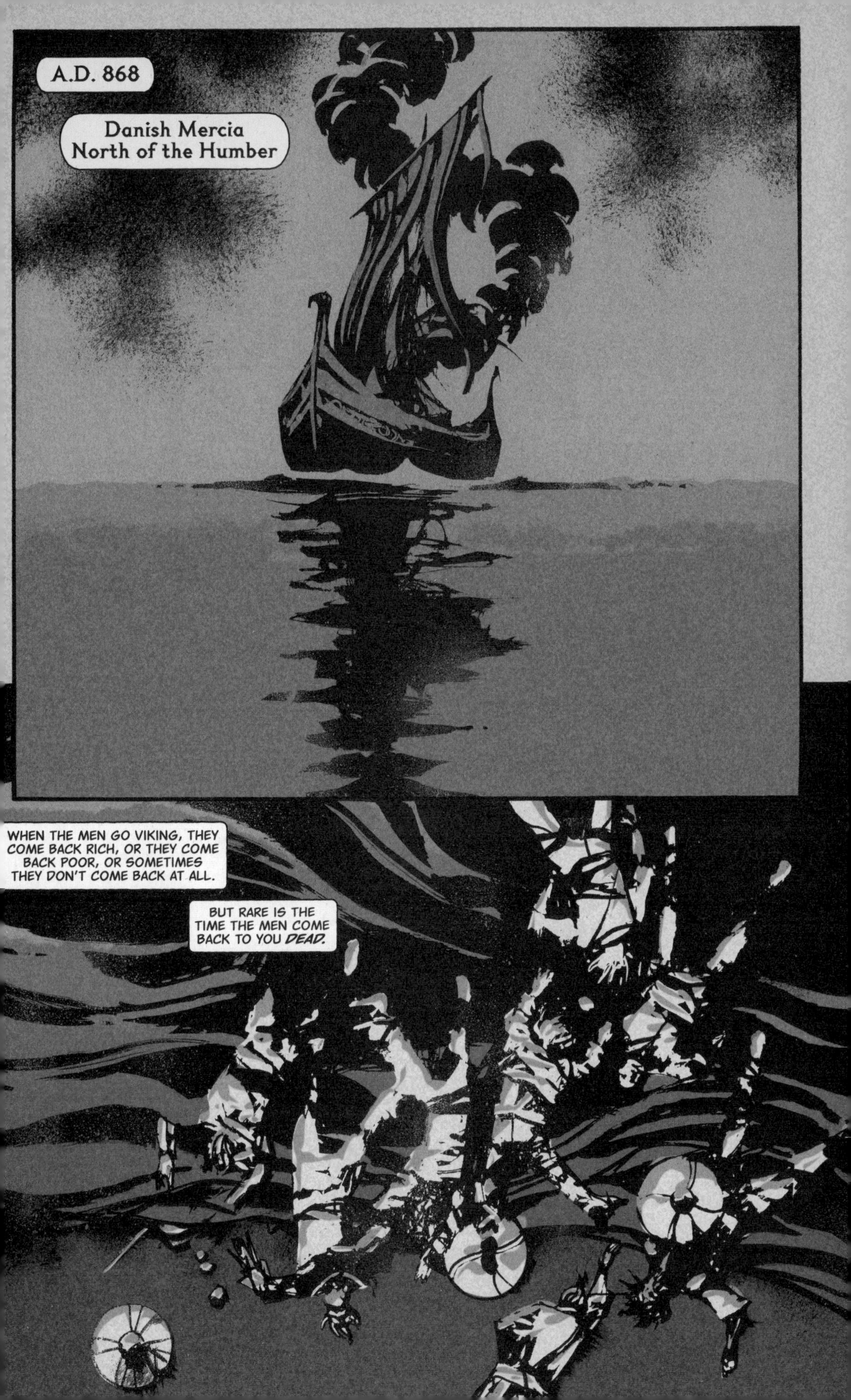
A.D. 868
Danish Mercia
North of the Humber
WHEN THE MEN GO VIKING, THEY COME BACK RICH, OR THEY COME BACK POOR, OR SOMETIMES THEY DON'T COME BACK AT ALL.
BUT RARE IS THE TIME THE MEN COME BACK TO YOU *DEAD.*

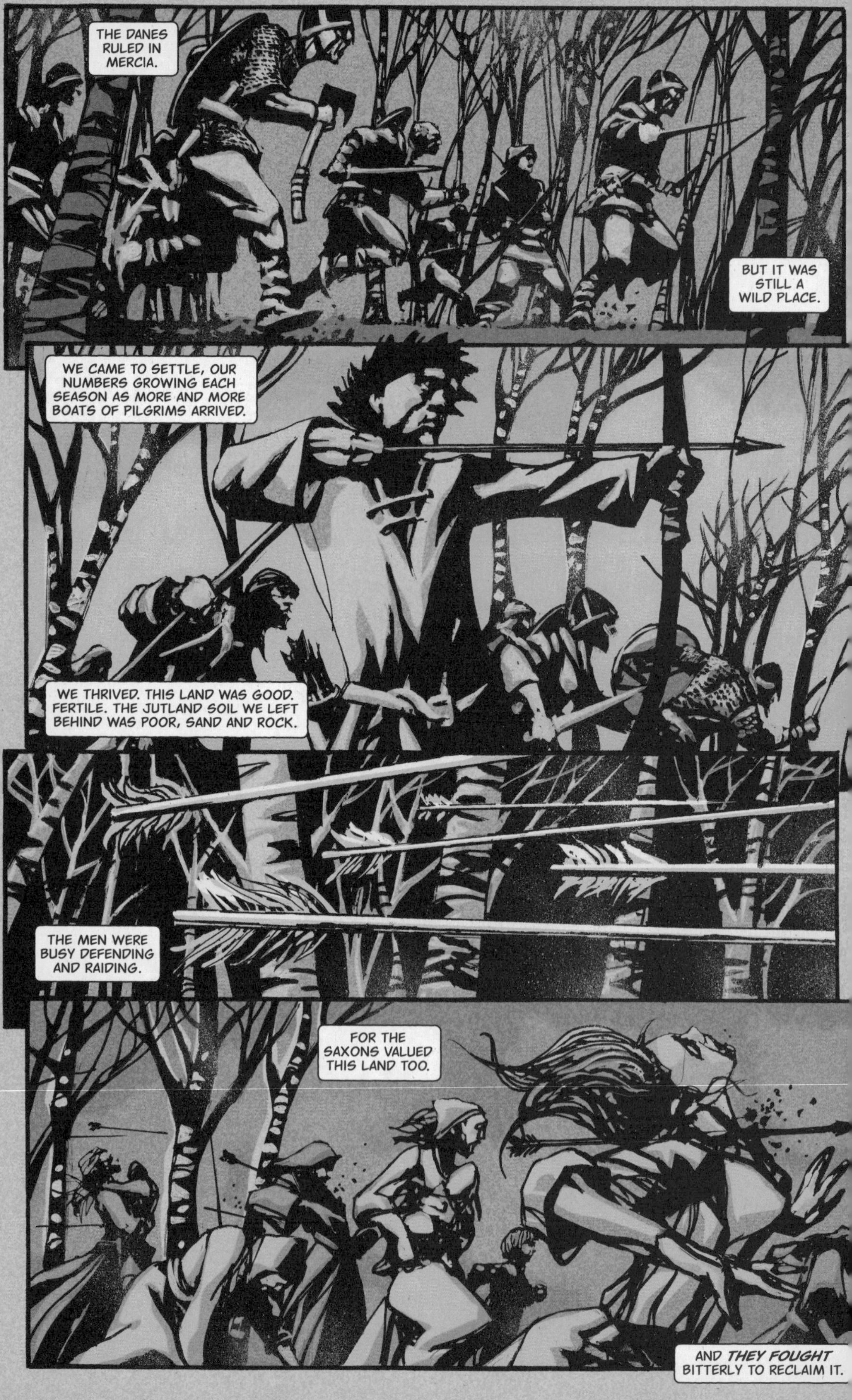
THE DANES RULED IN MERCIA.
BUT IT WAS STILL A WILD PLACE.
WE CAME TO SETTLE, OUR NUMBERS GROWING EACH SEASON AS MORE AND MORE BOATS OF PILGRIMS ARRIVED.
WE THRIVED. THIS LAND WAS GOOD. FERTILE. THE JUTLAND SOIL WE LEFT BEHIND WAS POOR, SAND AND ROCK.
THE MEN WERE BUSY DEFENDING AND RAIDING.
FOR THE SAXONS VALUED THIS LAND TOO.
AND *THEY FOUGHT* BITTERLY TO RECLAIM IT.

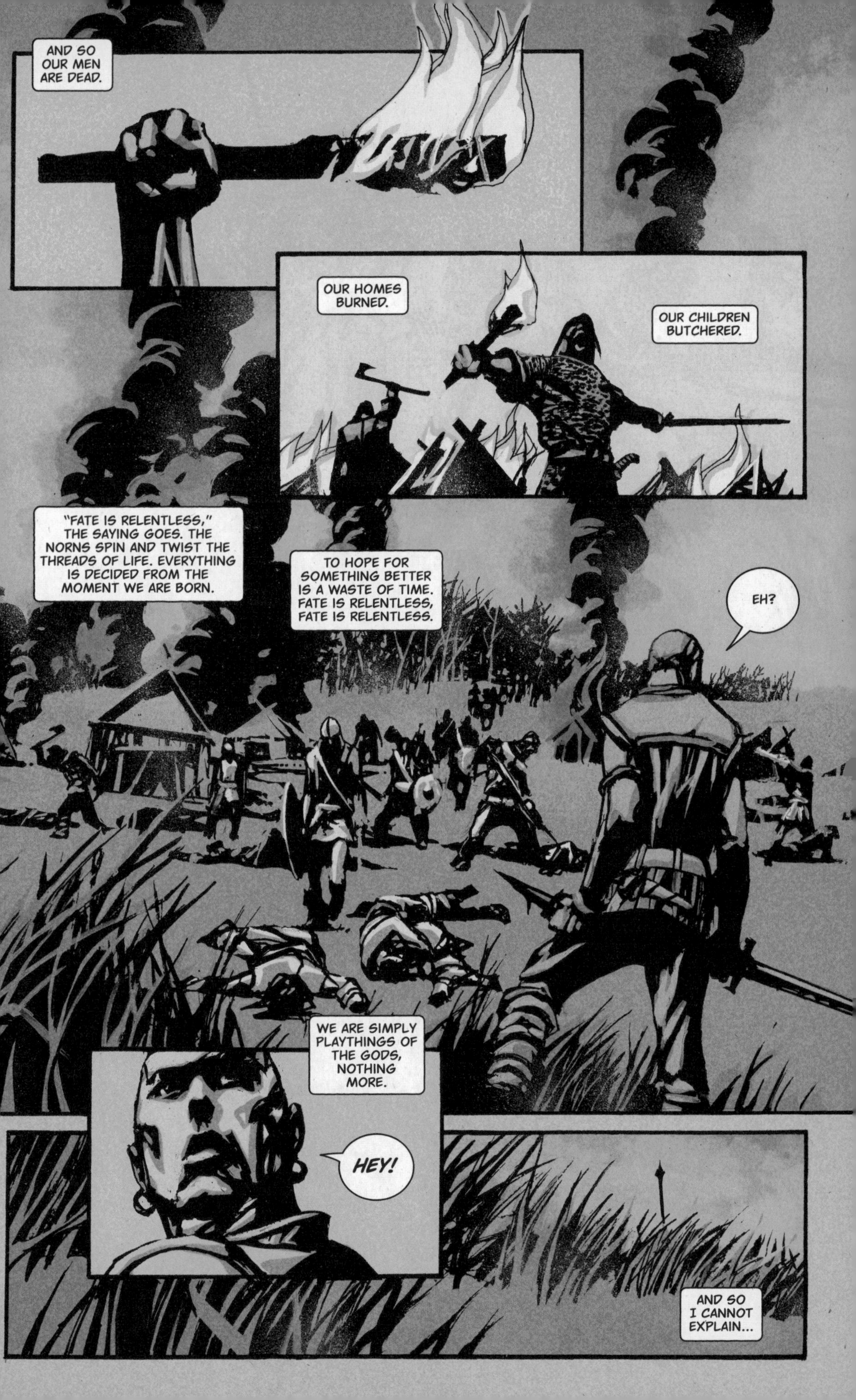
AND SO OUR MEN ARE DEAD.
OUR HOMES BURNED.
OUR CHILDREN BUTCHERED.
"FATE IS RELENTLESS," THE SAYING GOES. THE NORNS SPIN AND TWIST THE THREADS OF LIFE. EVERYTHING IS DECIDED FROM THE MOMENT WE ARE BORN.
TO HOPE FOR SOMETHING BETTER IS A WASTE OF TIME. FATE IS RELENTLESS, FATE IS RELENTLESS.
EH?
WE ARE SIMPLY PLAYTHINGS OF THE GODS, NOTHING MORE.
HEY!
AND SO I CANNOT EXPLAIN...

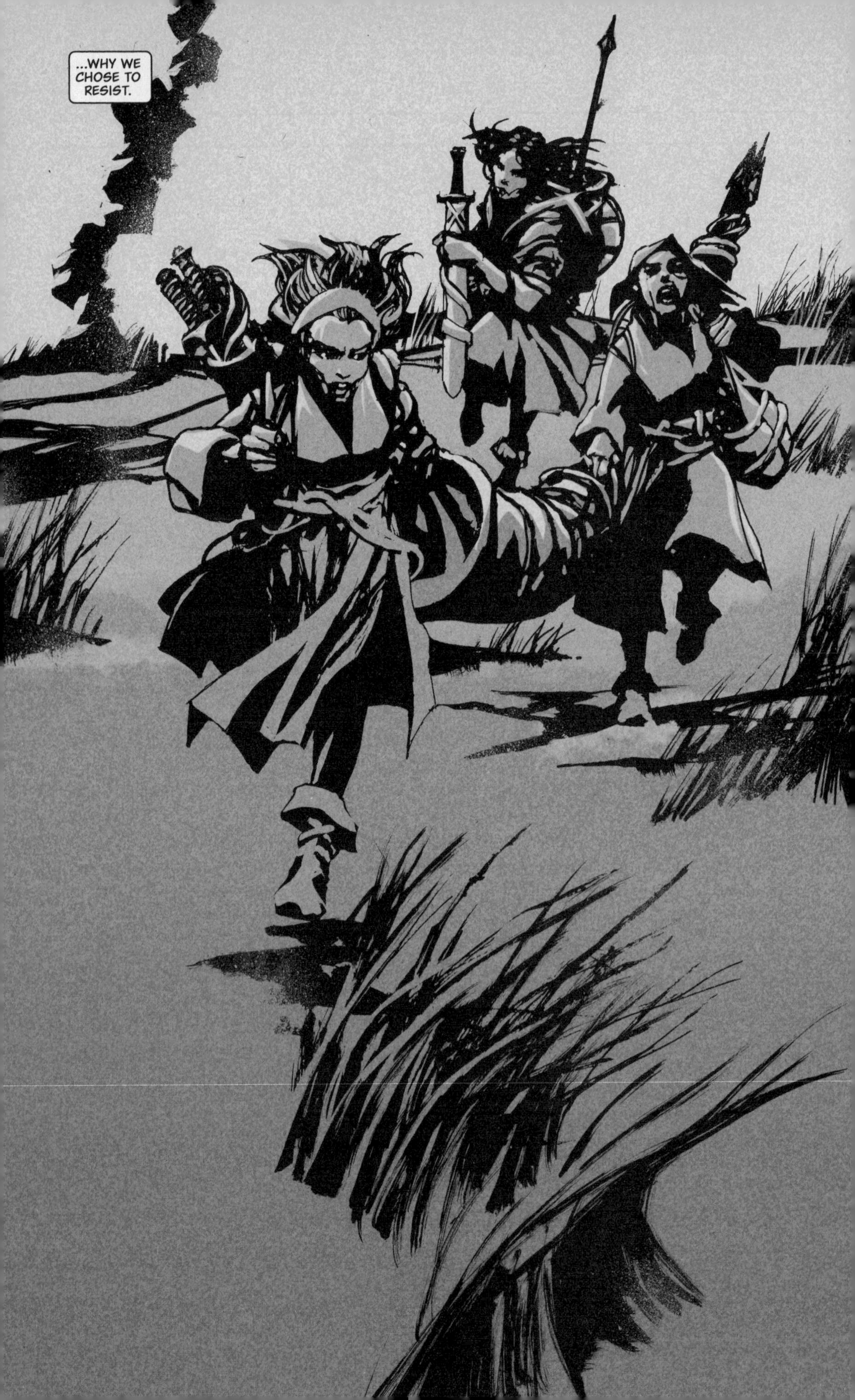
...WHY WE CHOSE TO RESIST.

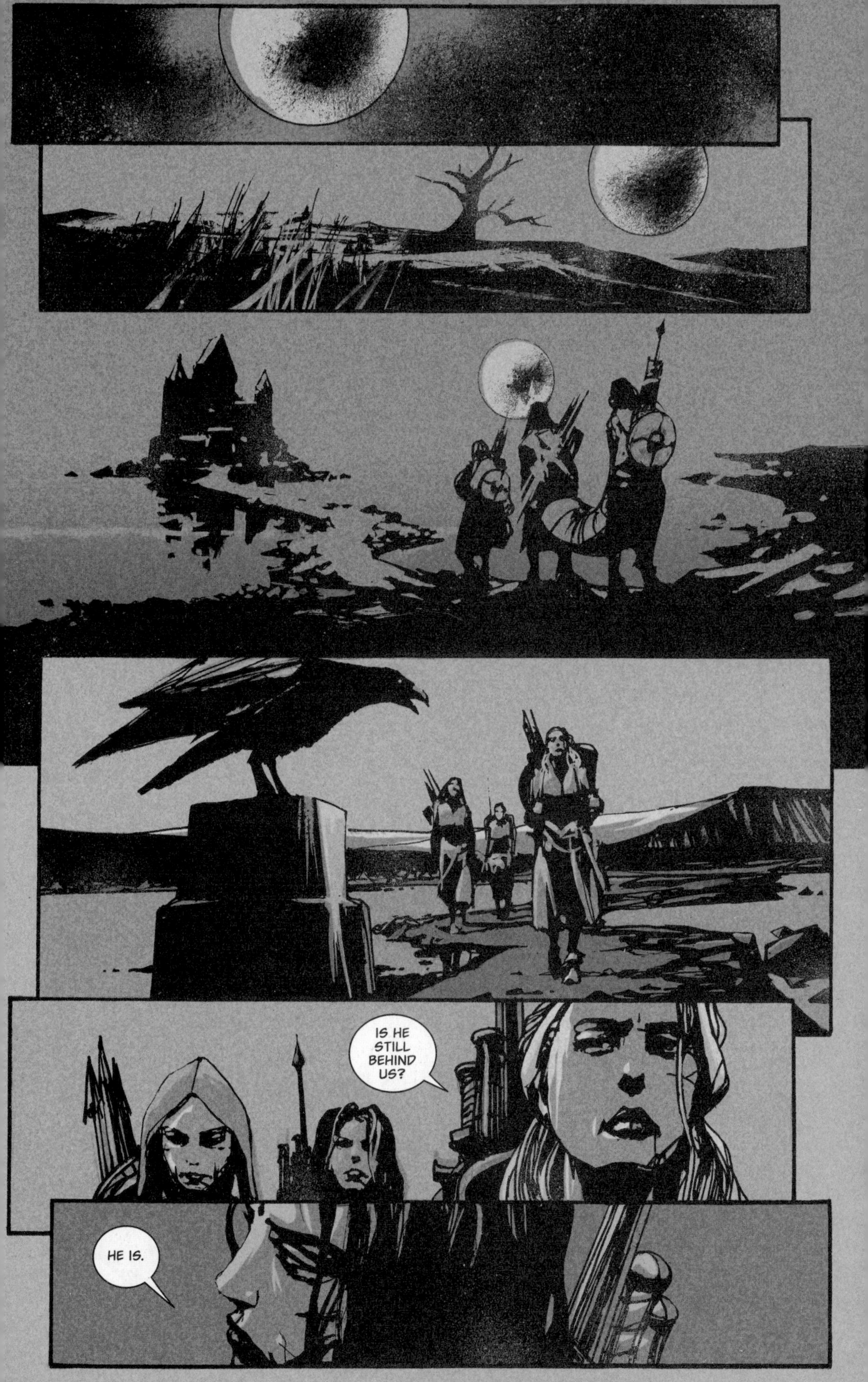
IS HE STILL BEHIND US?
HE IS.

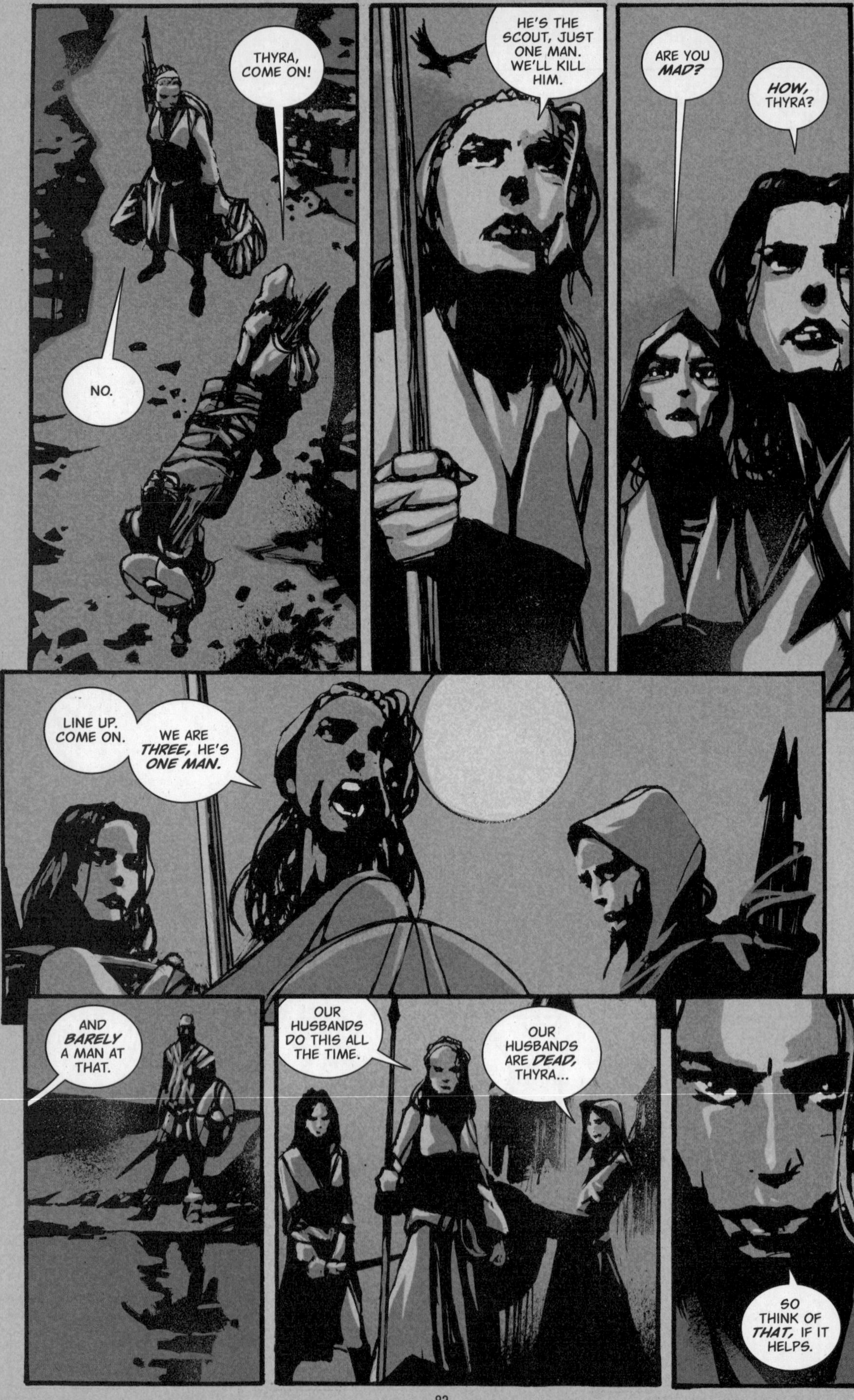
THYRA, COME ON!
NO.
HE'S THE SCOUT, JUST ONE MAN. WE'LL KILL HIM.
ARE YOU *MAD?*
HOW, THYRA?
LINE UP. COME ON.
WE ARE *THREE,* HE'S *ONE MAN.*
AND *BARELY* A MAN AT THAT.
OUR HUSBANDS DO THIS ALL THE TIME.
OUR HUSBANDS ARE *DEAD,* THYRA...
SO THINK OF *THAT,* IF IT HELPS.

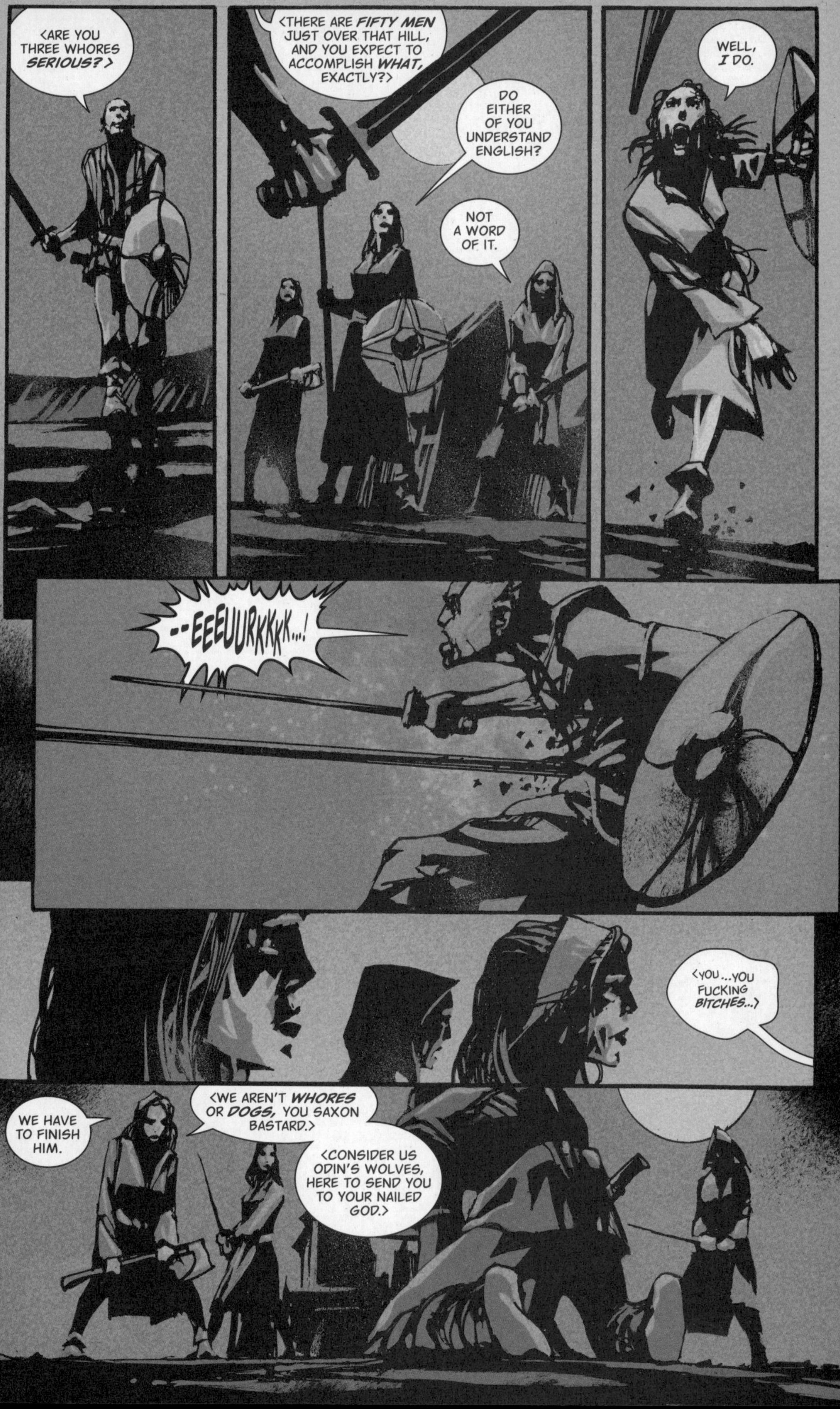
<ARE YOU THREE WHORES *SERIOUS?*>
<THERE ARE *FIFTY MEN* JUST OVER THAT HILL, AND YOU EXPECT TO ACCOMPLISH *WHAT,* EXACTLY?>
DO EITHER OF YOU UNDERSTAND ENGLISH?
NOT A WORD OF IT.
WELL, *I* DO.
--EEEUURKKKK...!
<YOU...YOU FUCKING *BITCHES...*>
WE HAVE TO FINISH HIM.
<WE AREN'T *WHORES* OR *DOGS,* YOU SAXON BASTARD.>
<CONSIDER US ODIN'S WOLVES, HERE TO SEND YOU TO YOUR NAILED GOD.>

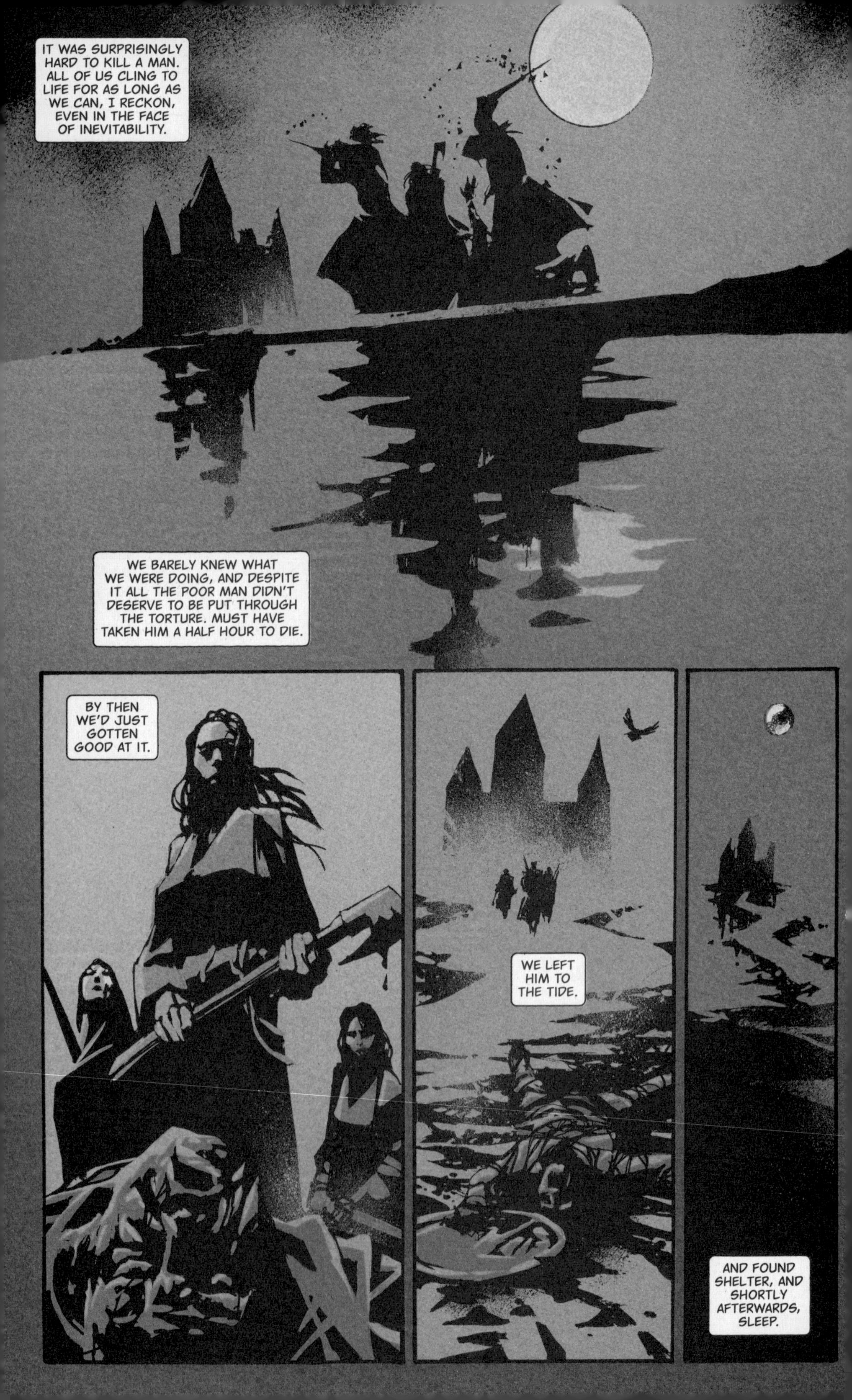
IT WAS SURPRISINGLY HARD TO KILL A MAN. ALL OF US CLING TO LIFE FOR AS LONG AS WE CAN, I RECKON, EVEN IN THE FACE OF INEVITABILITY.
WE BARELY KNEW WHAT WE WERE DOING, AND DESPITE IT ALL THE POOR MAN DIDN'T DESERVE TO BE PUT THROUGH THE TORTURE. MUST HAVE TAKEN HIM A HALF HOUR TO DIE.
BY THEN WE'D JUST GOTTEN GOOD AT IT.
WE LEFT HIM TO THE TIDE.
AND FOUND SHELTER, AND SHORTLY AFTERWARDS, SLEEP.

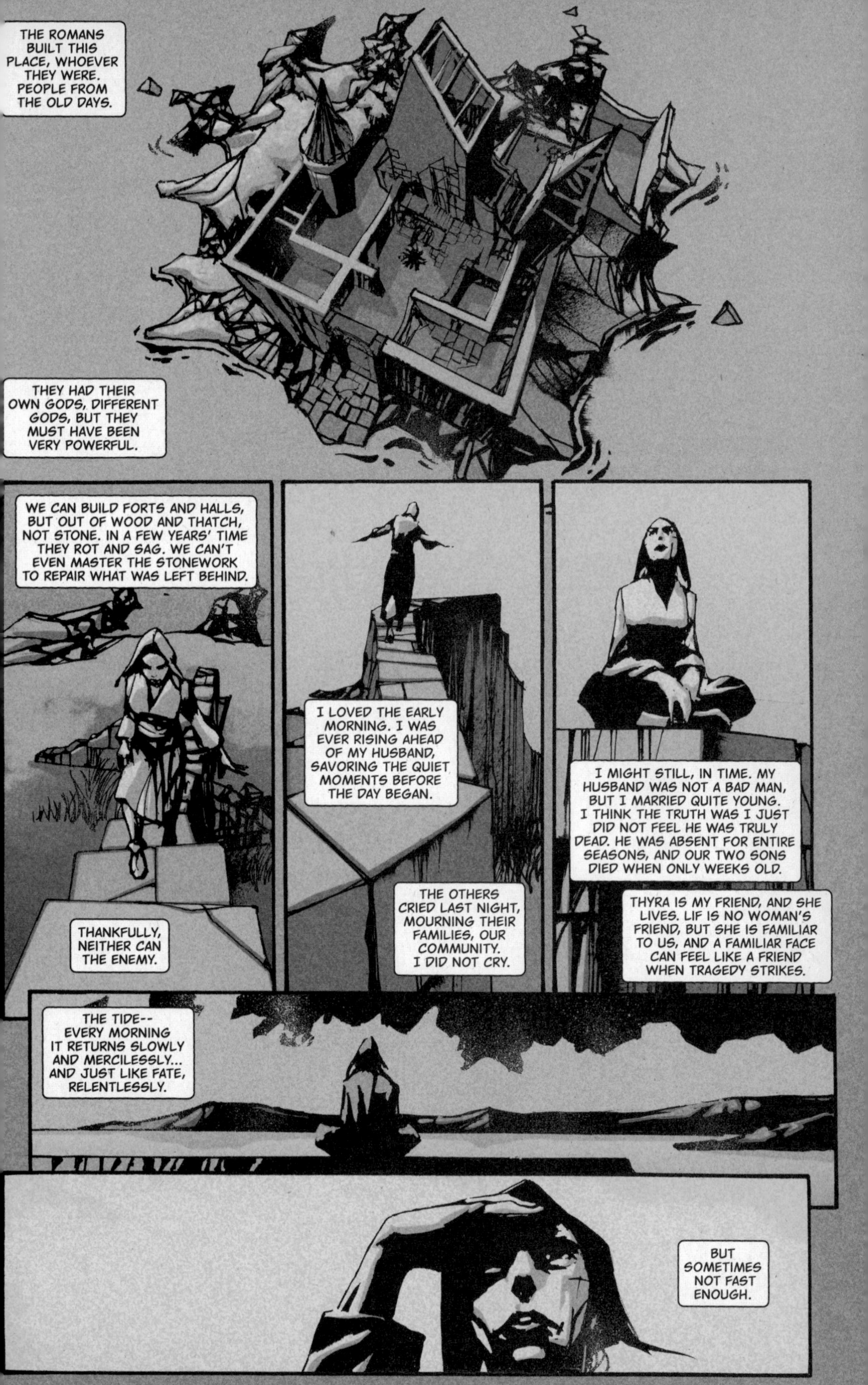

THE ROMANS BUILT THIS PLACE, WHOEVER THEY WERE. PEOPLE FROM THE OLD DAYS.
THEY HAD THEIR OWN GODS, DIFFERENT GODS, BUT THEY MUST HAVE BEEN VERY POWERFUL.
WE CAN BUILD FORTS AND HALLS, BUT OUT OF WOOD AND THATCH, NOT STONE. IN A FEW YEARS' TIME THEY ROT AND SAG. WE CAN'T EVEN MASTER THE STONEWORK TO REPAIR WHAT WAS LEFT BEHIND.
THANKFULLY, NEITHER CAN THE ENEMY.
I LOVED THE EARLY MORNING. I WAS EVER RISING AHEAD OF MY HUSBAND, SAVORING THE QUIET MOMENTS BEFORE THE DAY BEGAN.
THE OTHERS CRIED LAST NIGHT, MOURNING THEIR FAMILIES, OUR COMMUNITY. I DID NOT CRY.
I MIGHT STILL, IN TIME. MY HUSBAND WAS NOT A BAD MAN, BUT I MARRIED QUITE YOUNG. I THINK THE TRUTH WAS I JUST DID NOT FEEL HE WAS TRULY DEAD. HE WAS ABSENT FOR ENTIRE SEASONS, AND OUR TWO SONS DIED WHEN ONLY WEEKS OLD.
THYRA IS MY FRIEND, AND SHE LIVES. LIF IS NO WOMAN'S FRIEND, BUT SHE IS FAMILIAR TO US, AND A FAMILIAR FACE CAN FEEL LIKE A FRIEND WHEN TRAGEDY STRIKES.
THE TIDE-- EVERY MORNING IT RETURNS SLOWLY AND MERCILESSLY... AND JUST LIKE FATE, RELENTLESSLY.
BUT SOMETIMES NOT FAST ENOUGH.

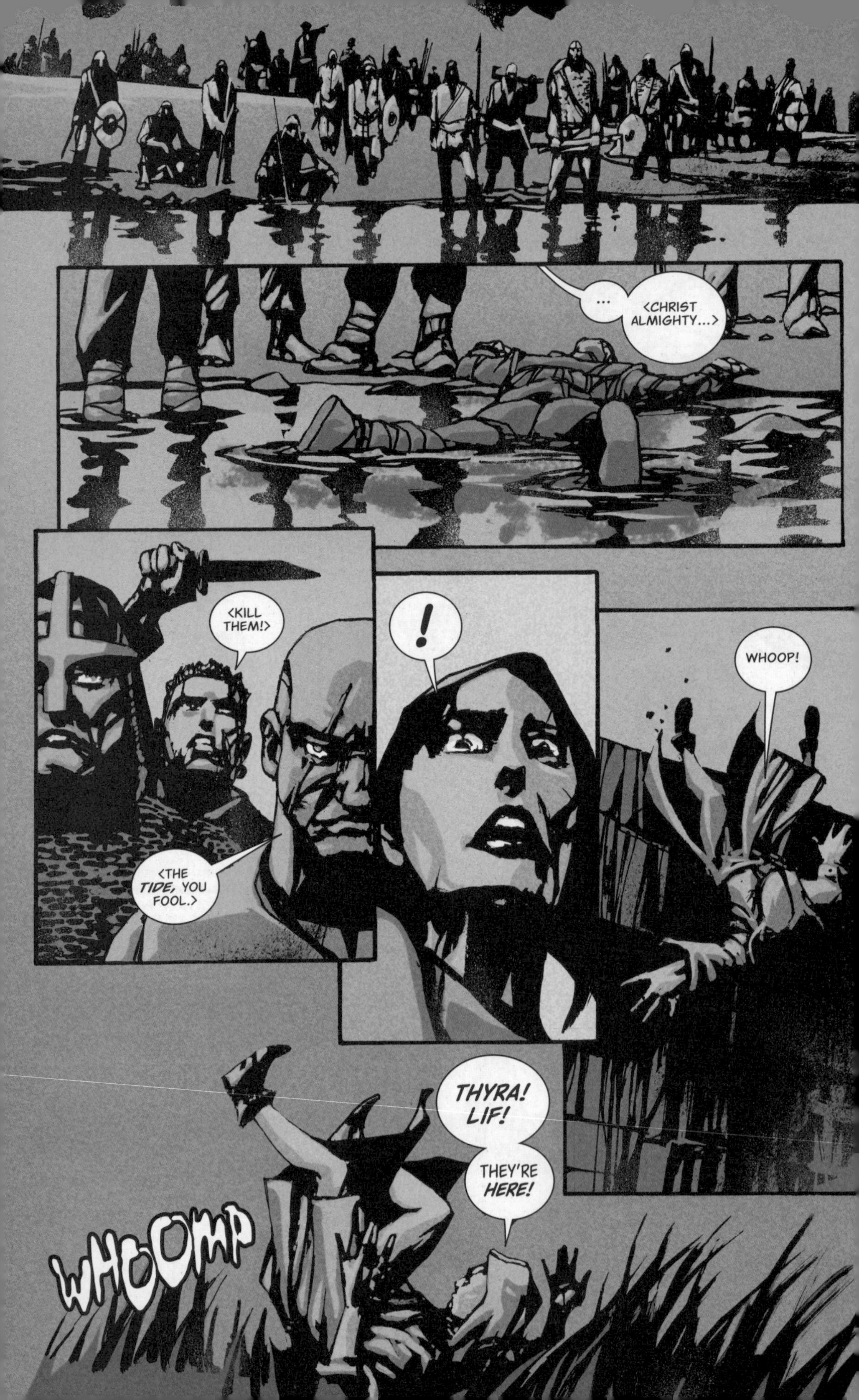
...
<CHRIST ALMIGHTY...>
<KILL THEM!>
<THE *TIDE,* YOU FOOL.>
!
WHOOP!
THYRA! LIF!
THEY'RE *HERE!*
WHOOMP

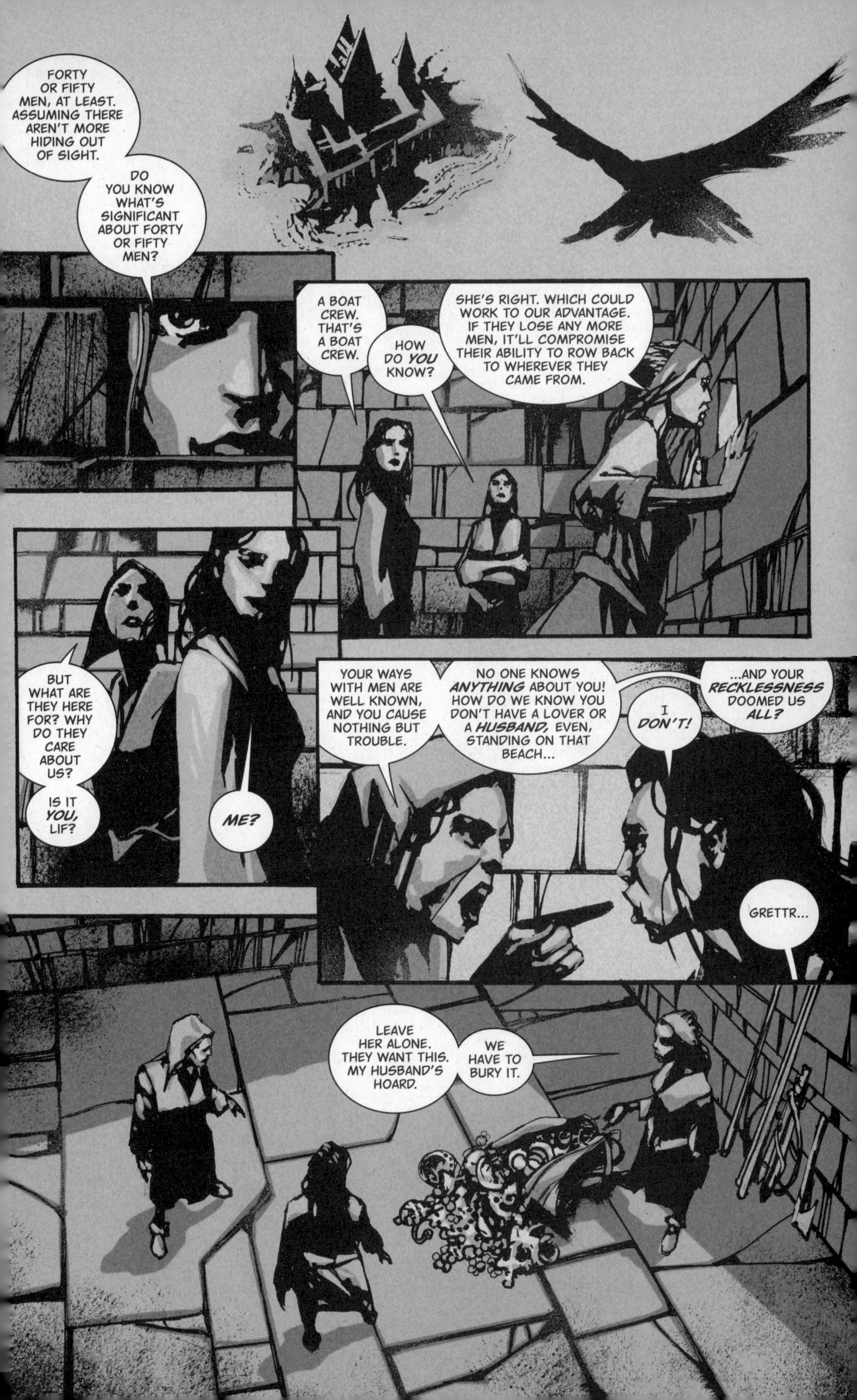
FORTY OR FIFTY MEN, AT LEAST. ASSUMING THERE AREN'T MORE HIDING OUT OF SIGHT.
DO YOU KNOW WHAT'S SIGNIFICANT ABOUT FORTY OR FIFTY MEN?
A BOAT CREW. THAT'S A BOAT CREW.
HOW DO *YOU* KNOW?
SHE'S RIGHT. WHICH COULD WORK TO OUR ADVANTAGE. IF THEY LOSE ANY MORE MEN, IT'LL COMPROMISE THEIR ABILITY TO ROW BACK TO WHEREVER THEY CAME FROM.
BUT WHAT ARE THEY HERE FOR? WHY DO THEY CARE ABOUT US?
IS IT *YOU,* LIF?
ME?
YOUR WAYS WITH MEN ARE WELL KNOWN, AND YOU CAUSE NOTHING BUT TROUBLE.
NO ONE KNOWS *ANYTHING* ABOUT YOU! HOW DO WE KNOW YOU DON'T HAVE A LOVER OR A *HUSBAND,* EVEN, STANDING ON THAT BEACH...
I *DON'T!*
...AND YOUR *RECKLESSNESS* DOOMED US *ALL?*
GRETTR...
LEAVE HER ALONE. THEY WANT THIS. MY HUSBAND'S HOARD.
WE HAVE TO BURY IT.

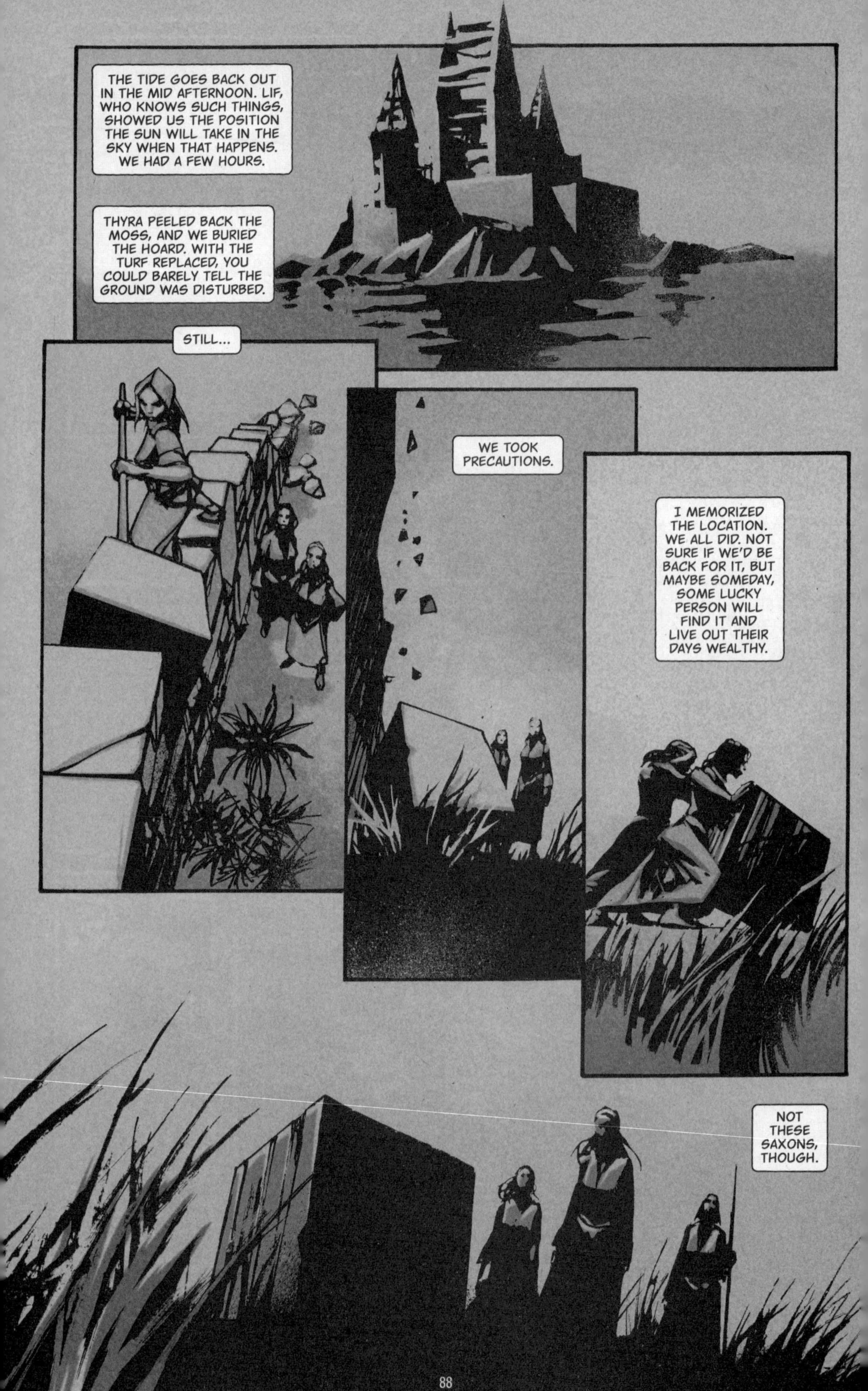
THE TIDE GOES BACK OUT IN THE MID AFTERNOON. LIF, WHO KNOWS SUCH THINGS, SHOWED US THE POSITION THE SUN WILL TAKE IN THE SKY WHEN THAT HAPPENS. WE HAD A FEW HOURS.
THYRA PEELED BACK THE MOSS, AND WE BURIED THE HOARD. WITH THE TURF REPLACED, YOU COULD BARELY TELL THE GROUND WAS DISTURBED.
STILL...
WE TOOK PRECAUTIONS.
I MEMORIZED THE LOCATION. WE ALL DID. NOT SURE IF WE'D BE BACK FOR IT, BUT MAYBE SOMEDAY, SOME LUCKY PERSON WILL FIND IT AND LIVE OUT THEIR DAYS WEALTHY.
NOT THESE SAXONS, THOUGH.

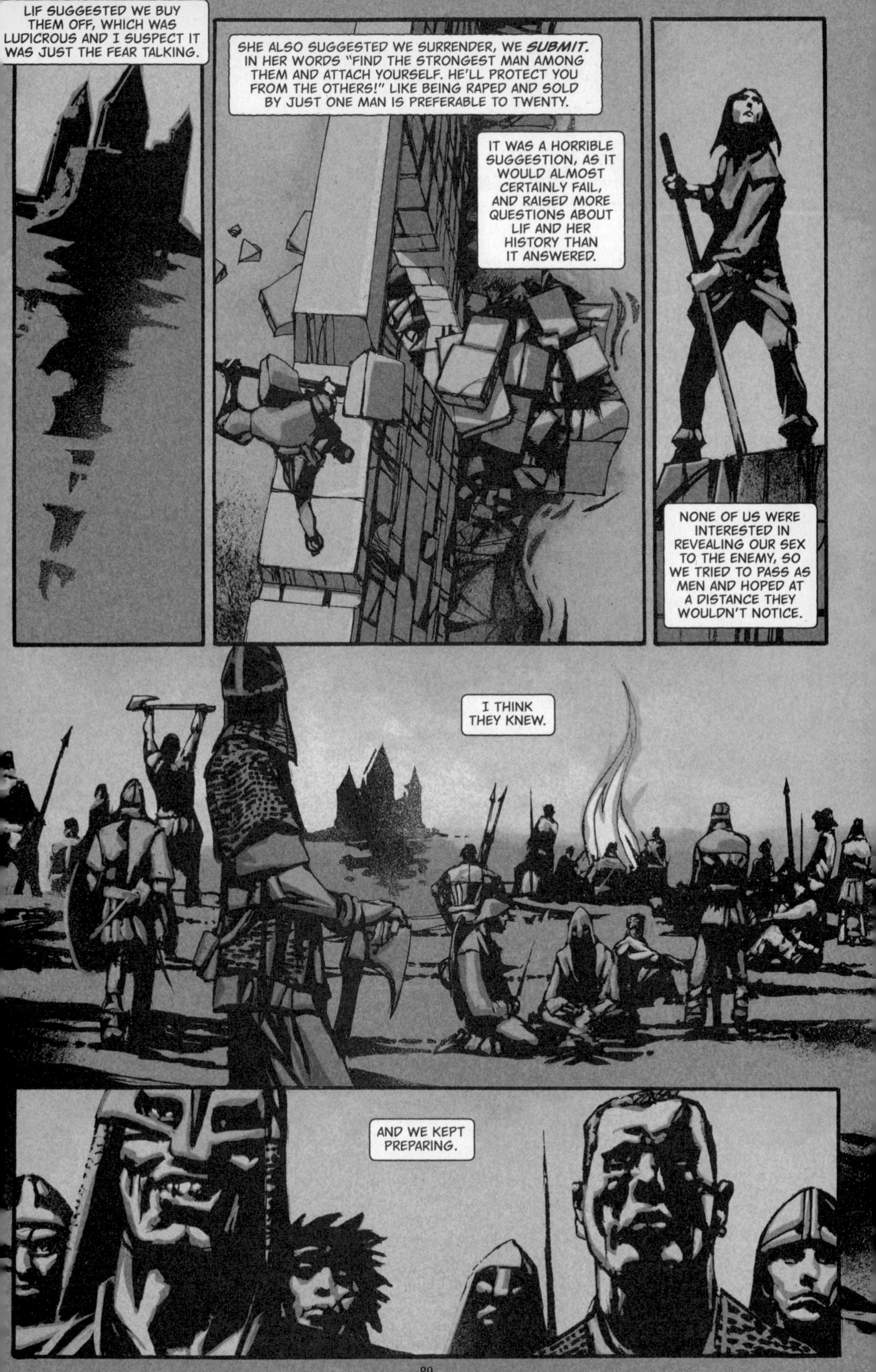
LIF SUGGESTED WE BUY THEM OFF, WHICH WAS LUDICROUS AND I SUSPECT IT WAS JUST THE FEAR TALKING.
SHE ALSO SUGGESTED WE SURRENDER, WE ***SUBMIT.*** IN HER WORDS "FIND THE STRONGEST MAN AMONG THEM AND ATTACH YOURSELF. HE'LL PROTECT YOU FROM THE OTHERS!" LIKE BEING RAPED AND SOLD BY JUST ONE MAN IS PREFERABLE TO TWENTY.
IT WAS A HORRIBLE SUGGESTION, AS IT WOULD ALMOST CERTAINLY FAIL, AND RAISED MORE QUESTIONS ABOUT LIF AND HER HISTORY THAN IT ANSWERED.
NONE OF US WERE INTERESTED IN REVEALING OUR SEX TO THE ENEMY, SO WE TRIED TO PASS AS MEN AND HOPED AT A DISTANCE THEY WOULDN'T NOTICE.
I THINK THEY KNEW.
AND WE KEPT PREPARING.

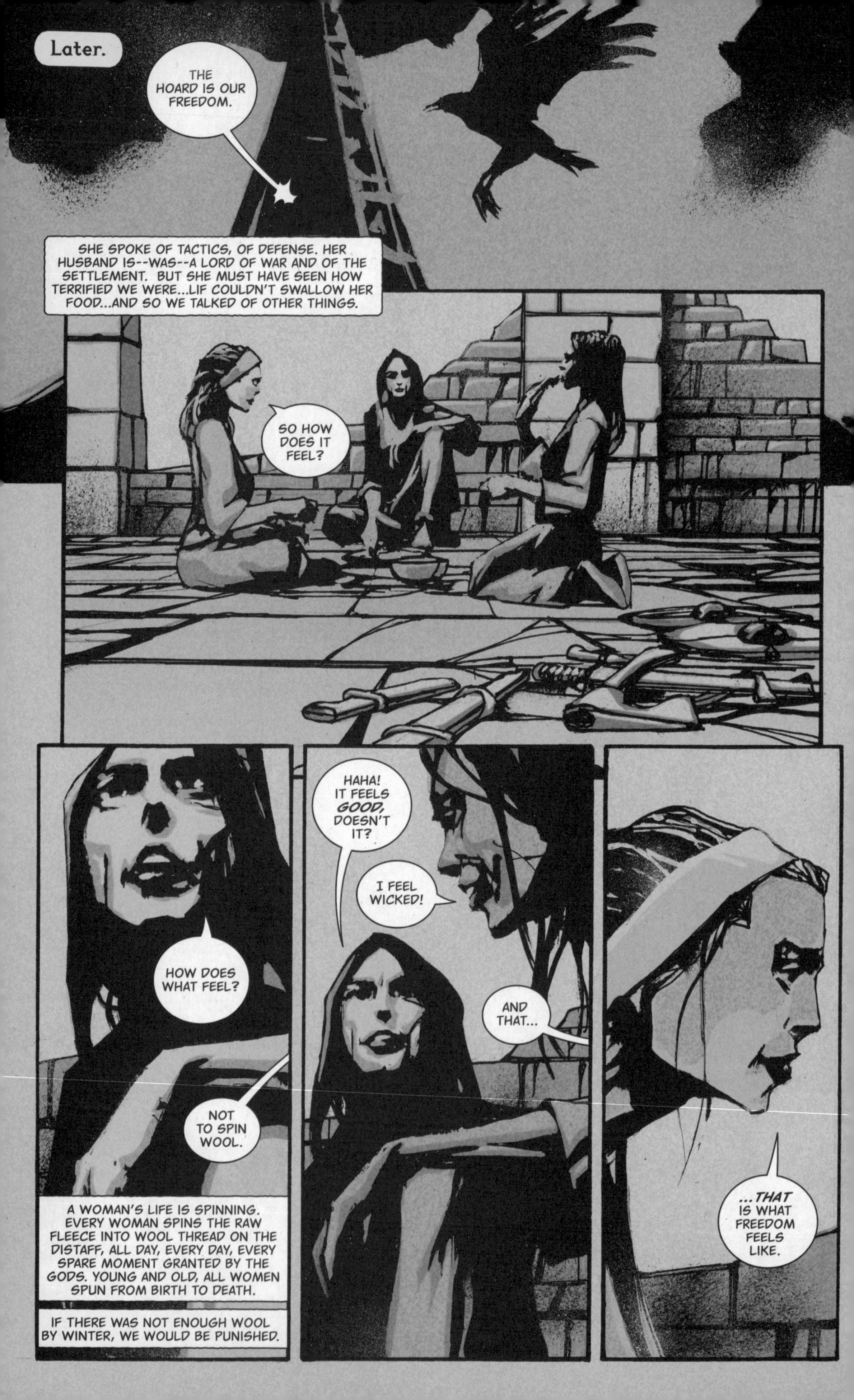
Later.
THE HOARD IS OUR FREEDOM.
SHE SPOKE OF TACTICS, OF DEFENSE. HER HUSBAND IS--WAS--A LORD OF WAR AND OF THE SETTLEMENT. BUT SHE MUST HAVE SEEN HOW TERRIFIED WE WERE...LIF COULDN'T SWALLOW HER FOOD...AND SO WE TALKED OF OTHER THINGS.
SO HOW DOES IT FEEL?
HOW DOES WHAT FEEL?
NOT TO SPIN WOOL.
A WOMAN'S LIFE IS SPINNING. EVERY WOMAN SPINS THE RAW FLEECE INTO WOOL THREAD ON THE DISTAFF, ALL DAY, EVERY DAY, EVERY SPARE MOMENT GRANTED BY THE GODS. YOUNG AND OLD, ALL WOMEN SPUN FROM BIRTH TO DEATH.
IF THERE WAS NOT ENOUGH WOOL BY WINTER, WE WOULD BE PUNISHED.
HAHA! IT FEELS *GOOD,* DOESN'T IT?
I FEEL WICKED!
AND THAT...
...*THAT* IS WHAT FREEDOM FEELS LIKE.

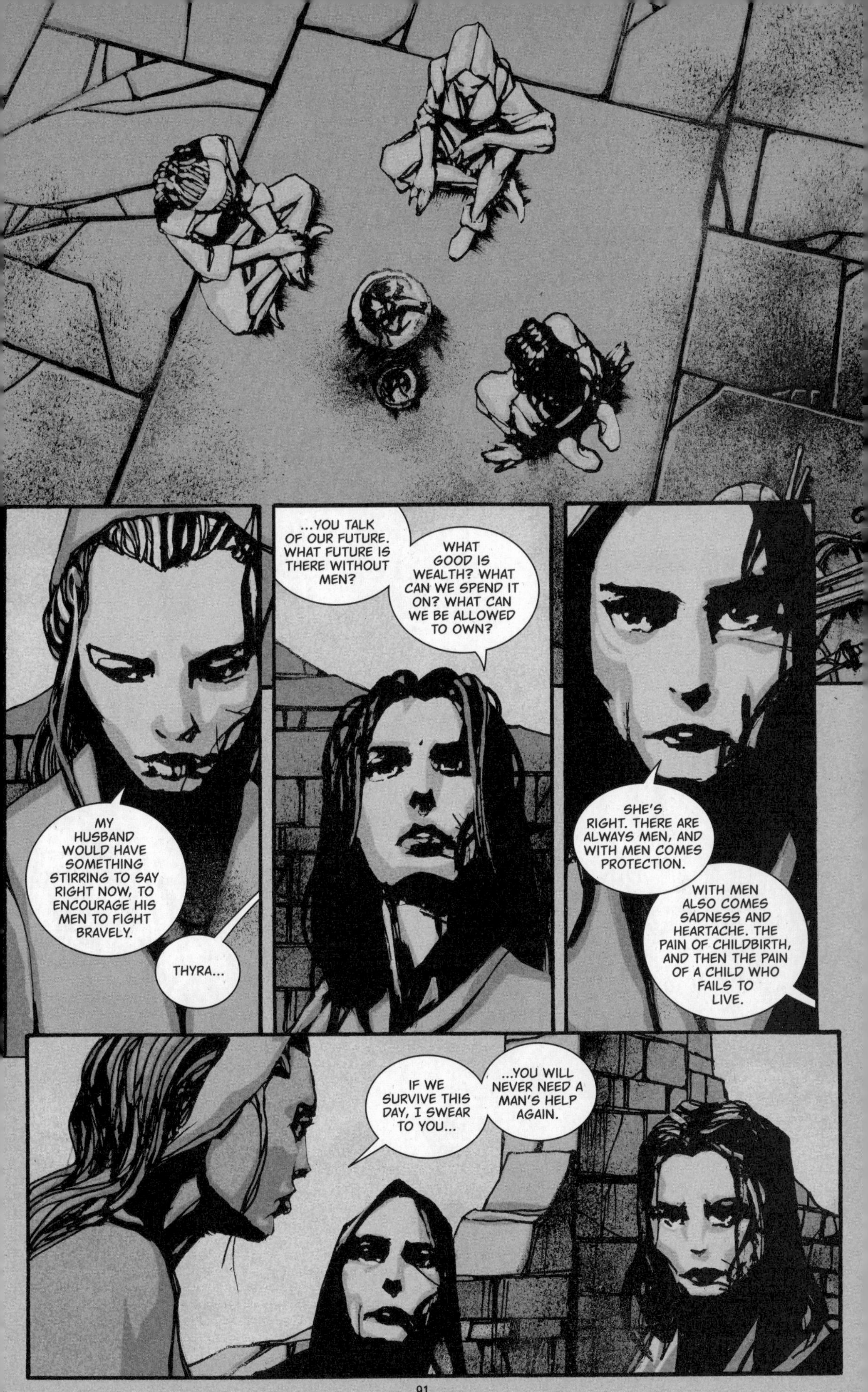
MY HUSBAND WOULD HAVE SOMETHING STIRRING TO SAY RIGHT NOW, TO ENCOURAGE HIS MEN TO FIGHT BRAVELY.
THYRA...
...YOU TALK OF OUR FUTURE. WHAT FUTURE IS THERE WITHOUT MEN?
WHAT GOOD IS WEALTH? WHAT CAN WE SPEND IT ON? WHAT CAN WE BE ALLOWED TO OWN?
SHE'S RIGHT. THERE ARE ALWAYS MEN, AND WITH MEN COMES PROTECTION.
WITH MEN ALSO COMES SADNESS AND HEARTACHE. THE PAIN OF CHILDBIRTH, AND THEN THE PAIN OF A CHILD WHO FAILS TO LIVE.
IF WE SURVIVE THIS DAY, I SWEAR TO YOU...
...YOU WILL NEVER NEED A MAN'S HELP AGAIN.

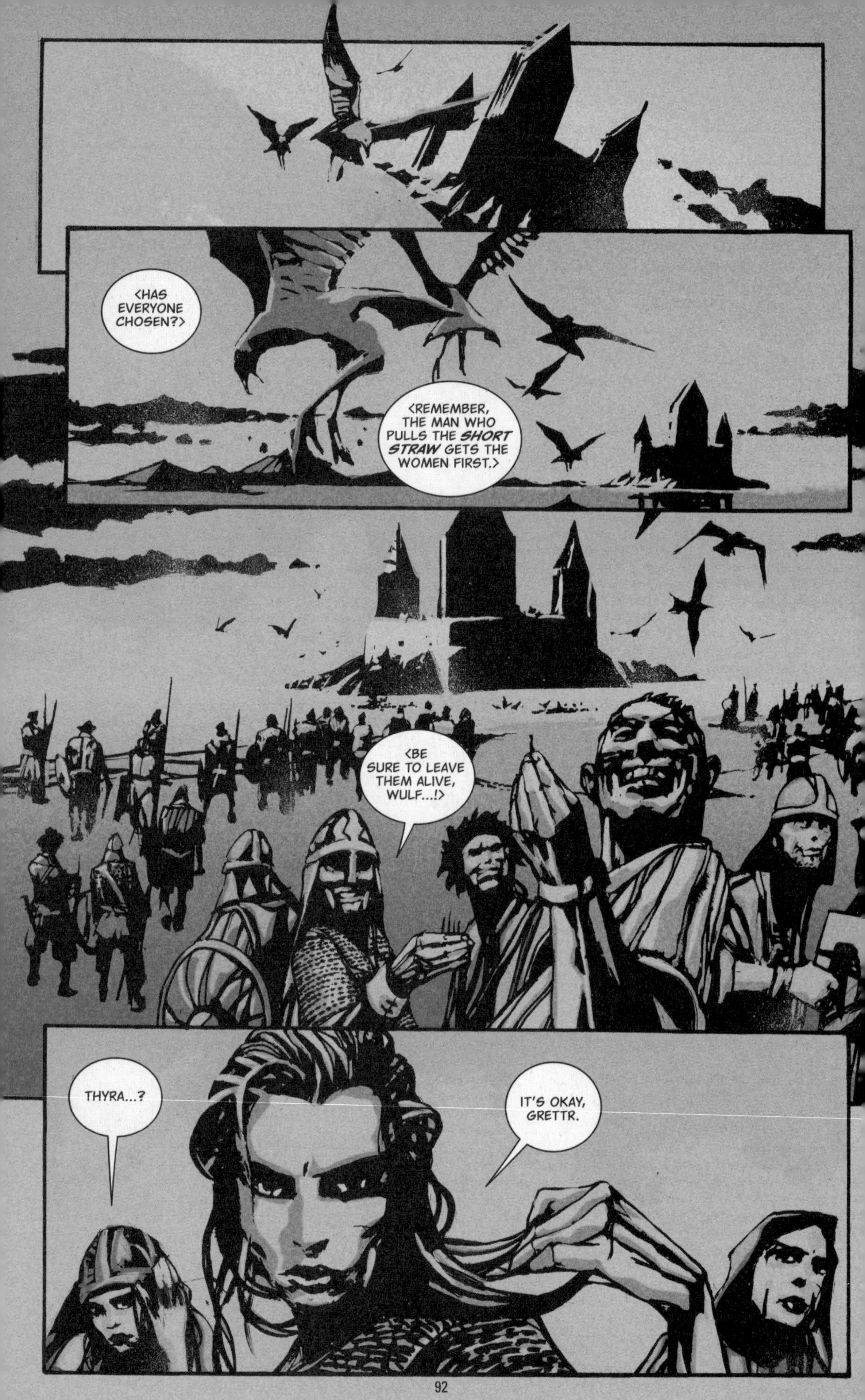
<HAS EVERYONE CHOSEN?>
<REMEMBER, THE MAN WHO PULLS THE SHORT STRAW GETS THE WOMEN FIRST.>
<BE SURE TO LEAVE THEM ALIVE, WULF...!>
THYRA...?
IT'S OKAY, GRETTR.

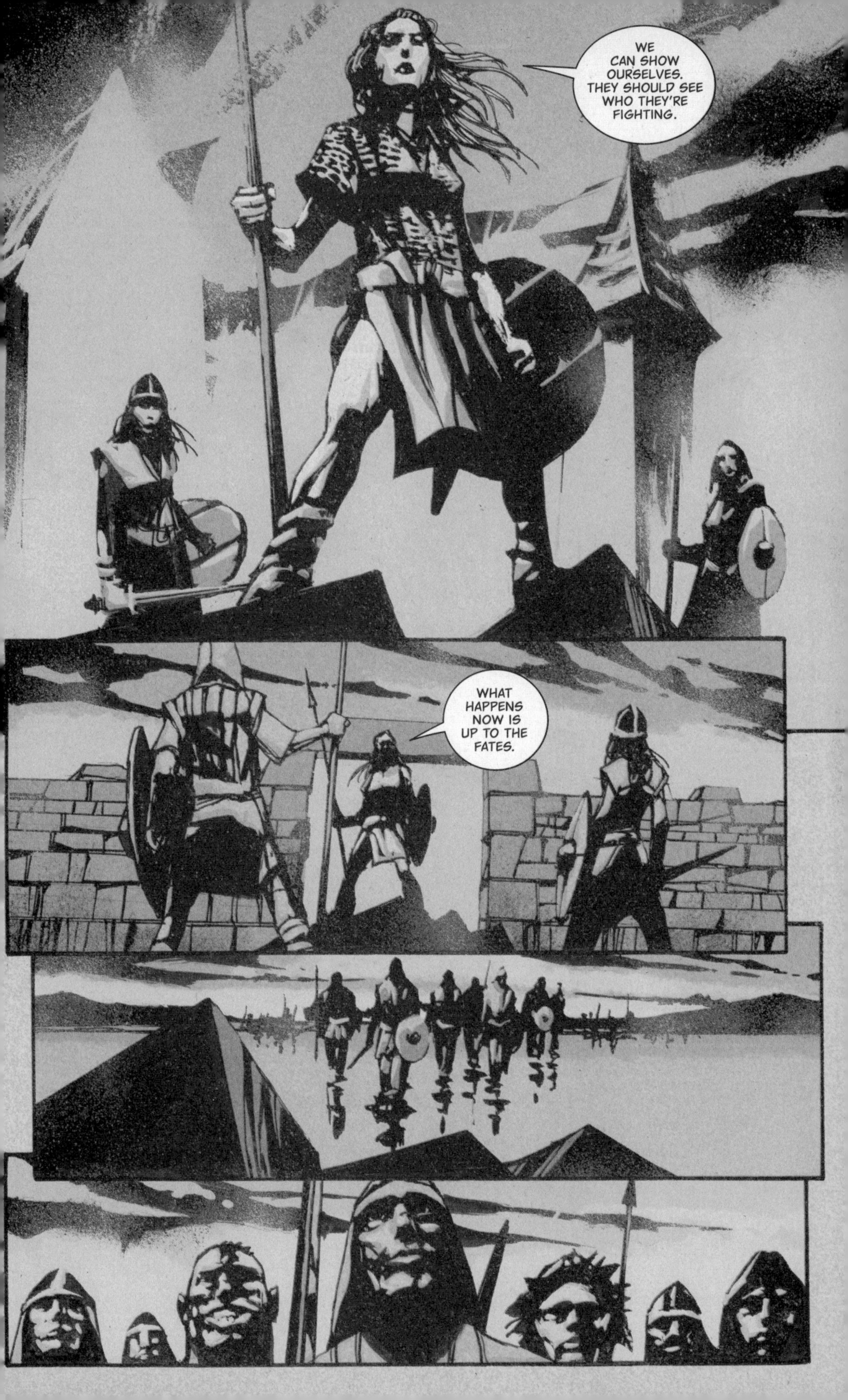
WE CAN SHOW OURSELVES. THEY SHOULD SEE WHO THEY'RE FIGHTING.
WHAT HAPPENS NOW IS UP TO THE FATES.

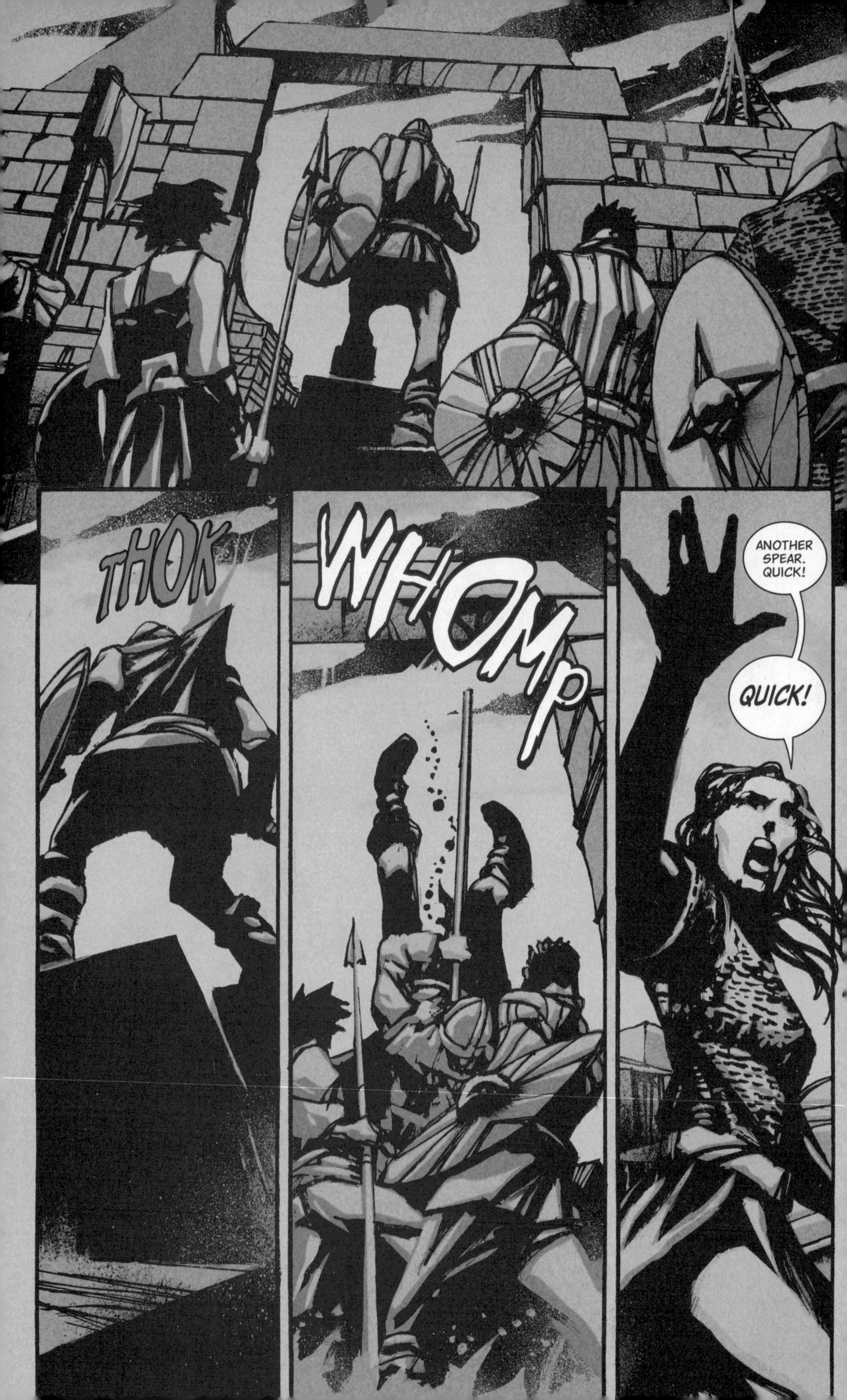
tHOK
WHOMp
ANOTHER SPEAR. QUICK!
QUICK!

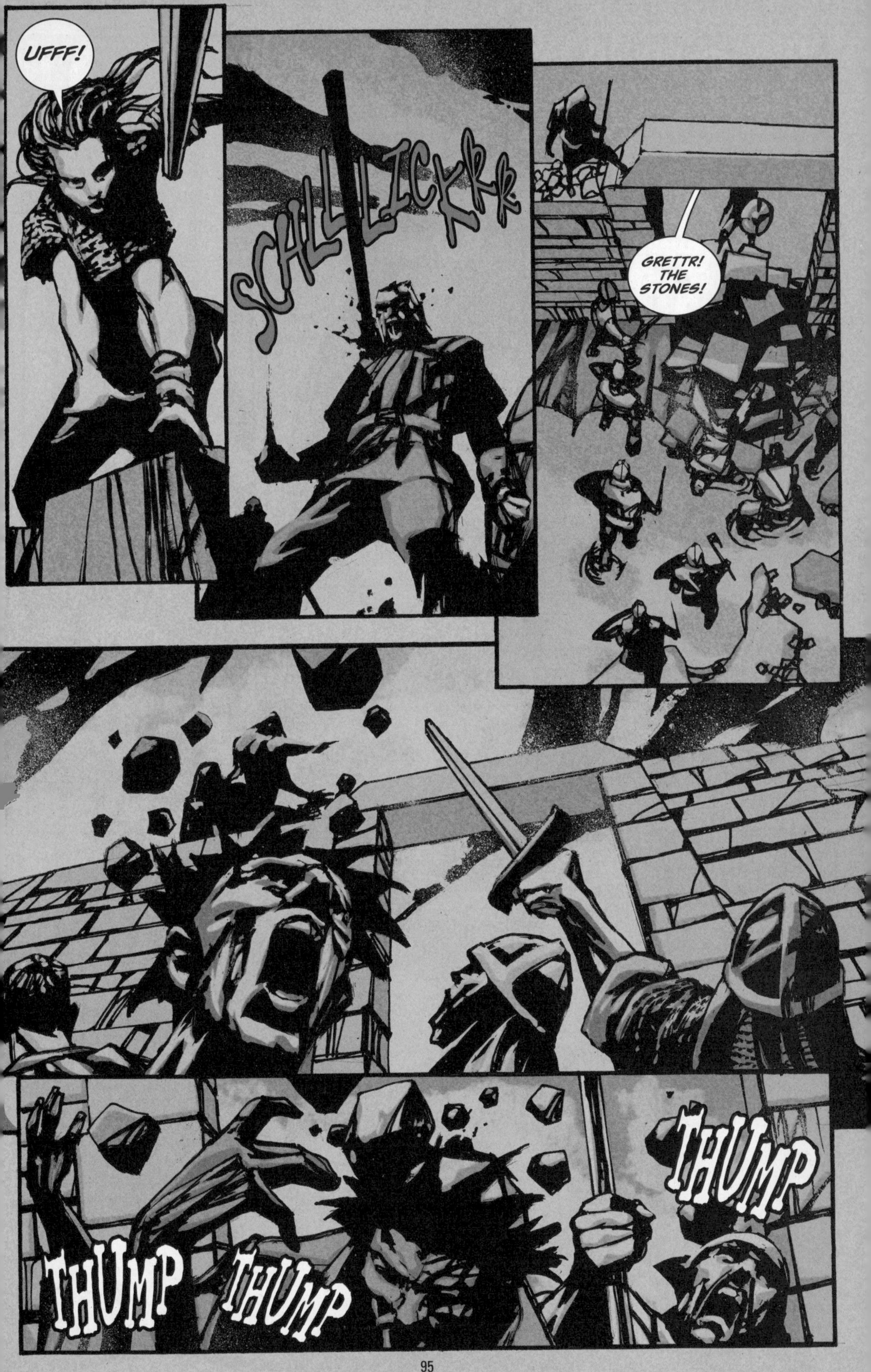
UFFF!
SCHLLICKRR
GRETTR! THE STONES!
THUMP
THUMP
THUMP

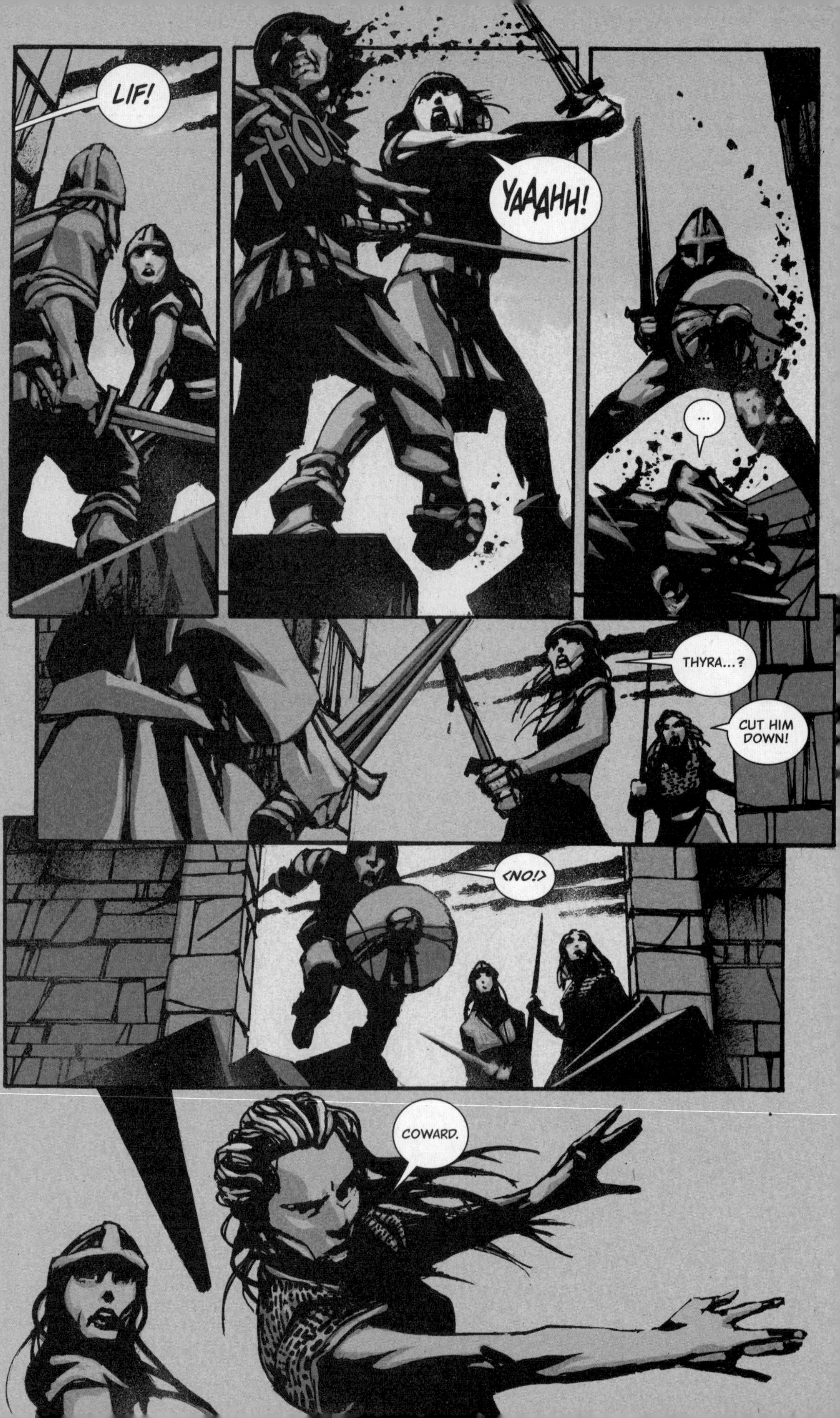
LIF!
YAAAHH!
...
THYRA...?
CUT HIM DOWN!
<NO!>
COWARD.

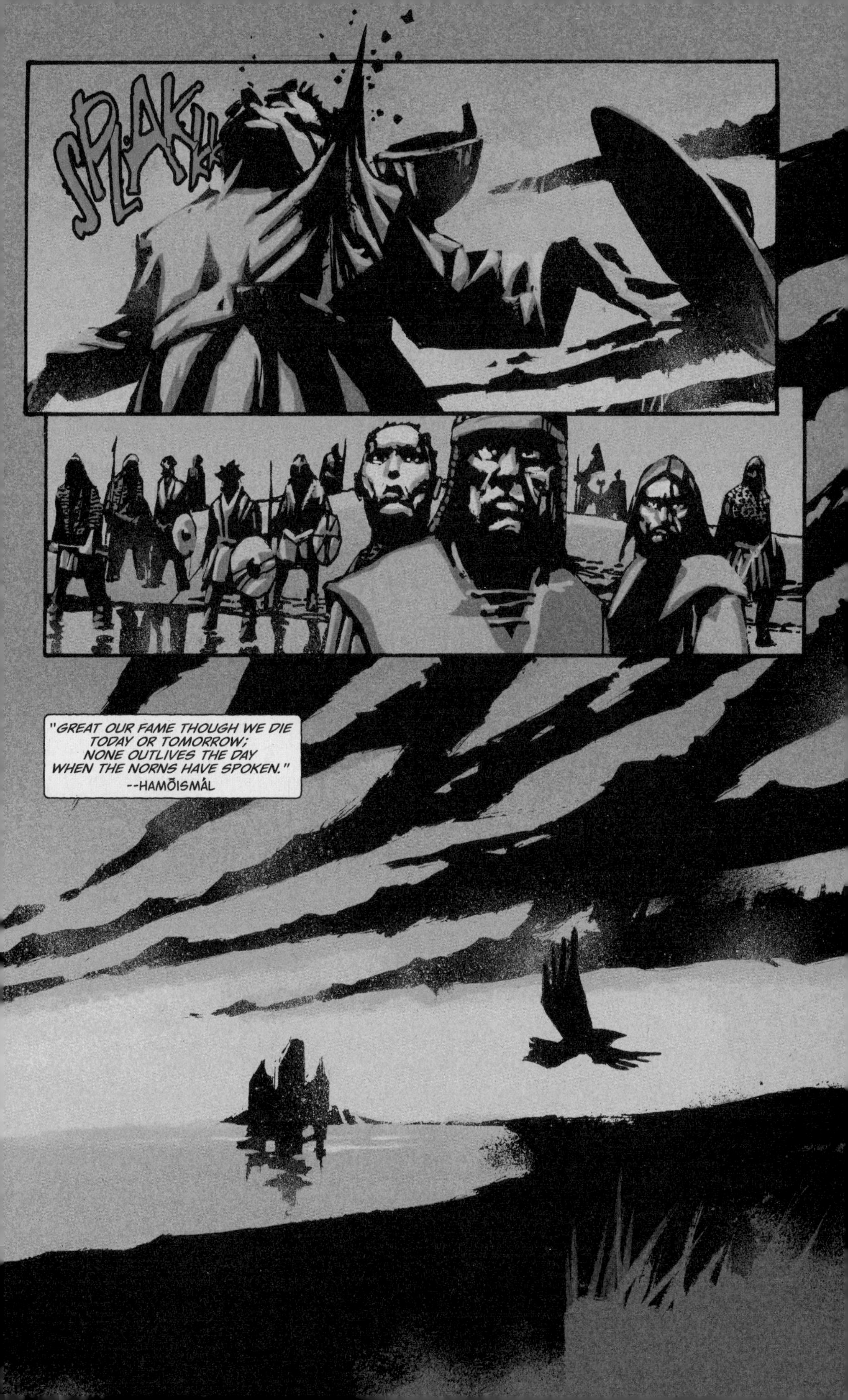
SPLAKK
"GREAT OUR FAME THOUGH WE DIE TODAY OR TOMORROW; NONE OUTLIVES THE DAY WHEN THE NORNS HAVE SPOKEN."
--HAMÕISMÁL

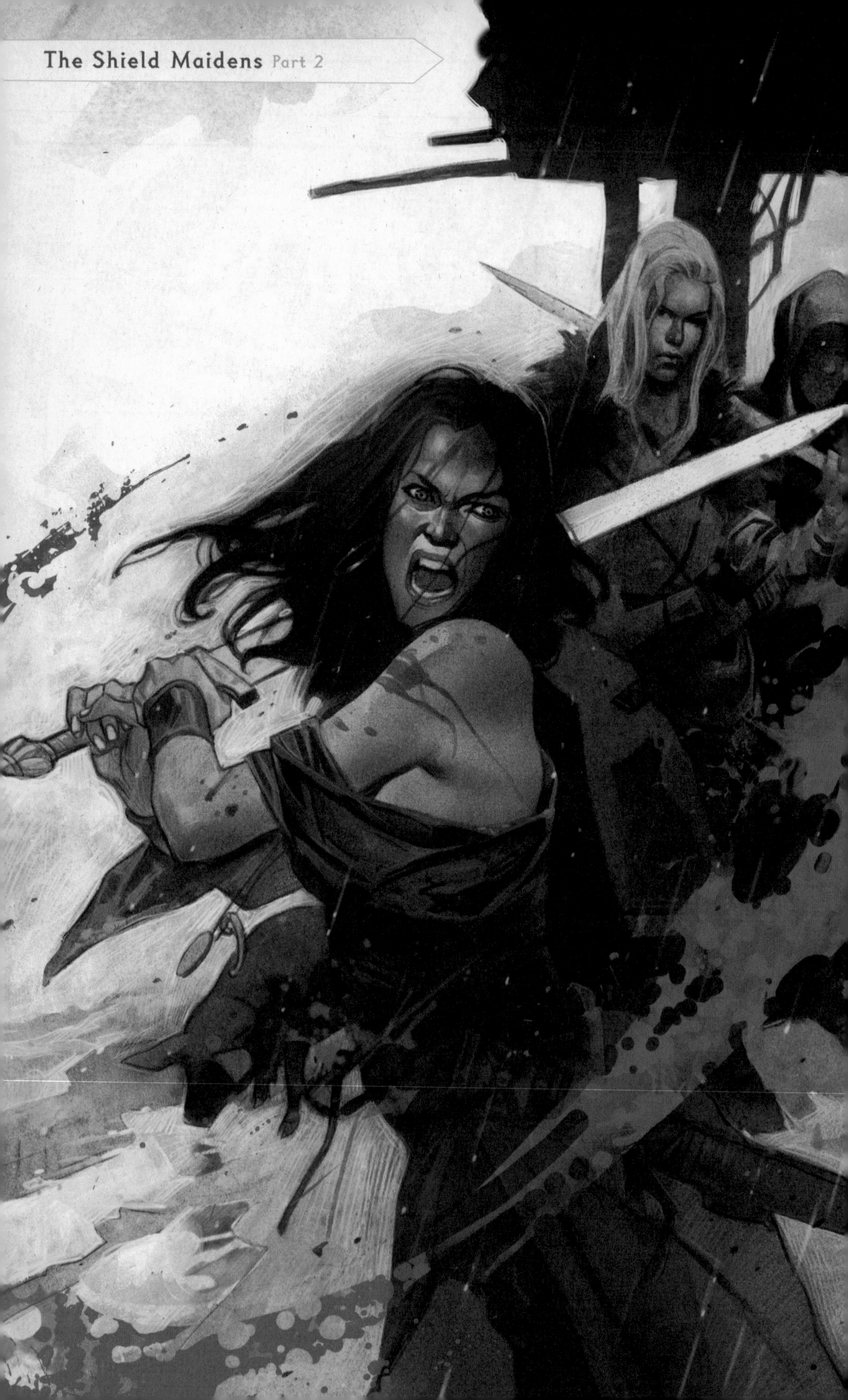

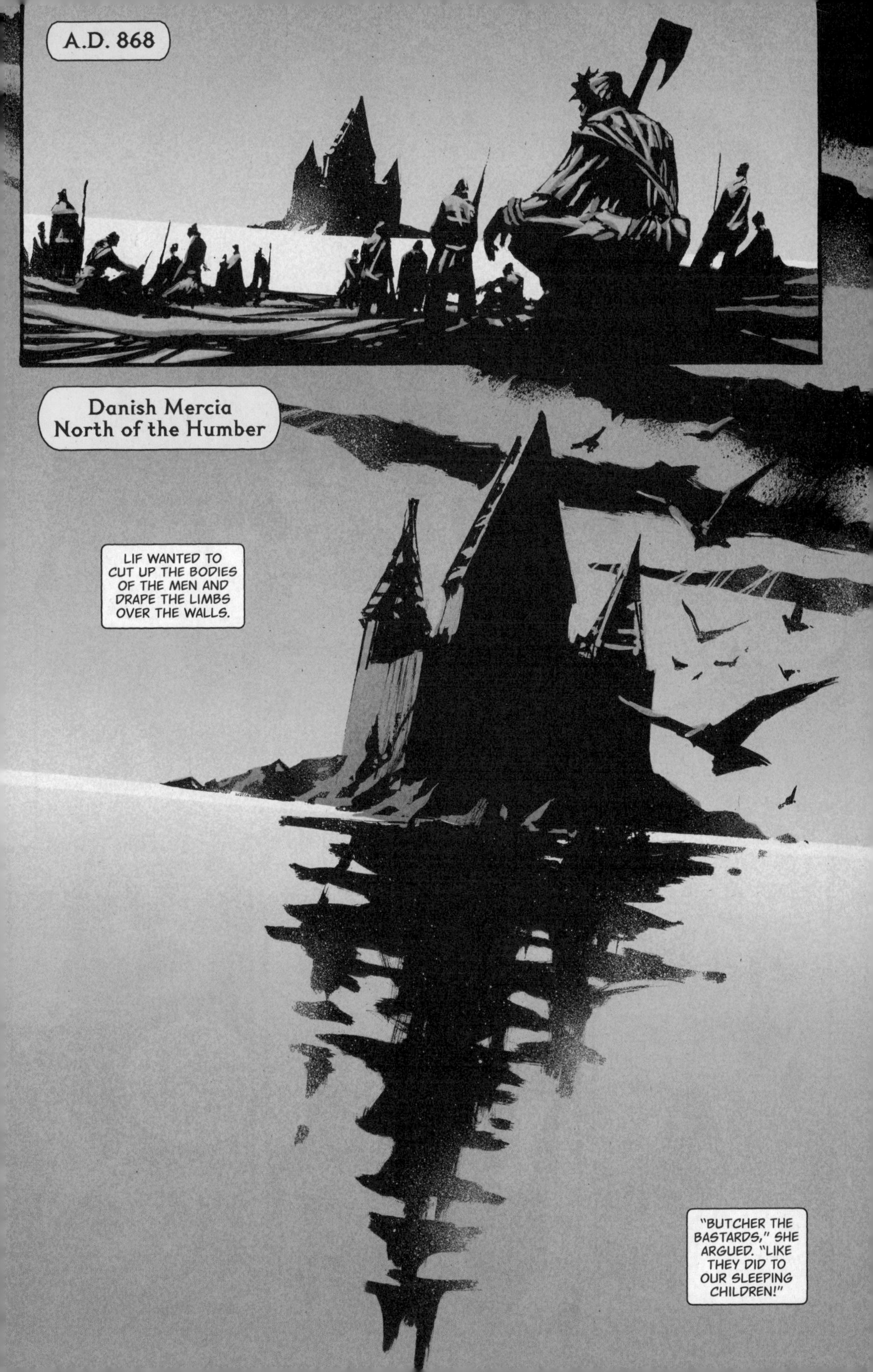
A.D. 868
Danish Mercia
North of the Humber
LIF WANTED TO CUT UP THE BODIES OF THE MEN AND DRAPE THE LIMBS OVER THE WALLS.
"BUTCHER THE BASTARDS," SHE ARGUED. "LIKE THEY DID TO OUR SLEEPING CHILDREN!"

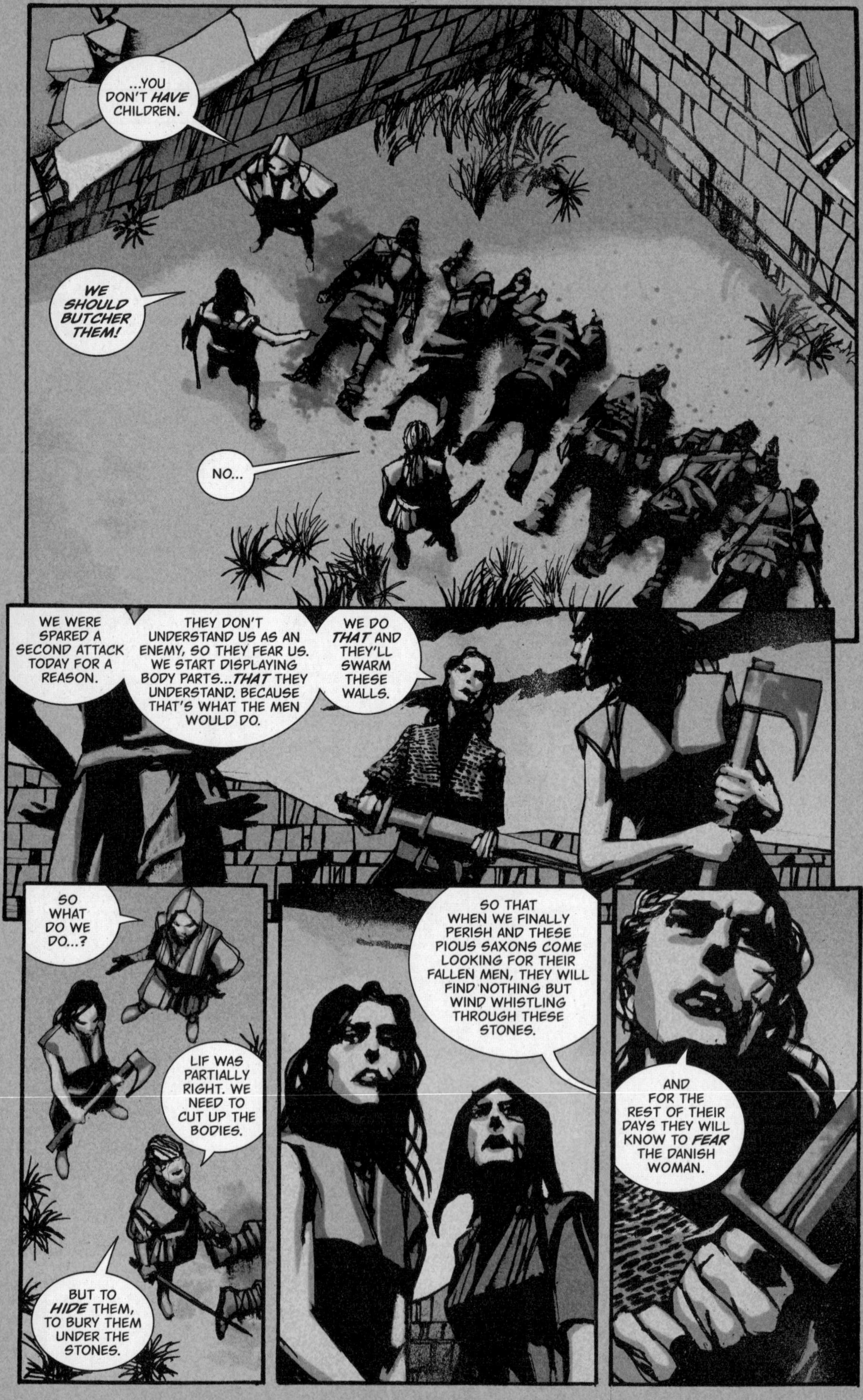
...YOU DON'T *HAVE* CHILDREN.
WE SHOULD BUTCHER THEM!
NO...
WE WERE SPARED A SECOND ATTACK TODAY FOR A REASON.
THEY DON'T UNDERSTAND US AS AN ENEMY, SO THEY FEAR US. WE START DISPLAYING BODY PARTS...*THAT* THEY UNDERSTAND. BECAUSE THAT'S WHAT THE MEN WOULD DO.
WE DO *THAT* AND THEY'LL SWARM THESE WALLS.
SO WHAT DO WE DO...?
LIF WAS PARTIALLY RIGHT. WE NEED TO CUT UP THE BODIES.
BUT TO *HIDE* THEM, TO BURY THEM UNDER THE STONES.
SO THAT WHEN WE FINALLY PERISH AND THESE PIOUS SAXONS COME LOOKING FOR THEIR FALLEN MEN, THEY WILL FIND NOTHING BUT WIND WHISTLING THROUGH THESE STONES.
AND FOR THE REST OF THEIR DAYS THEY WILL KNOW TO *FEAR* THE DANISH WOMAN.

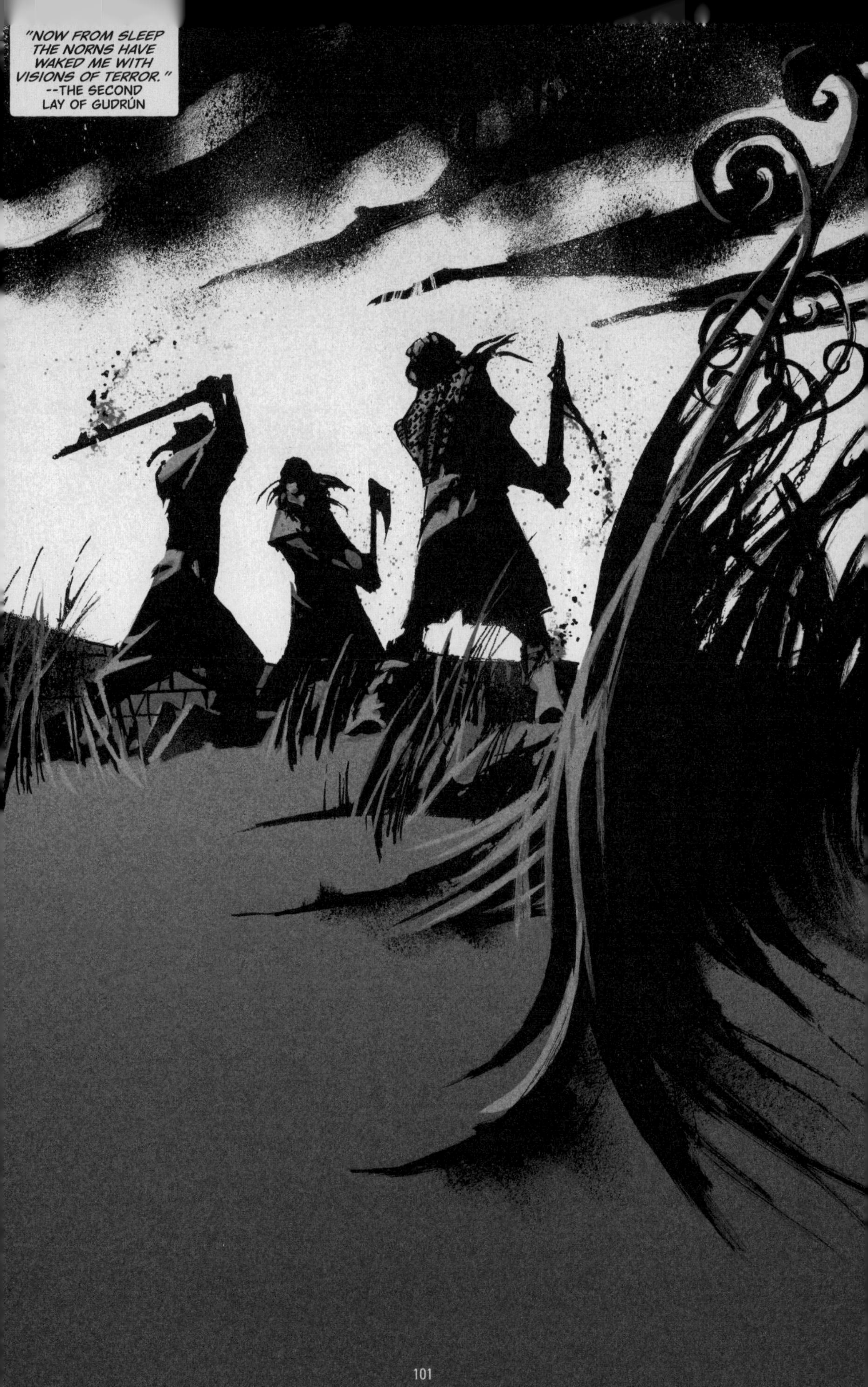
"NOW FROM SLEEP THE NORNS HAVE WAKED ME WITH VISIONS OF TERROR."
--THE SECOND LAY OF GUDRÚN

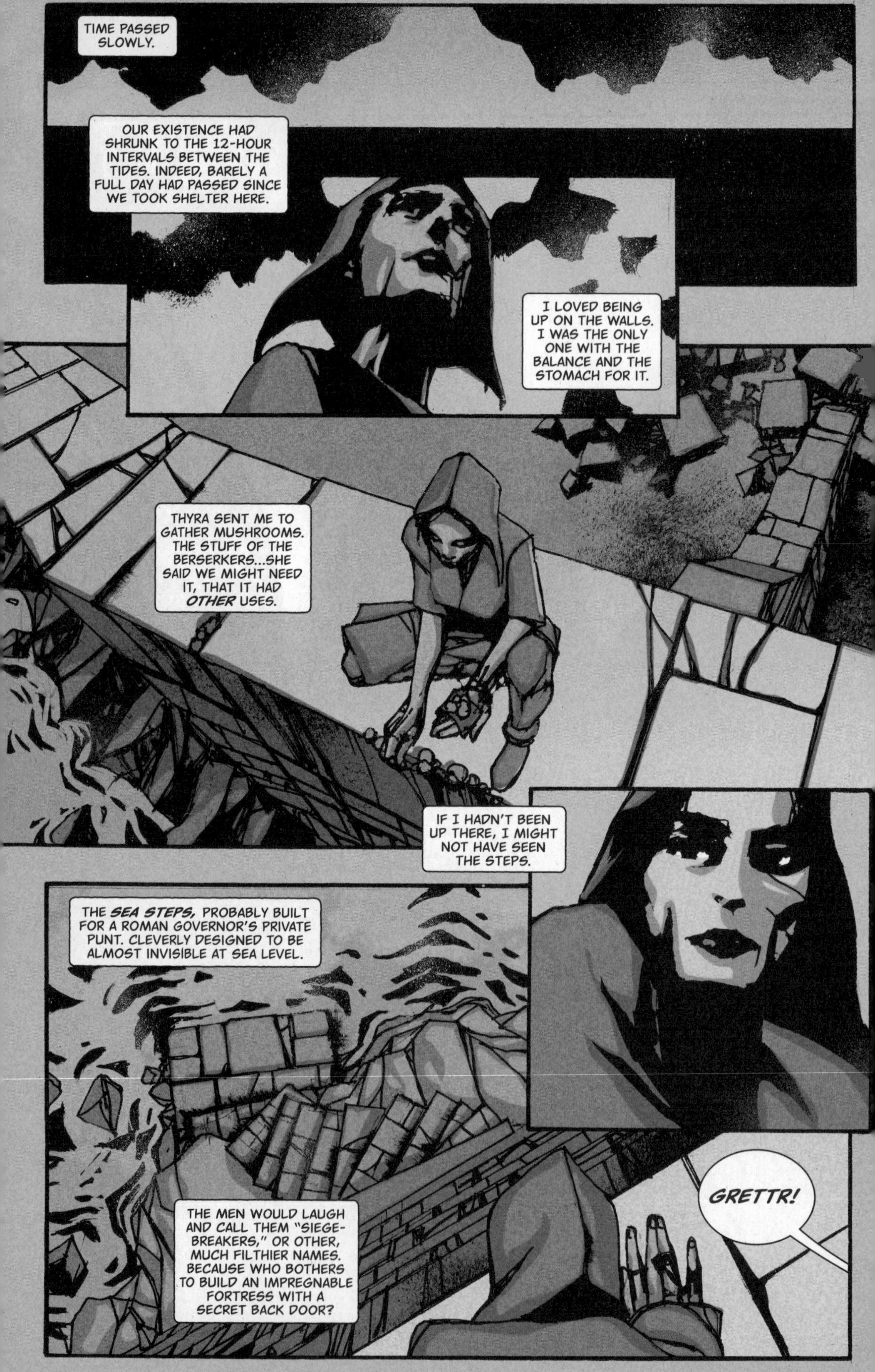
TIME PASSED SLOWLY.
OUR EXISTENCE HAD SHRUNK TO THE 12-HOUR INTERVALS BETWEEN THE TIDES. INDEED, BARELY A FULL DAY HAD PASSED SINCE WE TOOK SHELTER HERE.
I LOVED BEING UP ON THE WALLS. I WAS THE ONLY ONE WITH THE BALANCE AND THE STOMACH FOR IT.
THYRA SENT ME TO GATHER MUSHROOMS. THE STUFF OF THE BERSERKERS...SHE SAID WE MIGHT NEED IT, THAT IT HAD *OTHER* USES.
IF I HADN'T BEEN UP THERE, I MIGHT NOT HAVE SEEN THE STEPS.
THE *SEA STEPS,* PROBABLY BUILT FOR A ROMAN GOVERNOR'S PRIVATE PUNT. CLEVERLY DESIGNED TO BE ALMOST INVISIBLE AT SEA LEVEL.
THE MEN WOULD LAUGH AND CALL THEM "SIEGE-BREAKERS," OR OTHER, MUCH FILTHIER NAMES. BECAUSE WHO BOTHERS TO BUILD AN IMPREGNABLE FORTRESS WITH A SECRET BACK DOOR?
GRETTR!

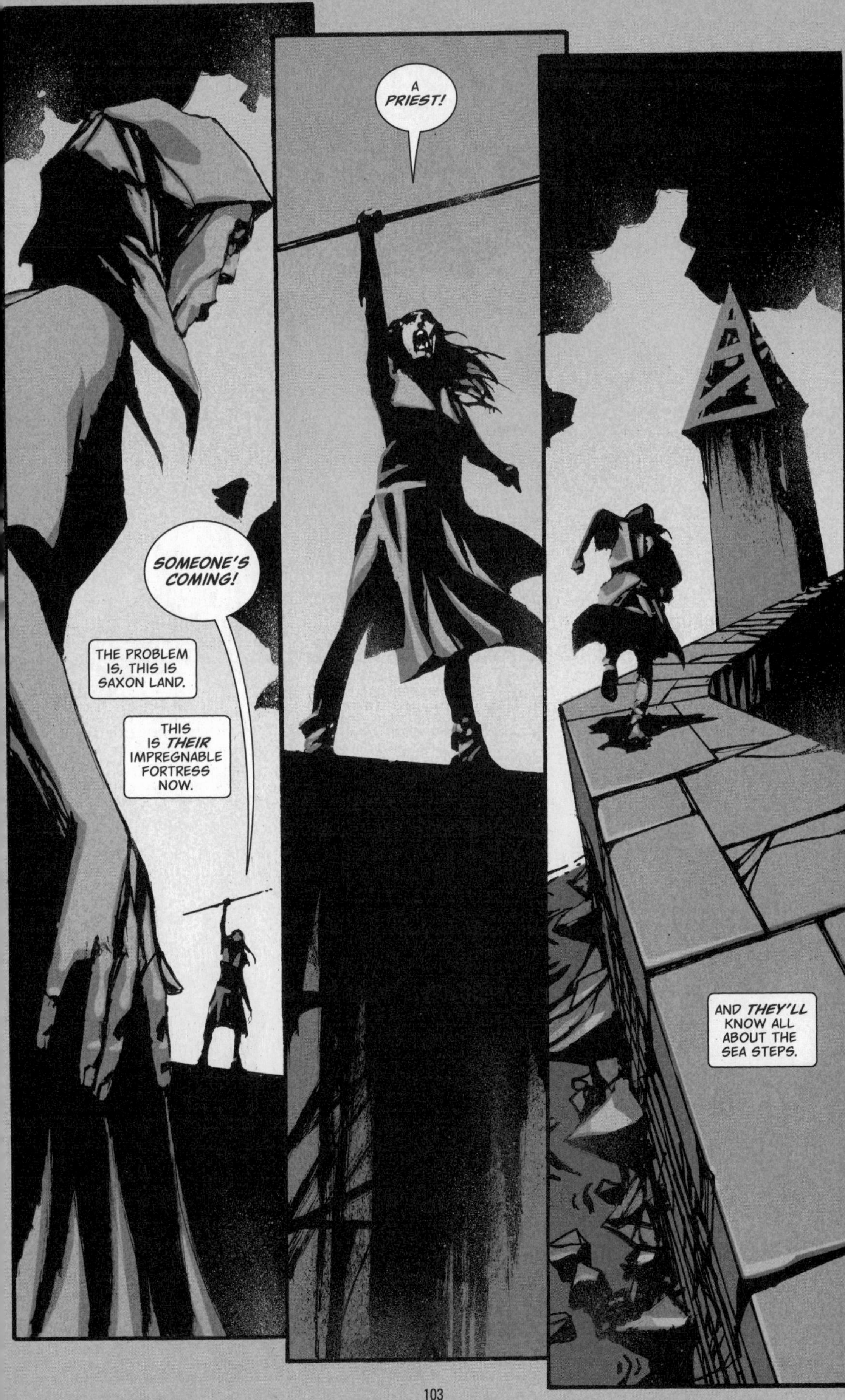
THE PROBLEM IS, THIS IS SAXON LAND.
THIS IS THEIR IMPREGNABLE FORTRESS NOW.
SOMEONE'S COMING!
A PRIEST!
AND THEY'LL KNOW ALL ABOUT THE SEA STEPS.

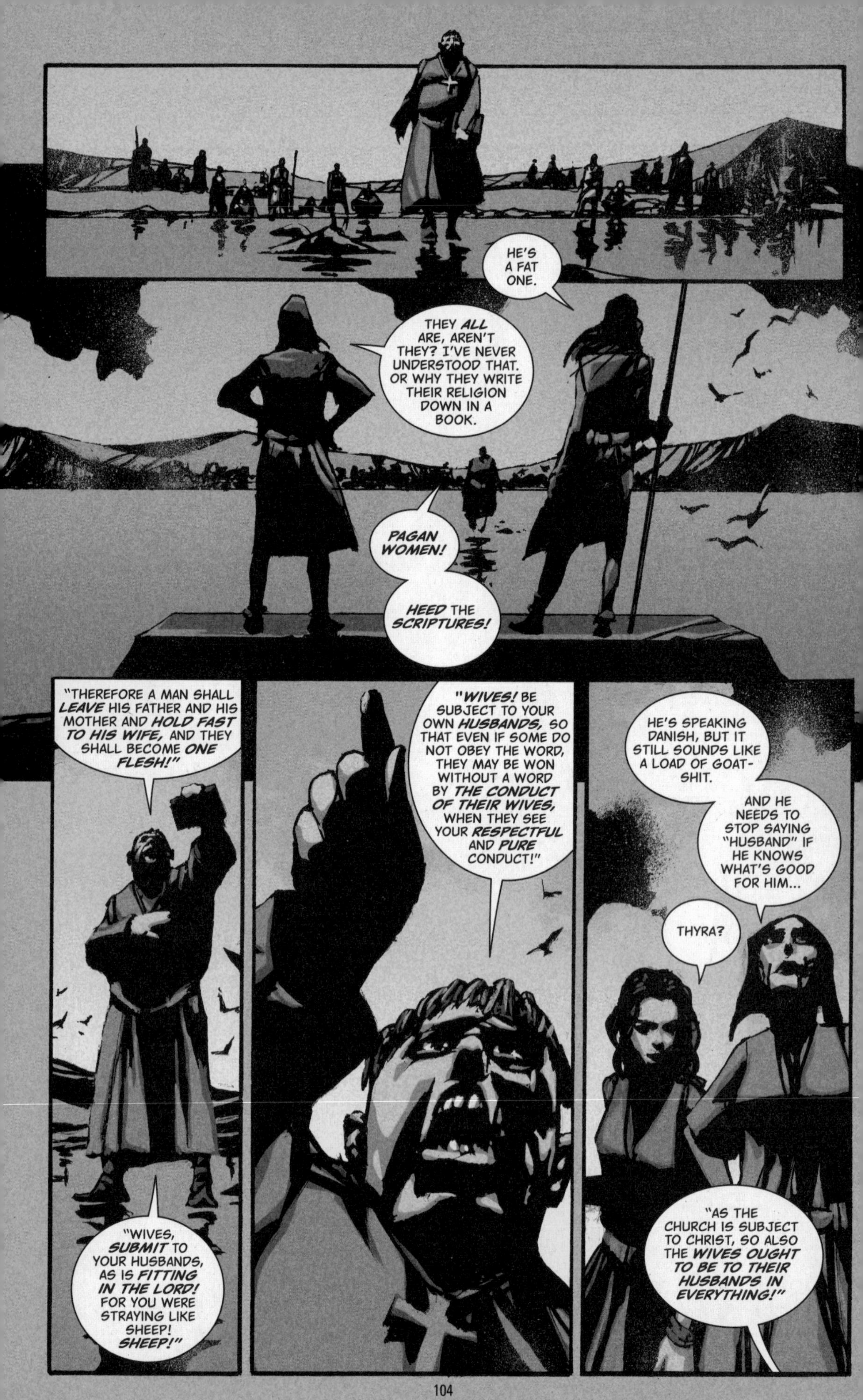
HE'S A FAT ONE.
THEY ALL ARE, AREN'T THEY? I'VE NEVER UNDERSTOOD THAT. OR WHY THEY WRITE THEIR RELIGION DOWN IN A BOOK.
PAGAN WOMEN!
HEED THE SCRIPTURES!
"THEREFORE A MAN SHALL LEAVE HIS FATHER AND HIS MOTHER AND HOLD FAST TO HIS WIFE, AND THEY SHALL BECOME ONE FLESH!"
"WIVES, SUBMIT TO YOUR HUSBANDS, AS IS FITTING IN THE LORD! FOR YOU WERE STRAYING LIKE SHEEP! SHEEP!"
"WIVES! BE SUBJECT TO YOUR OWN HUSBANDS, SO THAT EVEN IF SOME DO NOT OBEY THE WORD, THEY MAY BE WON WITHOUT A WORD BY THE CONDUCT OF THEIR WIVES, WHEN THEY SEE YOUR RESPECTFUL AND PURE CONDUCT!"
HE'S SPEAKING DANISH, BUT IT STILL SOUNDS LIKE A LOAD OF GOAT-SHIT.
AND HE NEEDS TO STOP SAYING "HUSBAND" IF HE KNOWS WHAT'S GOOD FOR HIM...
THYRA?
"AS THE CHURCH IS SUBJECT TO CHRIST, SO ALSO THE WIVES OUGHT TO BE TO THEIR HUSBANDS IN EVERYTHING!"

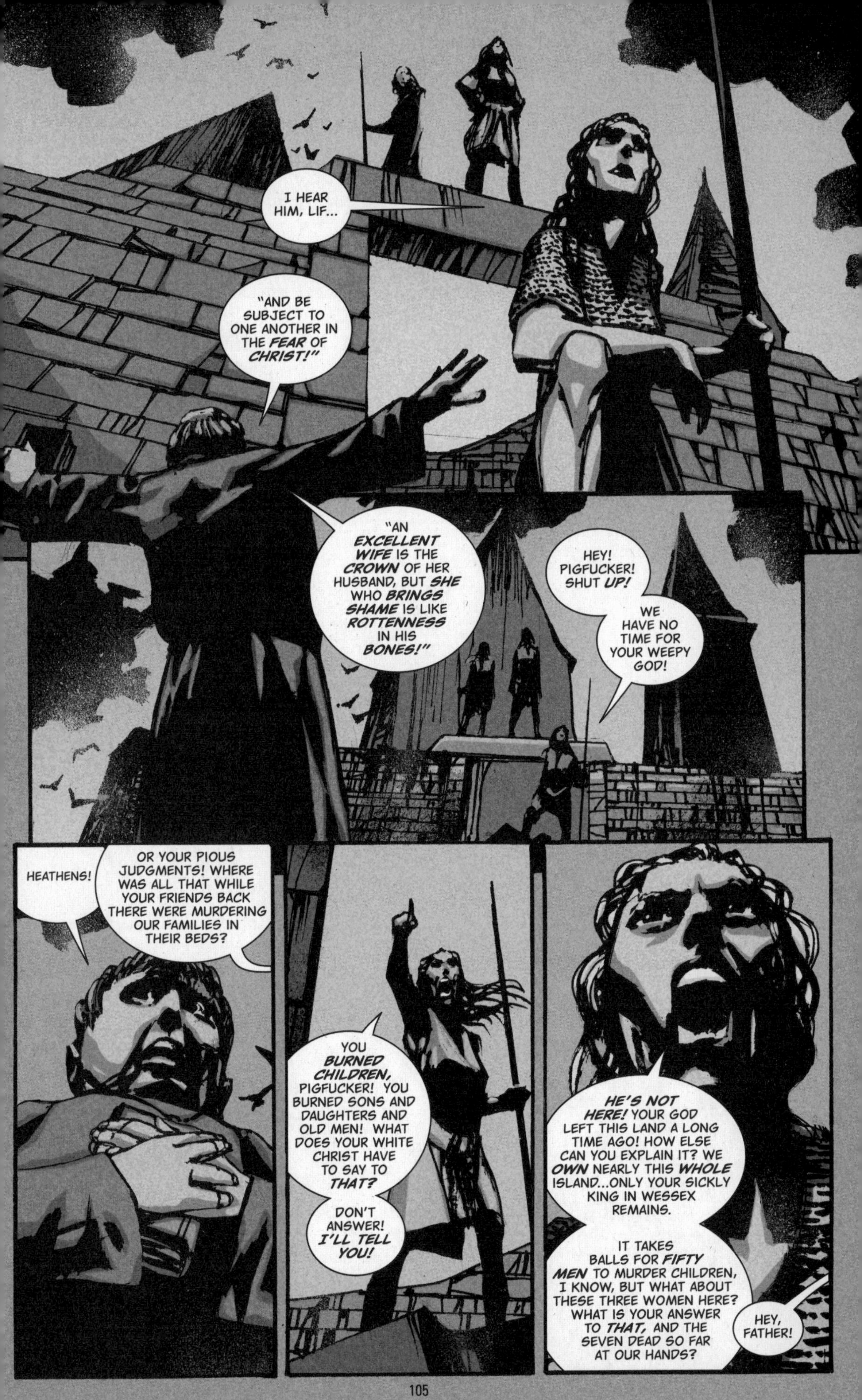
I HEAR HIM, LIF...
"AND BE SUBJECT TO ONE ANOTHER IN THE FEAR OF CHRIST!"
"AN EXCELLENT WIFE IS THE CROWN OF HER HUSBAND, BUT SHE WHO BRINGS SHAME IS LIKE ROTTENNESS IN HIS BONES!"
HEY! PIGFUCKER! SHUT UP!
WE HAVE NO TIME FOR YOUR WEEPY GOD!
HEATHENS!
OR YOUR PIOUS JUDGMENTS! WHERE WAS ALL THAT WHILE YOUR FRIENDS BACK THERE WERE MURDERING OUR FAMILIES IN THEIR BEDS?
YOU BURNED CHILDREN, PIGFUCKER! YOU BURNED SONS AND DAUGHTERS AND OLD MEN! WHAT DOES YOUR WHITE CHRIST HAVE TO SAY TO THAT?
DON'T ANSWER! I'LL TELL YOU!
HE'S NOT HERE! YOUR GOD LEFT THIS LAND A LONG TIME AGO! HOW ELSE CAN YOU EXPLAIN IT? WE OWN NEARLY THIS WHOLE ISLAND...ONLY YOUR SICKLY KING IN WESSEX REMAINS.
IT TAKES BALLS FOR FIFTY MEN TO MURDER CHILDREN, I KNOW, BUT WHAT ABOUT THESE THREE WOMEN HERE? WHAT IS YOUR ANSWER TO THAT, AND THE SEVEN DEAD SO FAR AT OUR HANDS?
HEY, FATHER!

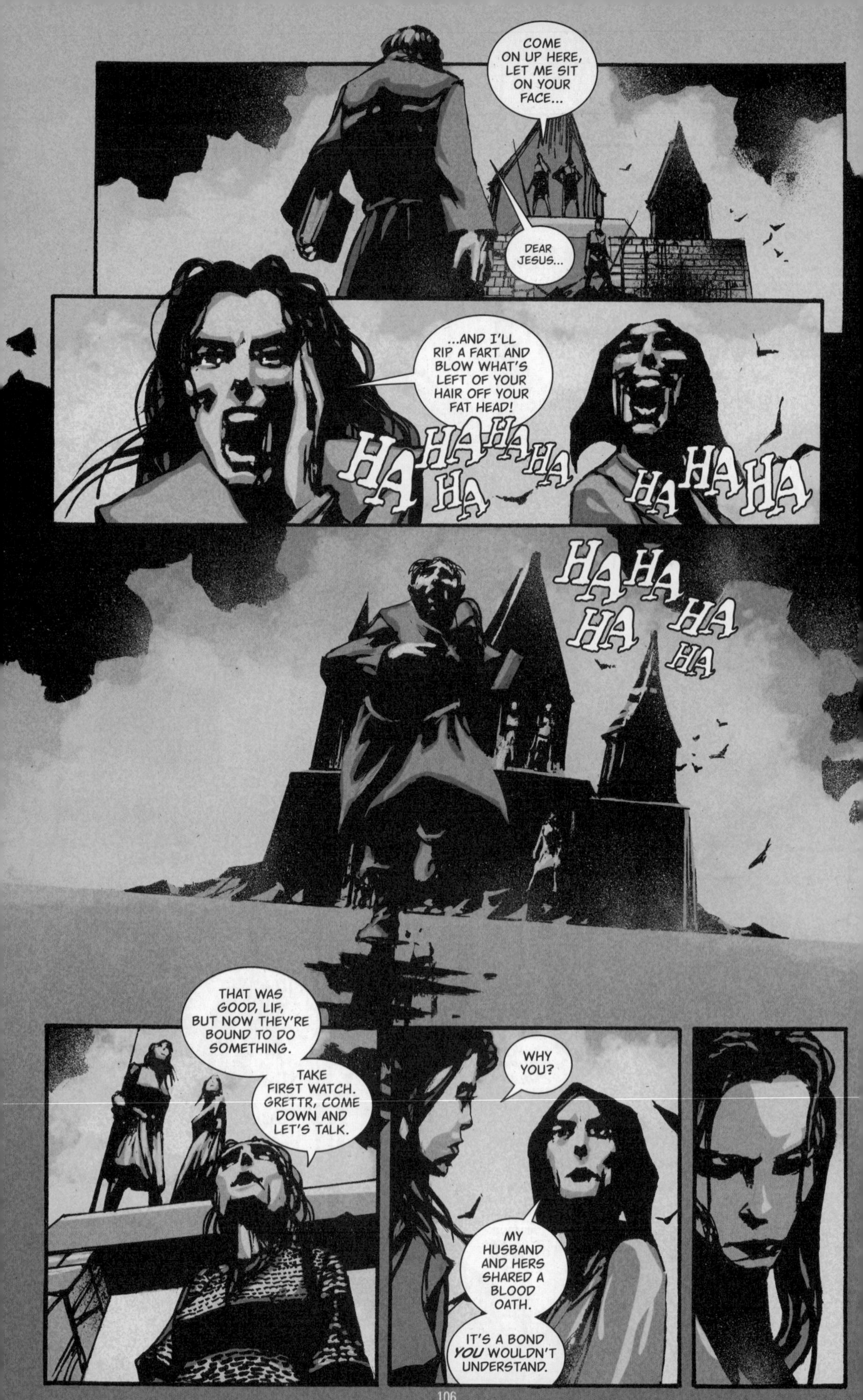
COME ON UP HERE, LET ME SIT ON YOUR FACE...
DEAR JESUS...
...AND I'LL RIP A FART AND BLOW WHAT'S LEFT OF YOUR HAIR OFF YOUR FAT HEAD!
HA HA HA HA HA HA
HA HA HA HA
HA HA HA HA HA HA
THAT WAS GOOD, LIF, BUT NOW THEY'RE BOUND TO DO SOMETHING.
TAKE FIRST WATCH. GRETTR, COME DOWN AND LET'S TALK.
WHY YOU?
MY HUSBAND AND HERS SHARED A BLOOD OATH.
IT'S A BOND *YOU* WOULDN'T UNDERSTAND.

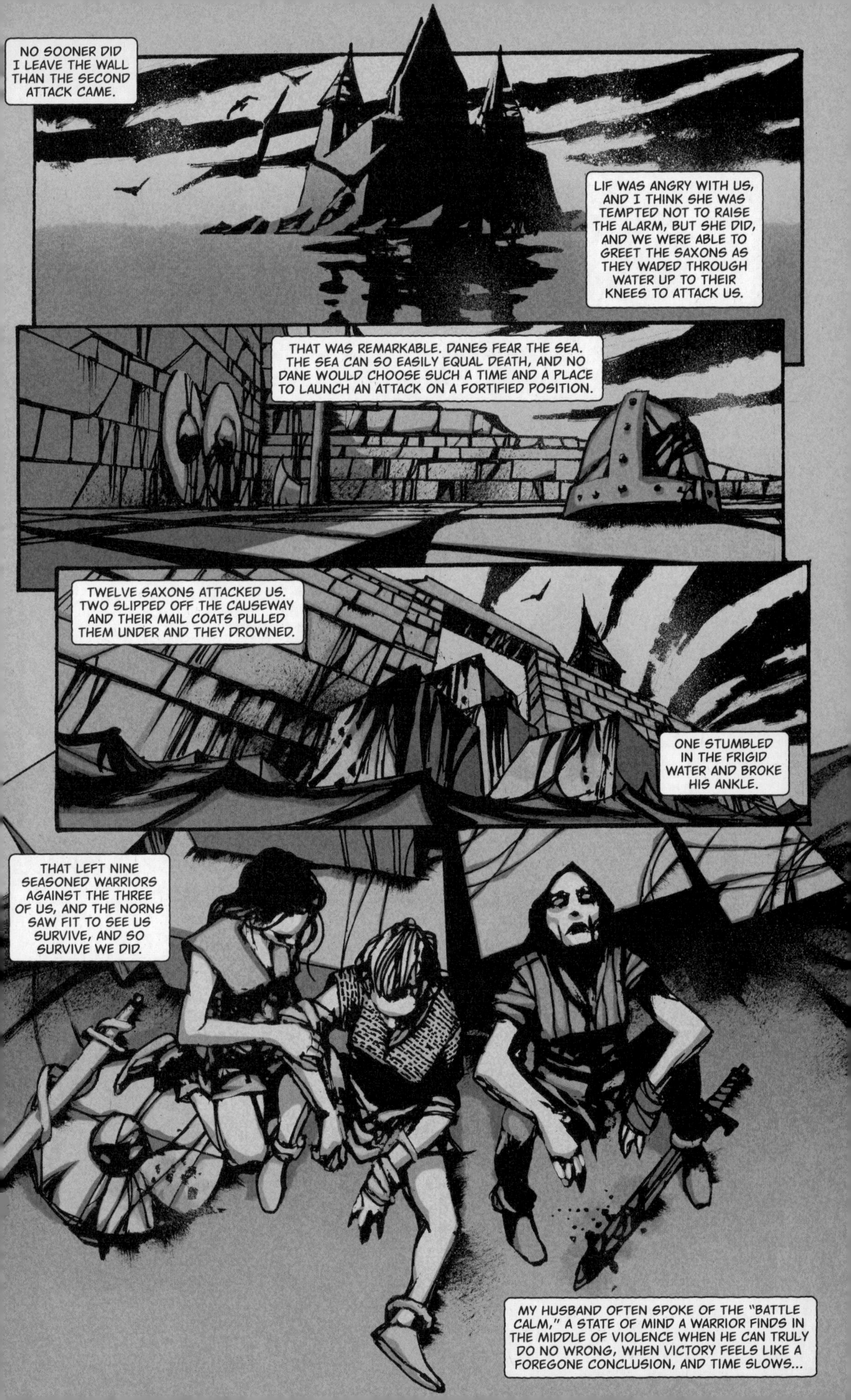
NO SOONER DID I LEAVE THE WALL THAN THE SECOND ATTACK CAME.
LIF WAS ANGRY WITH US, AND I THINK SHE WAS TEMPTED NOT TO RAISE THE ALARM, BUT SHE DID, AND WE WERE ABLE TO GREET THE SAXONS AS THEY WADED THROUGH WATER UP TO THEIR KNEES TO ATTACK US.
THAT WAS REMARKABLE. DANES FEAR THE SEA. THE SEA CAN SO EASILY EQUAL DEATH, AND NO DANE WOULD CHOOSE SUCH A TIME AND A PLACE TO LAUNCH AN ATTACK ON A FORTIFIED POSITION.
TWELVE SAXONS ATTACKED US. TWO SLIPPED OFF THE CAUSEWAY AND THEIR MAIL COATS PULLED THEM UNDER AND THEY DROWNED.
ONE STUMBLED IN THE FRIGID WATER AND BROKE HIS ANKLE.
THAT LEFT NINE SEASONED WARRIORS AGAINST THE THREE OF US, AND THE NORNS SAW FIT TO SEE US SURVIVE, AND SO SURVIVE WE DID.
MY HUSBAND OFTEN SPOKE OF THE "BATTLE CALM," A STATE OF MIND A WARRIOR FINDS IN THE MIDDLE OF VIOLENCE WHEN HE CAN TRULY DO NO WRONG, WHEN VICTORY FEELS LIKE A FOREGONE CONCLUSION, AND TIME SLOWS...

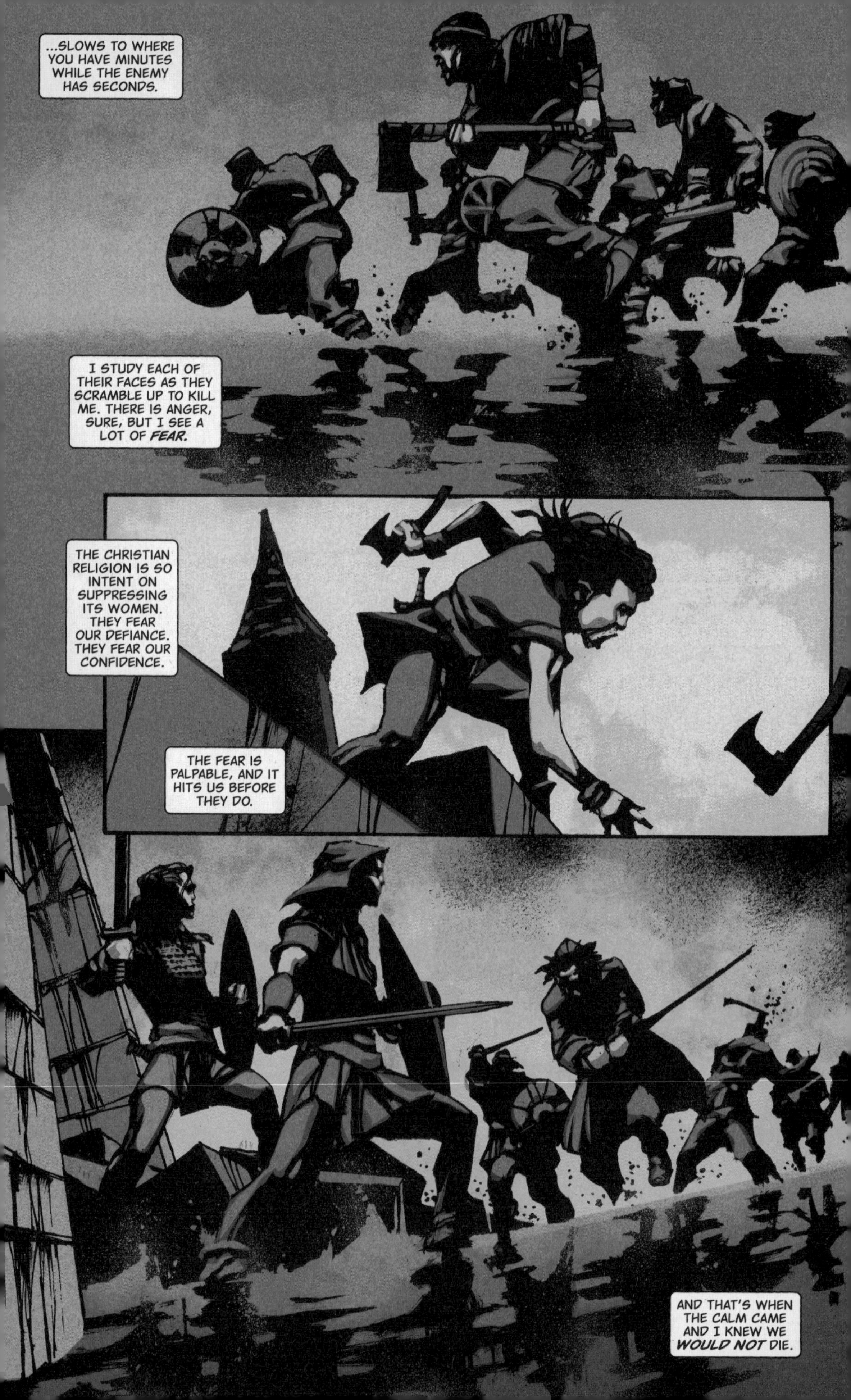
...SLOWS TO WHERE YOU HAVE MINUTES WHILE THE ENEMY HAS SECONDS.
I STUDY EACH OF THEIR FACES AS THEY SCRAMBLE UP TO KILL ME. THERE IS ANGER, SURE, BUT I SEE A LOT OF *FEAR.*
THE CHRISTIAN RELIGION IS SO INTENT ON SUPPRESSING ITS WOMEN. THEY FEAR OUR DEFIANCE. THEY FEAR OUR CONFIDENCE.
THE FEAR IS PALPABLE, AND IT HITS US BEFORE THEY DO.
AND THAT'S WHEN THE CALM CAME AND I KNEW WE ***WOULD NOT*** DIE.

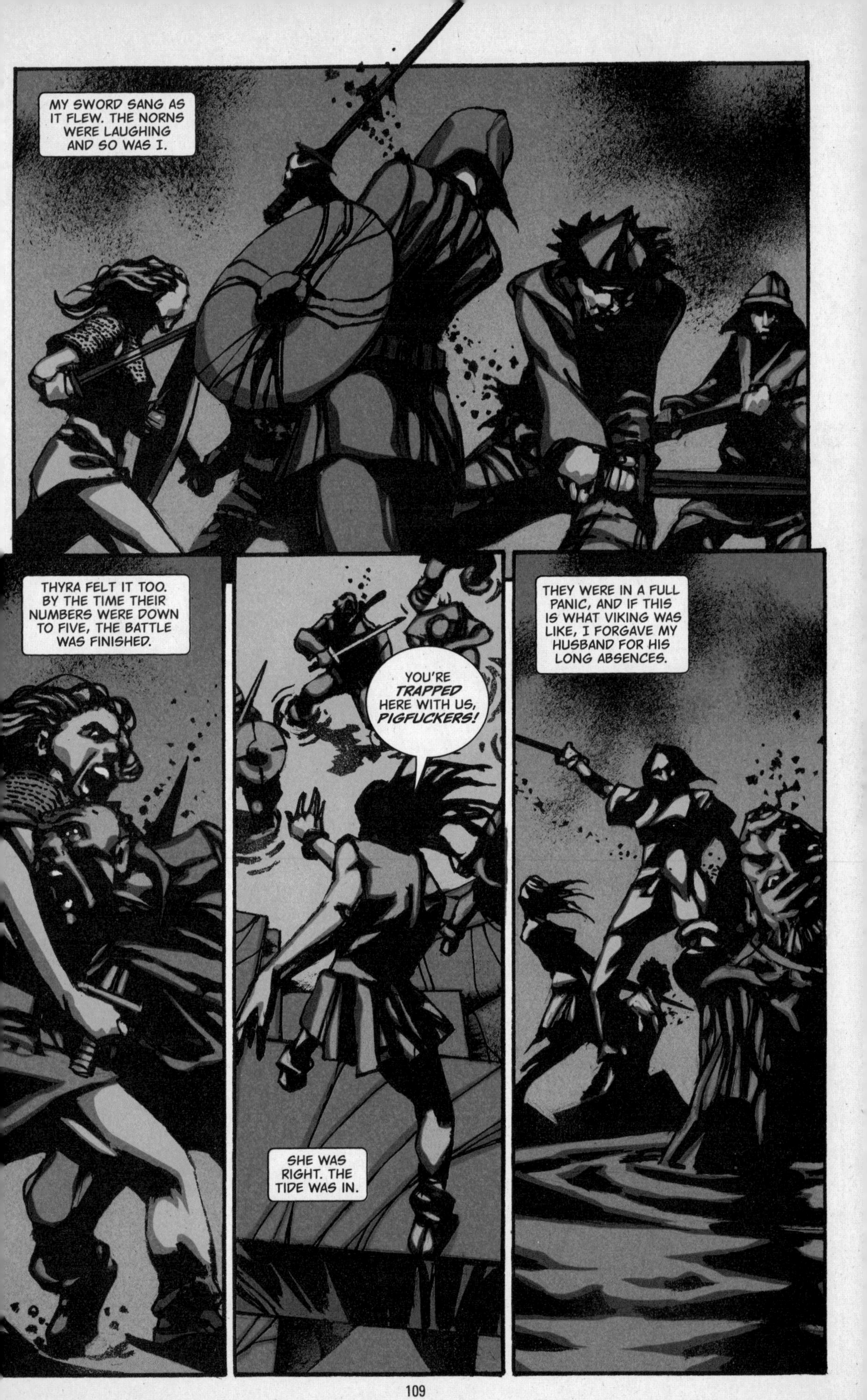
MY SWORD SANG AS IT FLEW. THE NORNS WERE LAUGHING AND SO WAS I.
THYRA FELT IT TOO. BY THE TIME THEIR NUMBERS WERE DOWN TO FIVE, THE BATTLE WAS FINISHED.
YOU'RE *TRAPPED* HERE WITH US, *PIGFUCKERS!*
SHE WAS RIGHT. THE TIDE WAS IN.
THEY WERE IN A FULL PANIC, AND IF THIS IS WHAT VIKING WAS LIKE, I FORGAVE MY HUSBAND FOR HIS LONG ABSENCES.

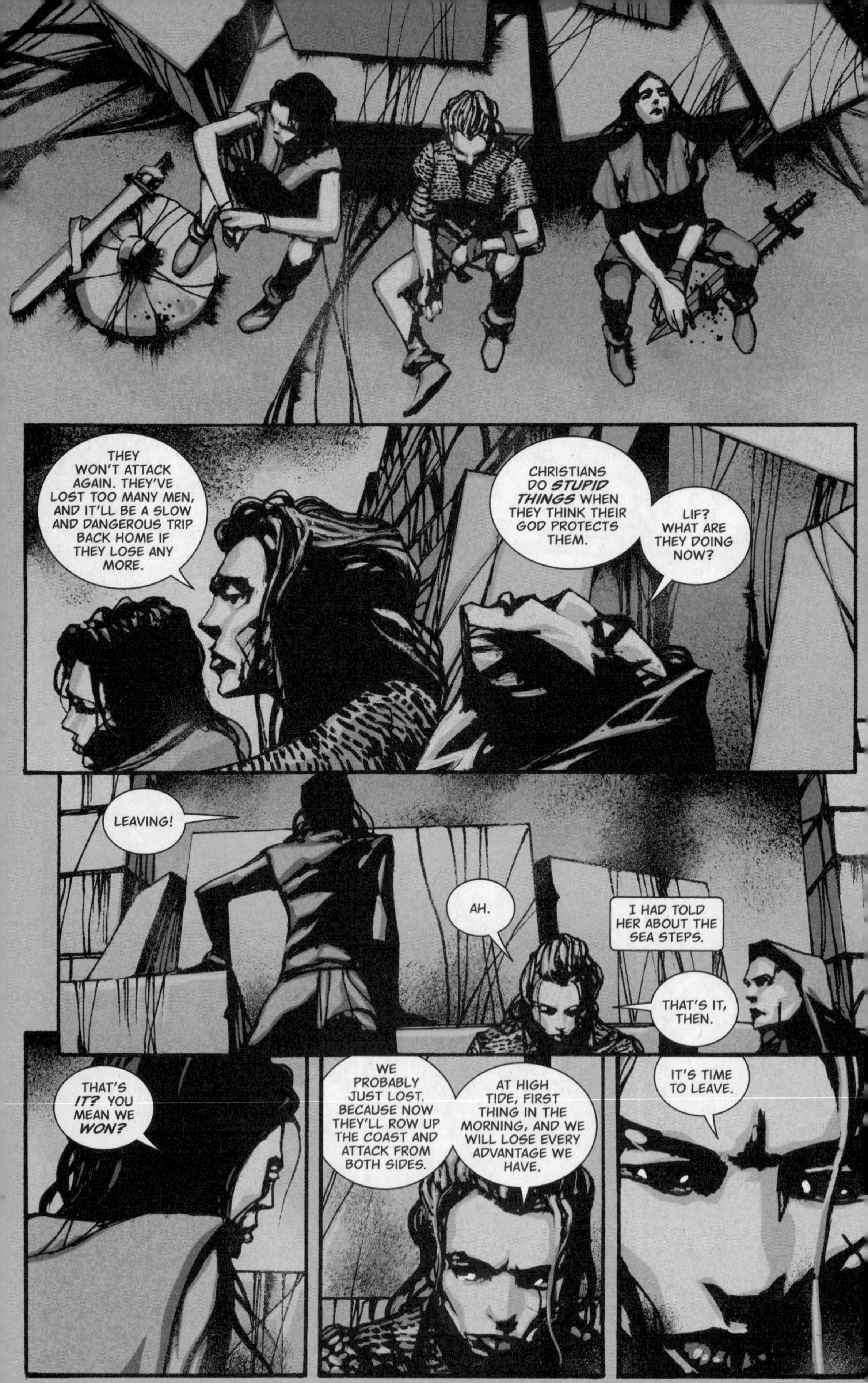
THEY WON'T ATTACK AGAIN. THEY'VE LOST TOO MANY MEN, AND IT'LL BE A SLOW AND DANGEROUS TRIP BACK HOME IF THEY LOSE ANY MORE.
CHRISTIANS DO *STUPID THINGS* WHEN THEY THINK THEIR GOD PROTECTS THEM.
LIF? WHAT ARE THEY DOING NOW?
LEAVING!
AH.
I HAD TOLD HER ABOUT THE SEA STEPS.
THAT'S IT, THEN.
THAT'S *IT?* YOU MEAN WE *WON?*
WE PROBABLY JUST LOST. BECAUSE NOW THEY'LL ROW UP THE COAST AND ATTACK FROM BOTH SIDES.
AT HIGH TIDE, FIRST THING IN THE MORNING, AND WE WILL LOSE EVERY ADVANTAGE WE HAVE.
IT'S TIME TO LEAVE.

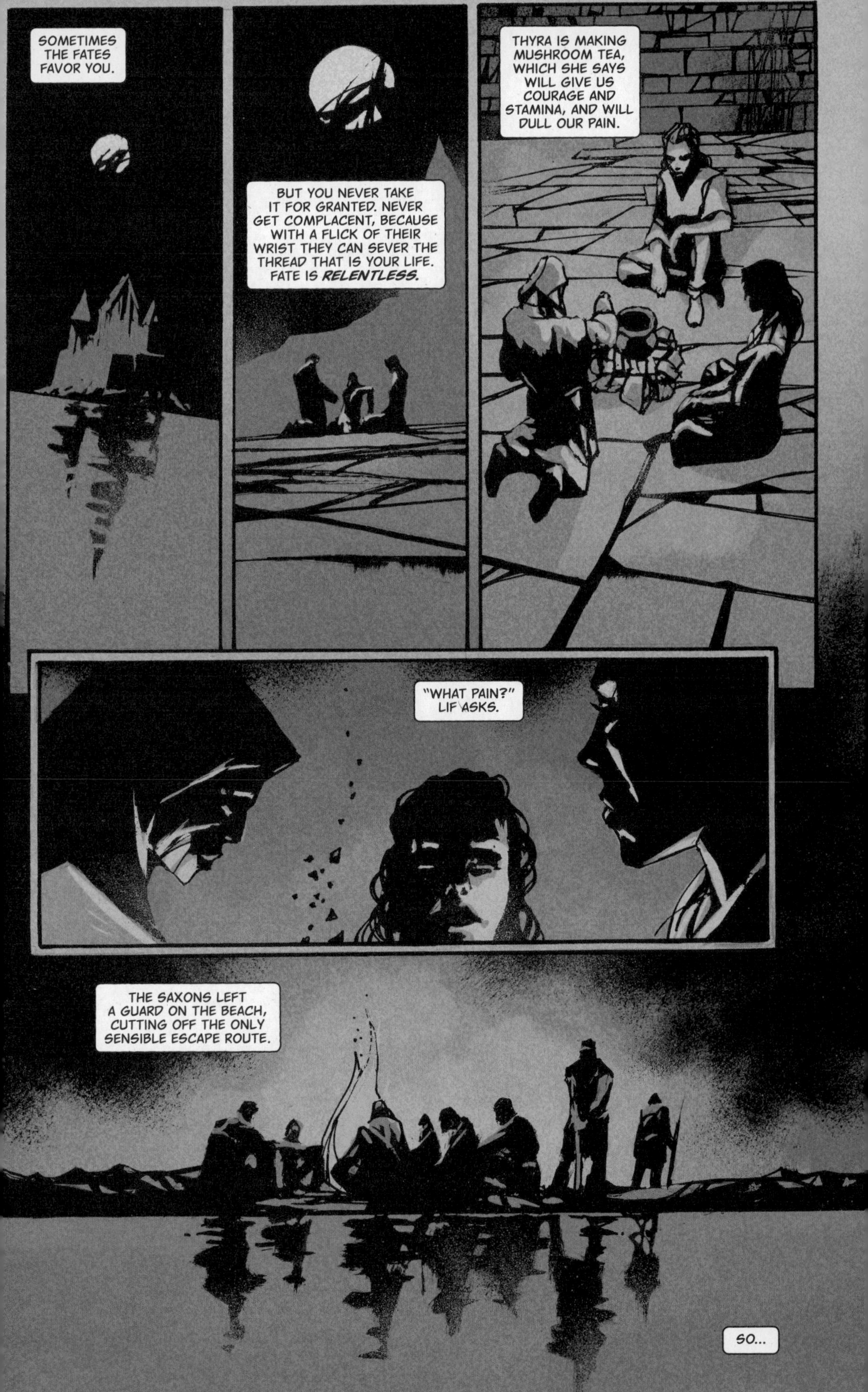
SOMETIMES THE FATES FAVOR YOU.
BUT YOU NEVER TAKE IT FOR GRANTED. NEVER GET COMPLACENT, BECAUSE WITH A FLICK OF THEIR WRIST THEY CAN SEVER THE THREAD THAT IS YOUR LIFE. FATE IS RELENTLESS.
THYRA IS MAKING MUSHROOM TEA, WHICH SHE SAYS WILL GIVE US COURAGE AND STAMINA, AND WILL DULL OUR PAIN.
"WHAT PAIN?" LIF ASKS.
THE SAXONS LEFT A GUARD ON THE BEACH, CUTTING OFF THE ONLY SENSIBLE ESCAPE ROUTE.
SO...

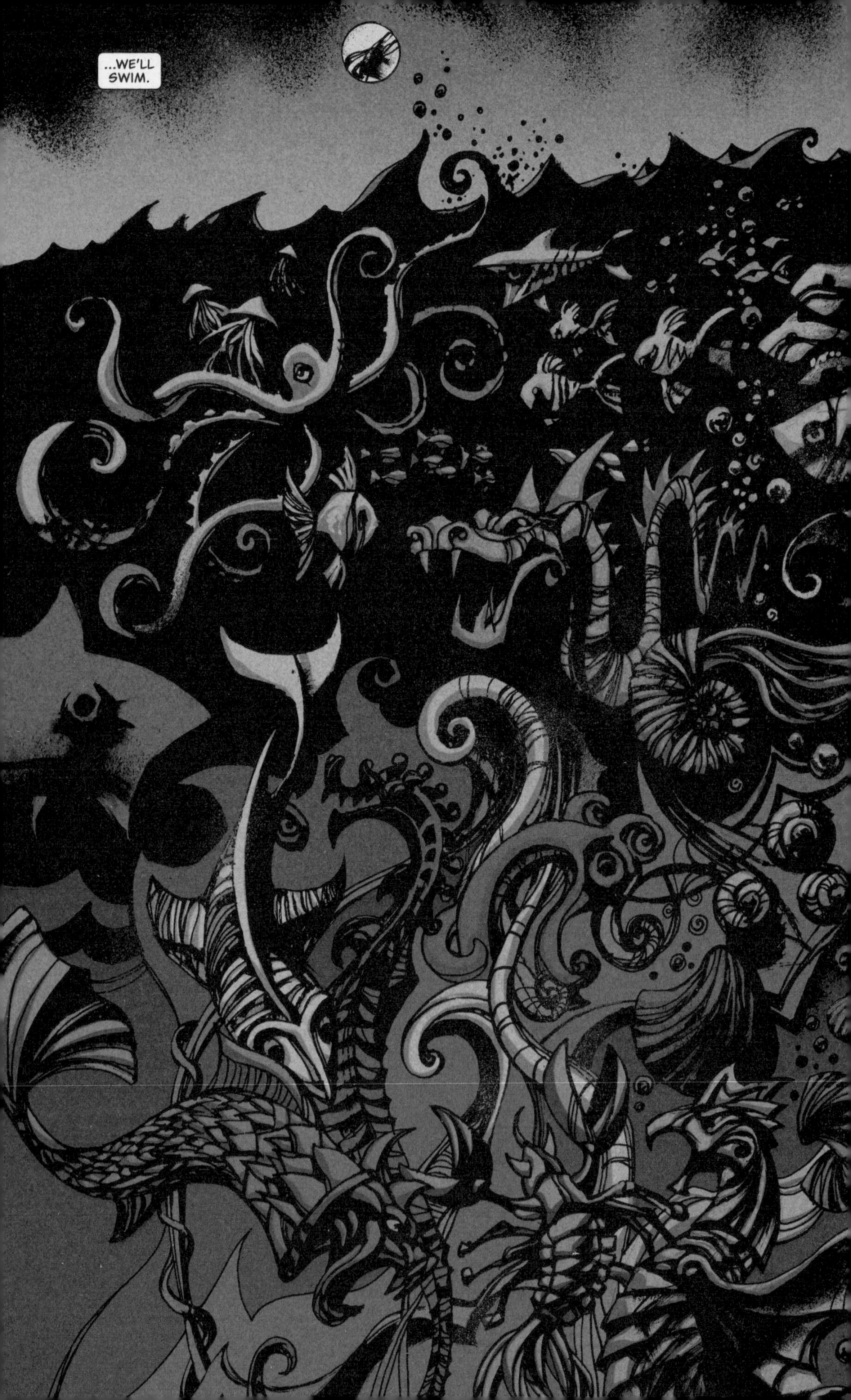
...WE'LL SWIM.

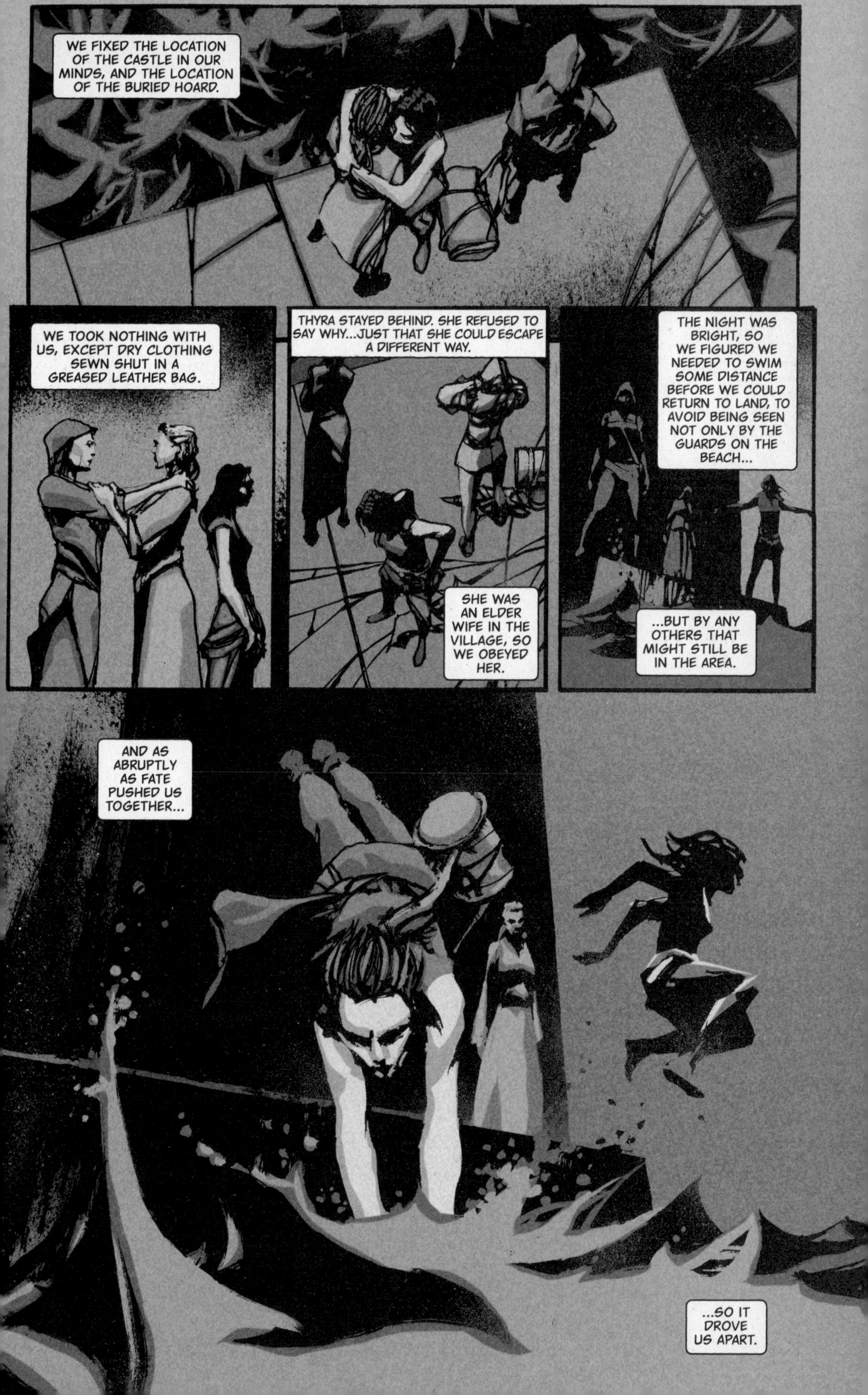
WE FIXED THE LOCATION OF THE CASTLE IN OUR MINDS, AND THE LOCATION OF THE BURIED HOARD.
WE TOOK NOTHING WITH US, EXCEPT DRY CLOTHING SEWN SHUT IN A GREASED LEATHER BAG.
THYRA STAYED BEHIND. SHE REFUSED TO SAY WHY...JUST THAT SHE COULD ESCAPE A DIFFERENT WAY.
SHE WAS AN ELDER WIFE IN THE VILLAGE, SO WE OBEYED HER.
THE NIGHT WAS BRIGHT, SO WE FIGURED WE NEEDED TO SWIM SOME DISTANCE BEFORE WE COULD RETURN TO LAND, TO AVOID BEING SEEN NOT ONLY BY THE GUARDS ON THE BEACH...
...BUT BY ANY OTHERS THAT MIGHT STILL BE IN THE AREA.
AND AS ABRUPTLY AS FATE PUSHED US TOGETHER...
...SO IT DROVE US APART.

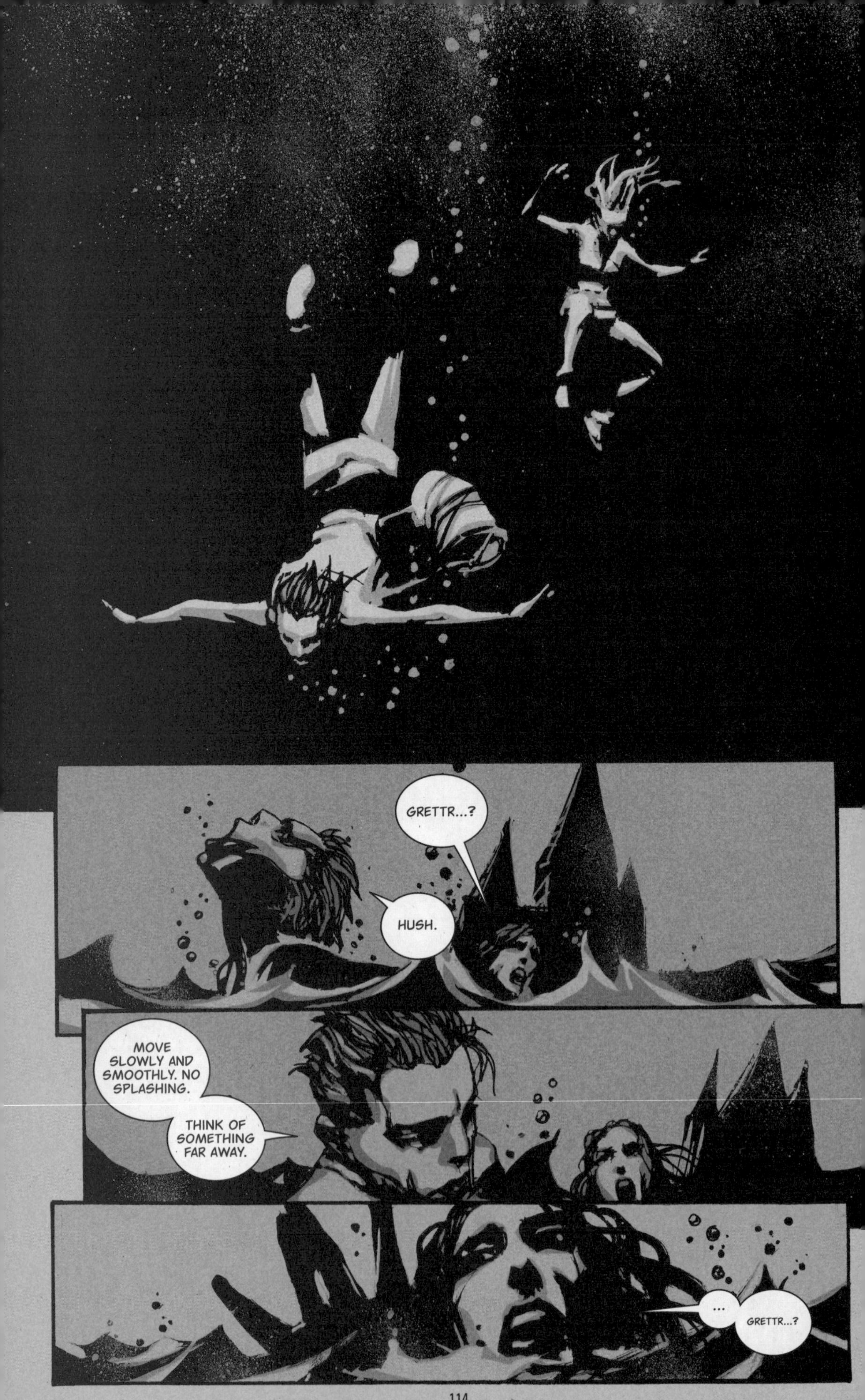
GRETTR...?
HUSH.
MOVE SLOWLY AND SMOOTHLY. NO SPLASHING.
THINK OF SOMETHING FAR AWAY.
...
GRETTR...?

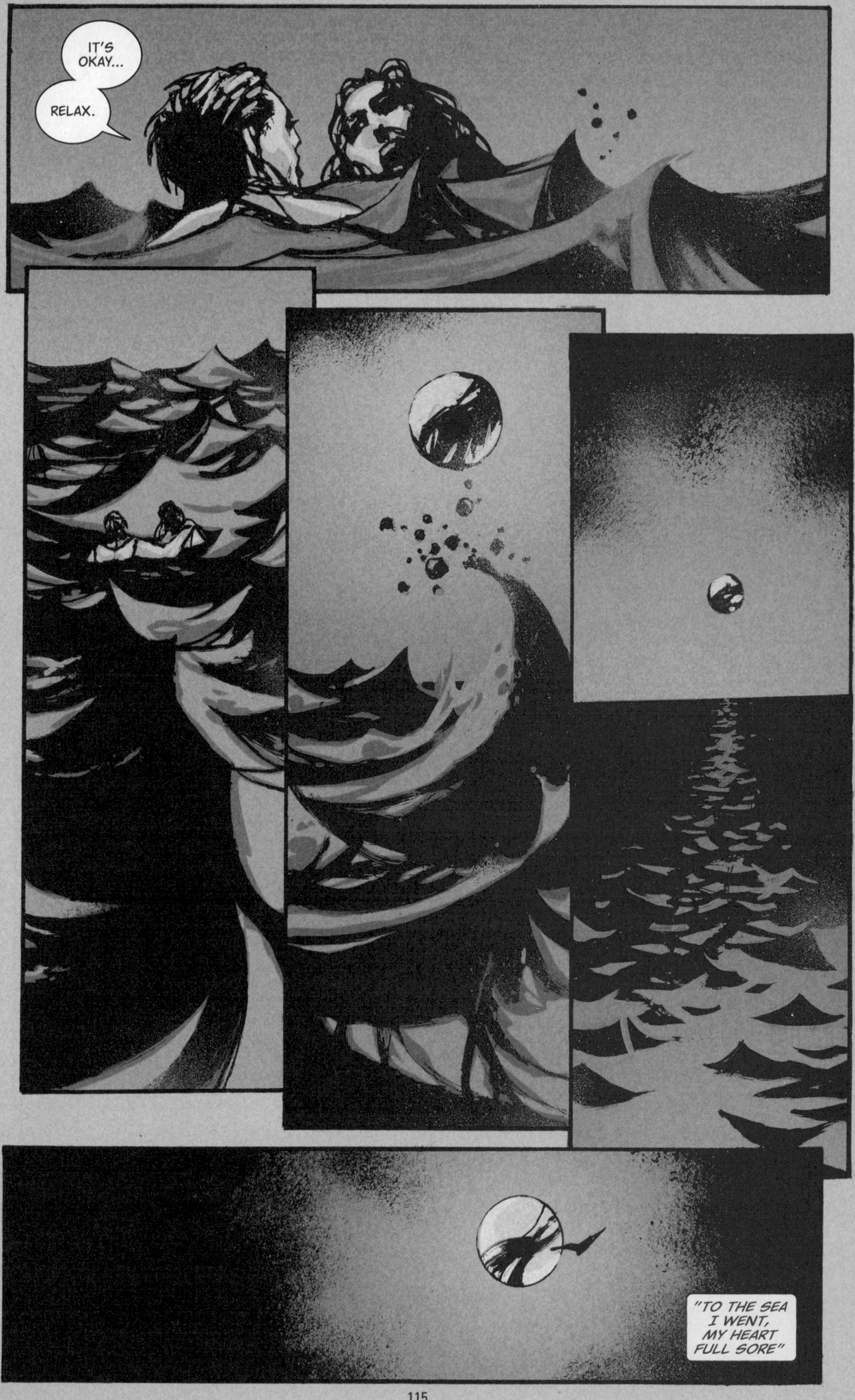
IT'S OKAY...
RELAX.
"TO THE SEA I WENT, MY HEART FULL SORE"

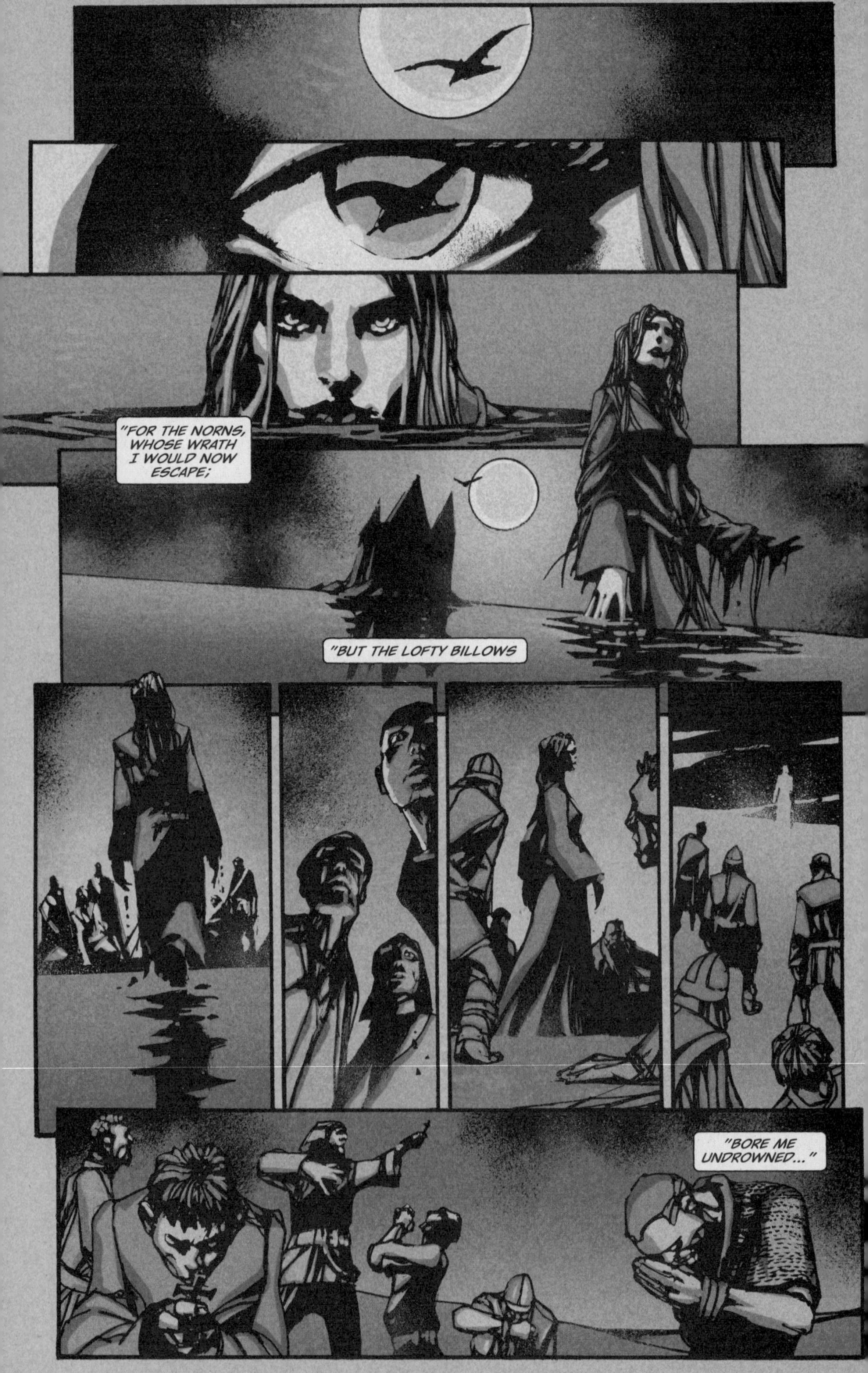
"FOR THE NORNS, WHOSE WRATH I WOULD NOW ESCAPE;
"BUT THE LOFTY BILLOWS
"BORE ME UNDROWNED..."

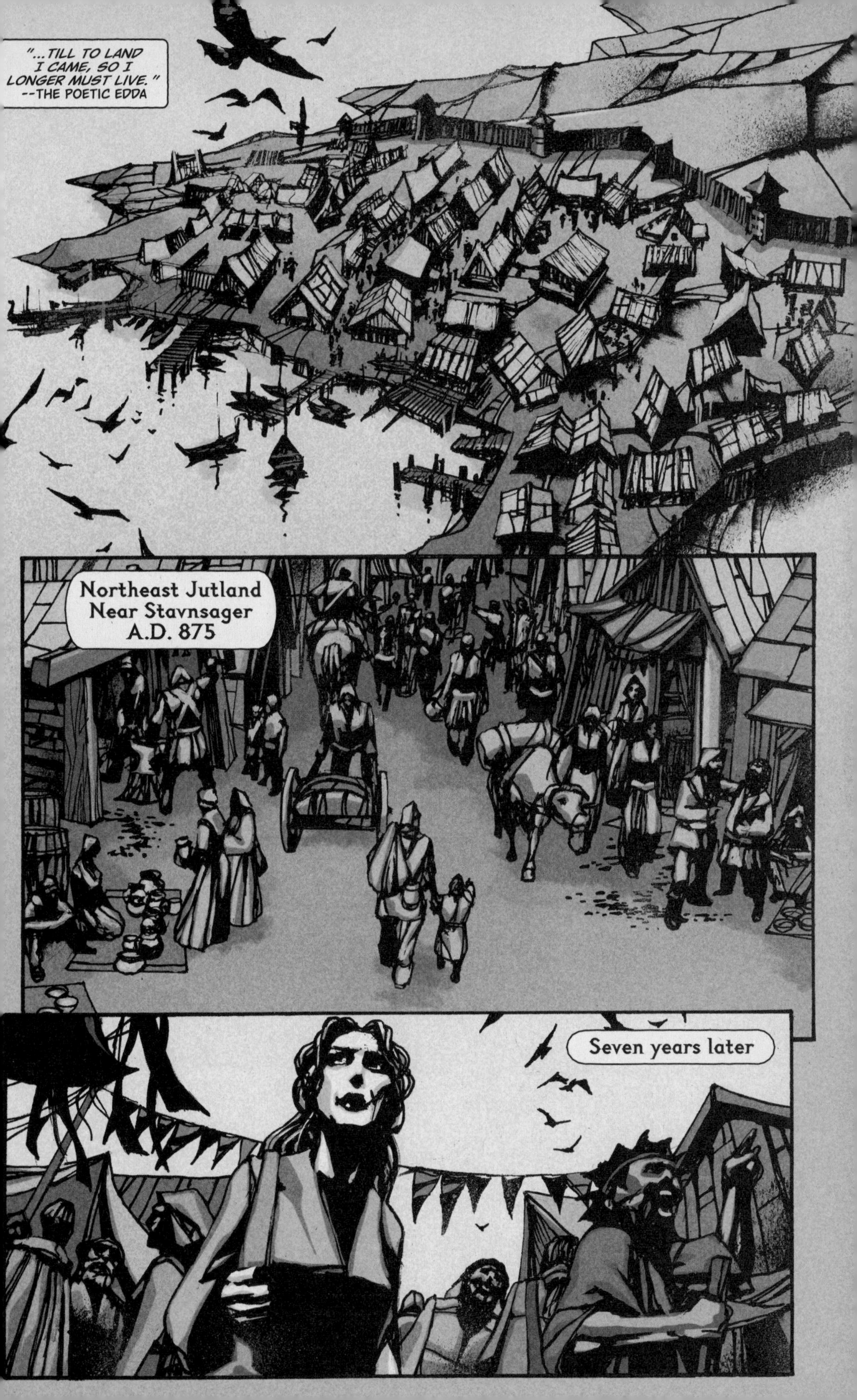
"...TILL TO LAND I CAME, SO I LONGER MUST LIVE."
--THE POETIC EDDA
Northeast Jutland
Near Stavnsager
A.D. 875
Seven years later

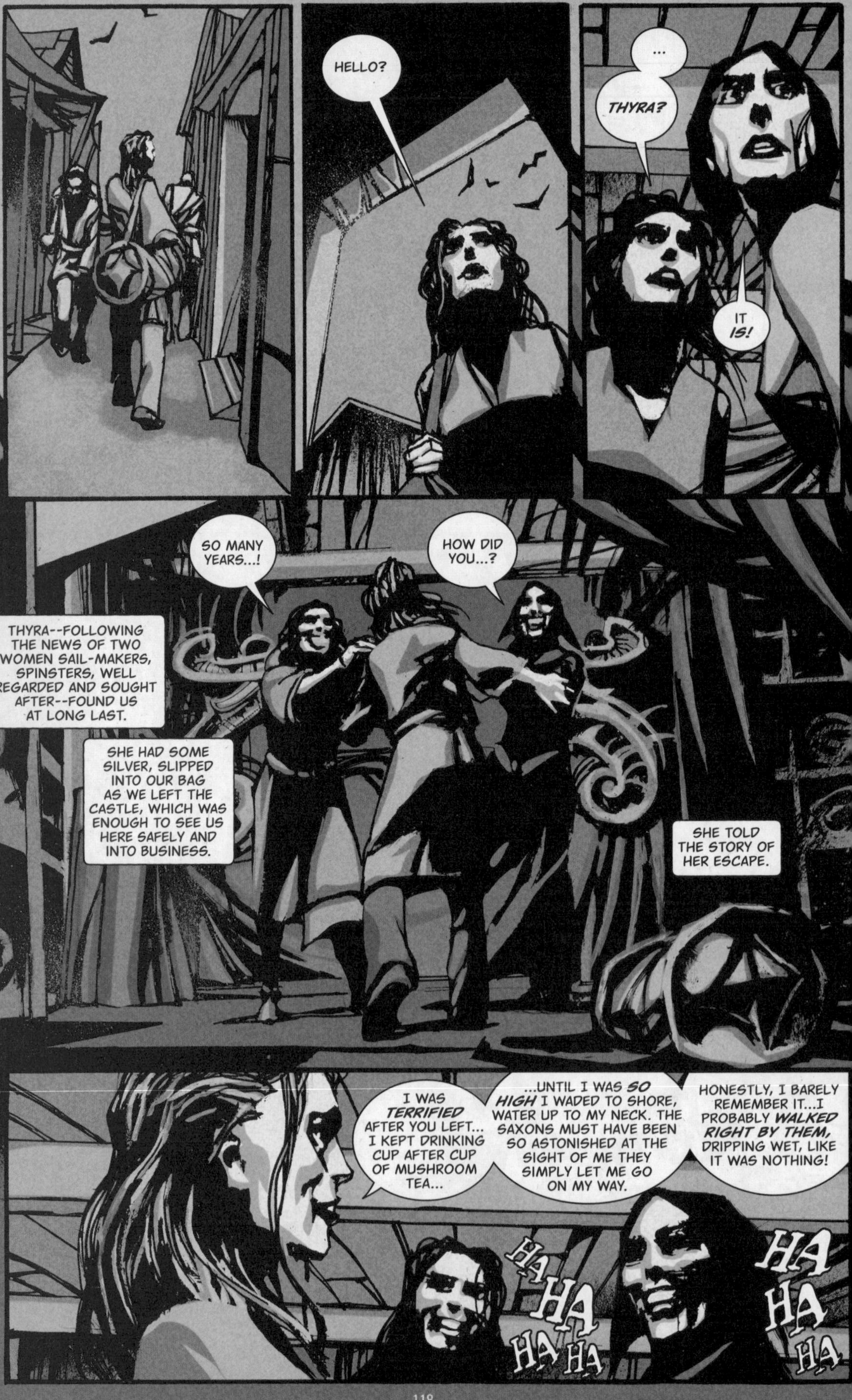
HELLO?
...
THYRA?
IT IS!
SO MANY YEARS...!
HOW DID YOU...?
THYRA--FOLLOWING THE NEWS OF TWO WOMEN SAIL-MAKERS, SPINSTERS, WELL REGARDED AND SOUGHT AFTER--FOUND US AT LONG LAST.
SHE HAD SOME SILVER, SLIPPED INTO OUR BAG AS WE LEFT THE CASTLE, WHICH WAS ENOUGH TO SEE US HERE SAFELY AND INTO BUSINESS.
SHE TOLD THE STORY OF HER ESCAPE.
I WAS TERRIFIED AFTER YOU LEFT... I KEPT DRINKING CUP AFTER CUP OF MUSHROOM TEA...
...UNTIL I WAS SO HIGH I WADED TO SHORE, WATER UP TO MY NECK. THE SAXONS MUST HAVE BEEN SO ASTONISHED AT THE SIGHT OF ME THEY SIMPLY LET ME GO ON MY WAY.
HONESTLY, I BARELY REMEMBER IT...I PROBABLY WALKED RIGHT BY THEM, DRIPPING WET, LIKE IT WAS NOTHING!
HA HA HA HA HA
HA HA HA

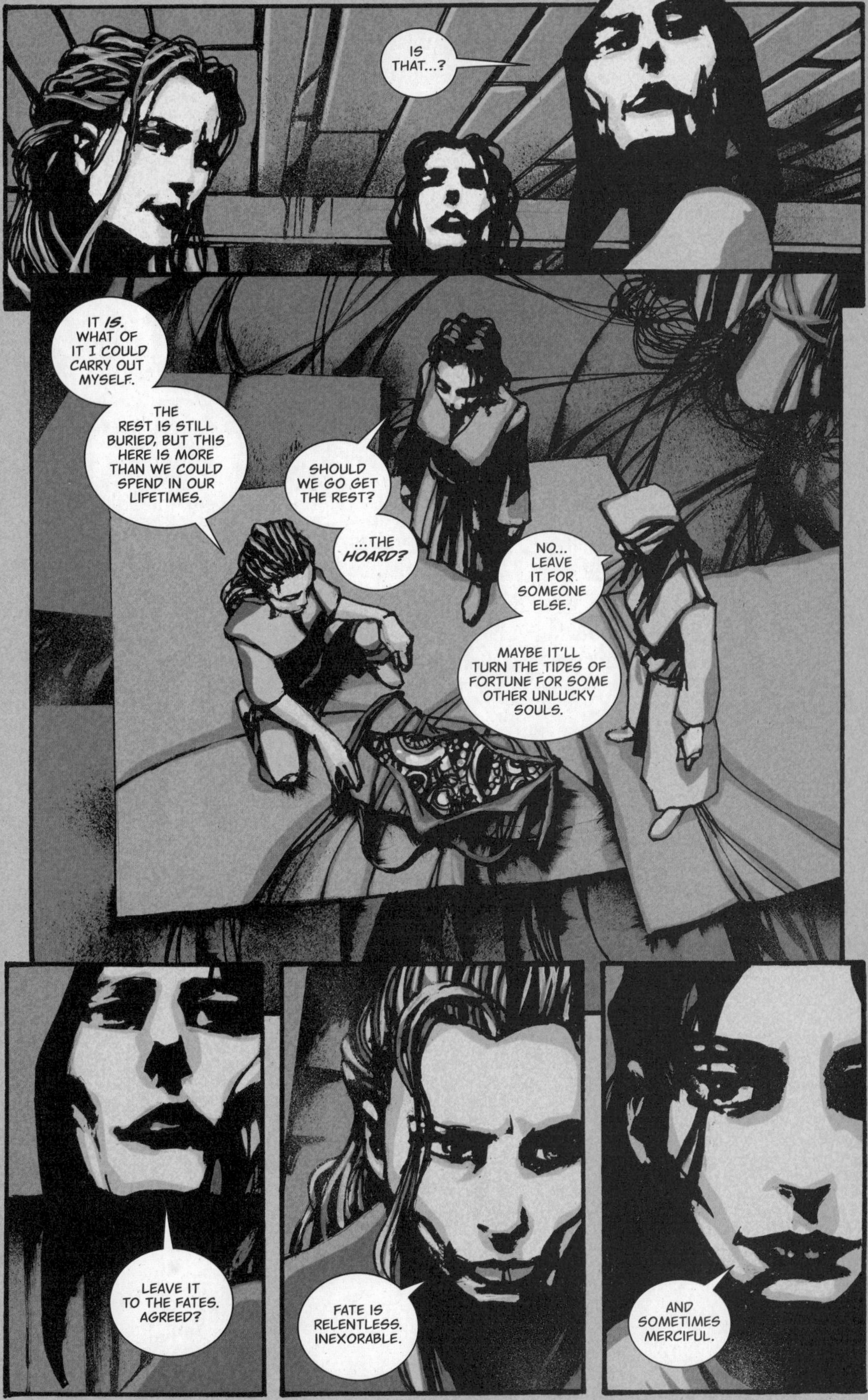
IS THAT...?
IT IS. WHAT OF IT I COULD CARRY OUT MYSELF.
THE REST IS STILL BURIED, BUT THIS HERE IS MORE THAN WE COULD SPEND IN OUR LIFETIMES.
SHOULD WE GO GET THE REST?
...THE HOARD?
NO... LEAVE IT FOR SOMEONE ELSE.
MAYBE IT'LL TURN THE TIDES OF FORTUNE FOR SOME OTHER UNLUCKY SOULS.
LEAVE IT TO THE FATES. AGREED?
FATE IS RELENTLESS. INEXORABLE.
AND SOMETIMES MERCIFUL.

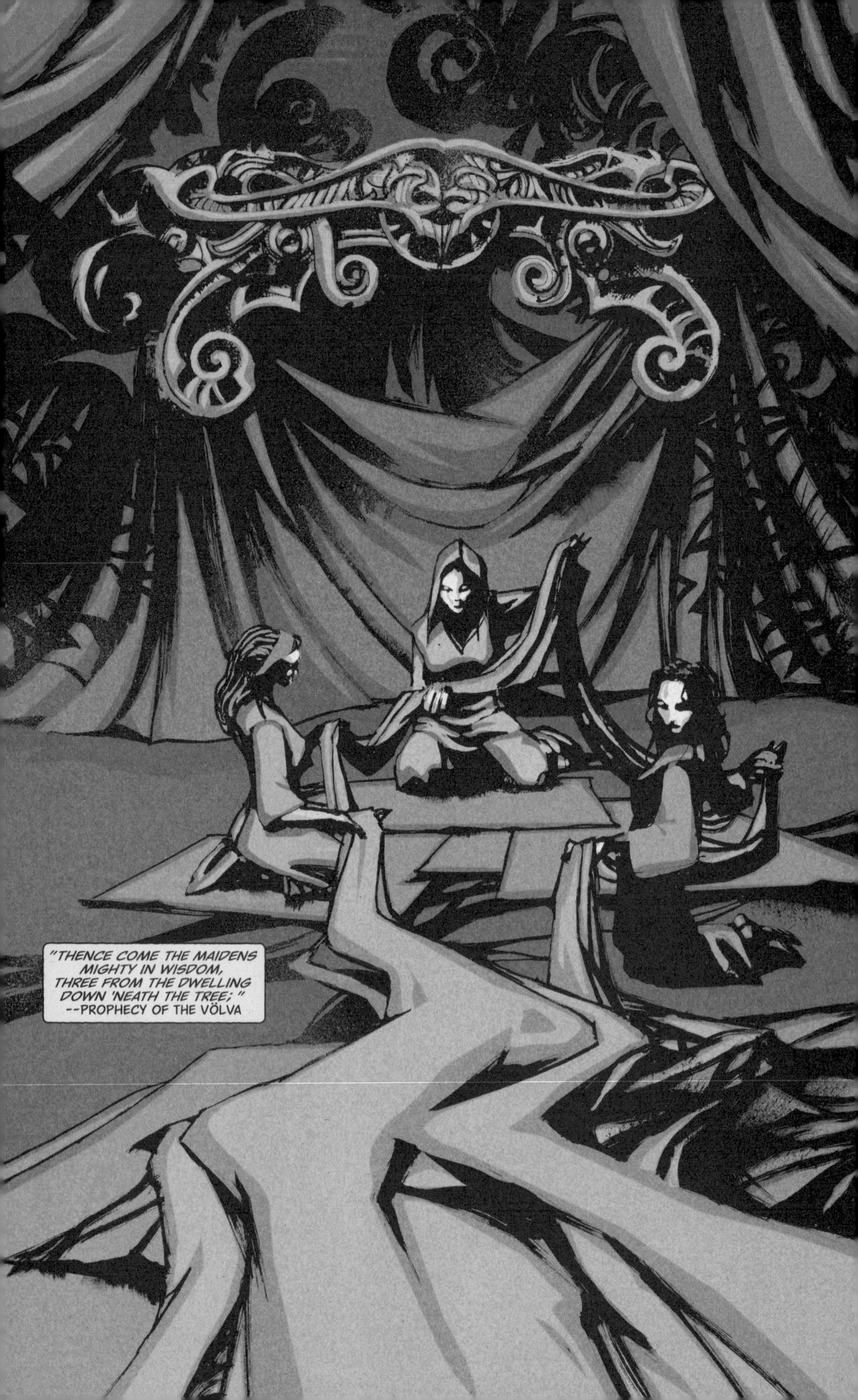
"THENCE COME THE MAIDENS
MIGHTY IN WISDOM,
THREE FROM THE DWELLING
DOWN 'NEATH THE TREE;"
--PROPHECY OF THE VÖLVA

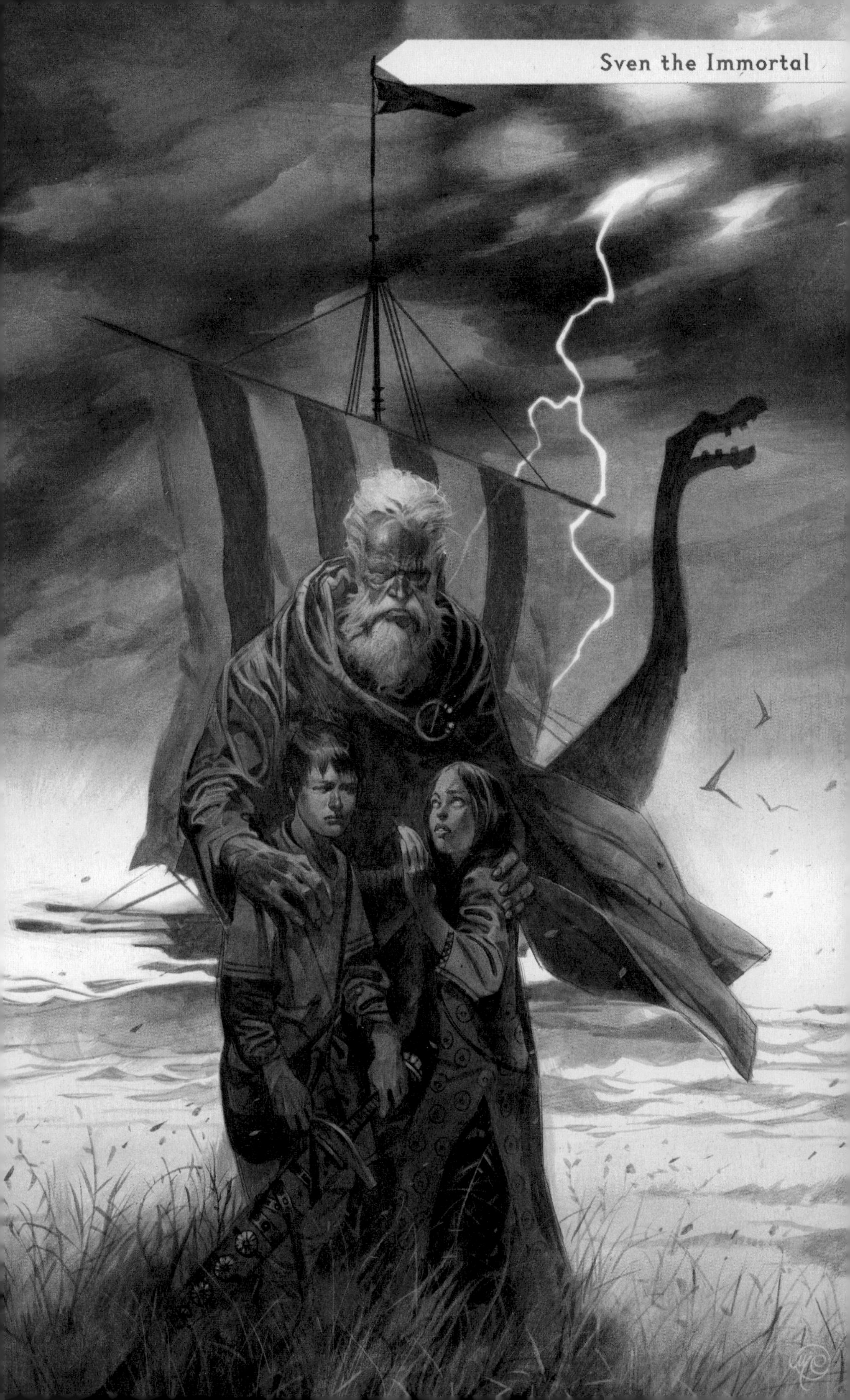
Sven the Immortal

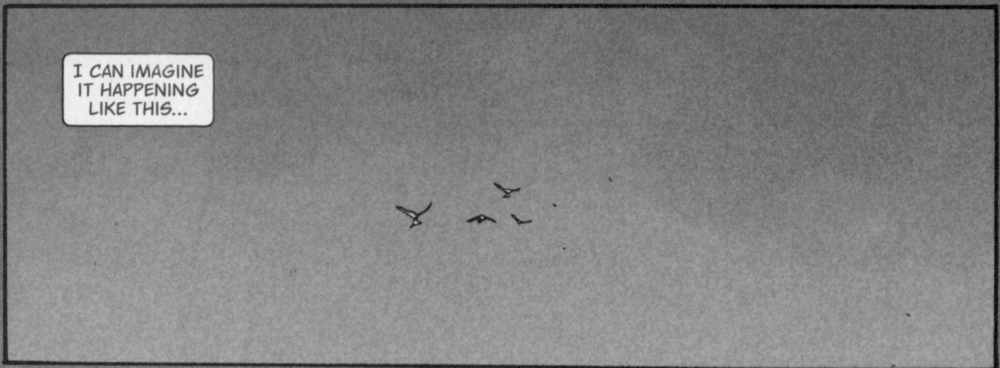
I CAN IMAGINE IT HAPPENING LIKE THIS...

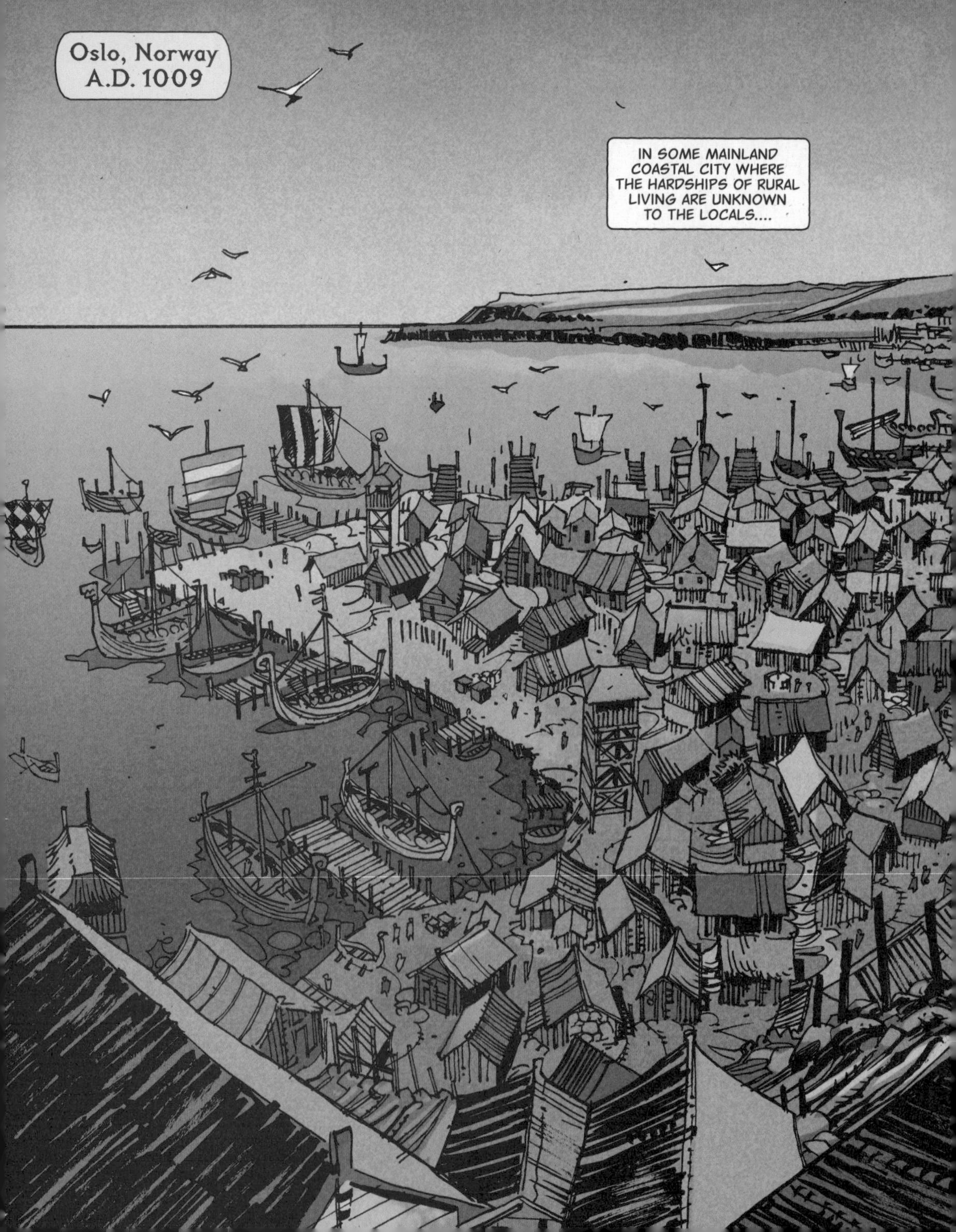
Oslo, Norway A.D. 1009
IN SOME MAINLAND COASTAL CITY WHERE THE HARDSHIPS OF RURAL LIVING ARE UNKNOWN TO THE LOCALS....

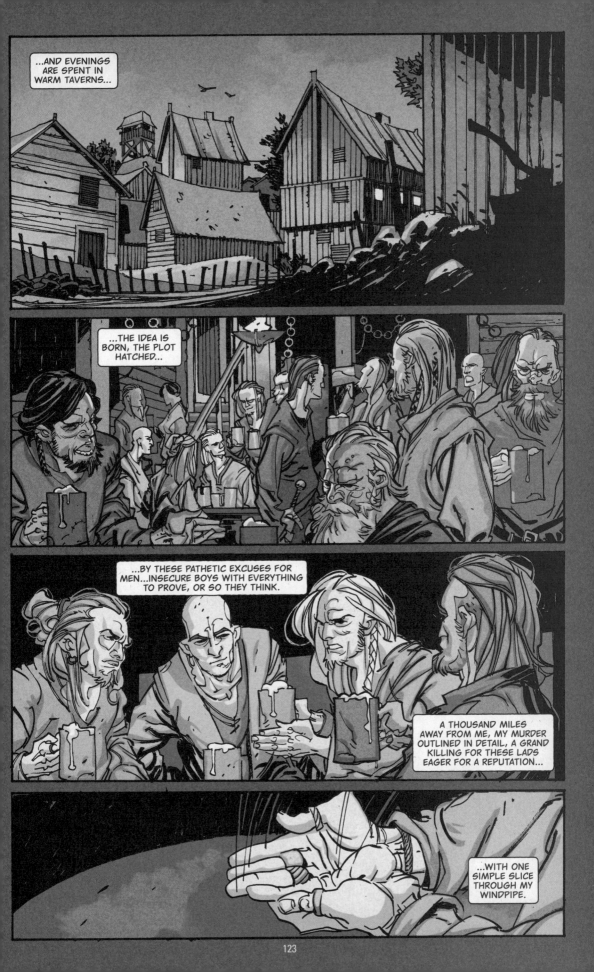

...AND EVENINGS ARE SPENT IN WARM TAVERNS...

...THE IDEA IS BORN, THE PLOT HATCHED...

...BY THESE PATHETIC EXCUSES FOR MEN...INSECURE BOYS WITH EVERYTHING TO PROVE, OR SO THEY THINK.

A THOUSAND MILES AWAY FROM ME, MY MURDER OUTLINED IN DETAIL, A GRAND KILLING FOR THESE LADS EAGER FOR A REPUTATION...

...WITH ONE SIMPLE SLICE THROUGH MY WINDPIPE.

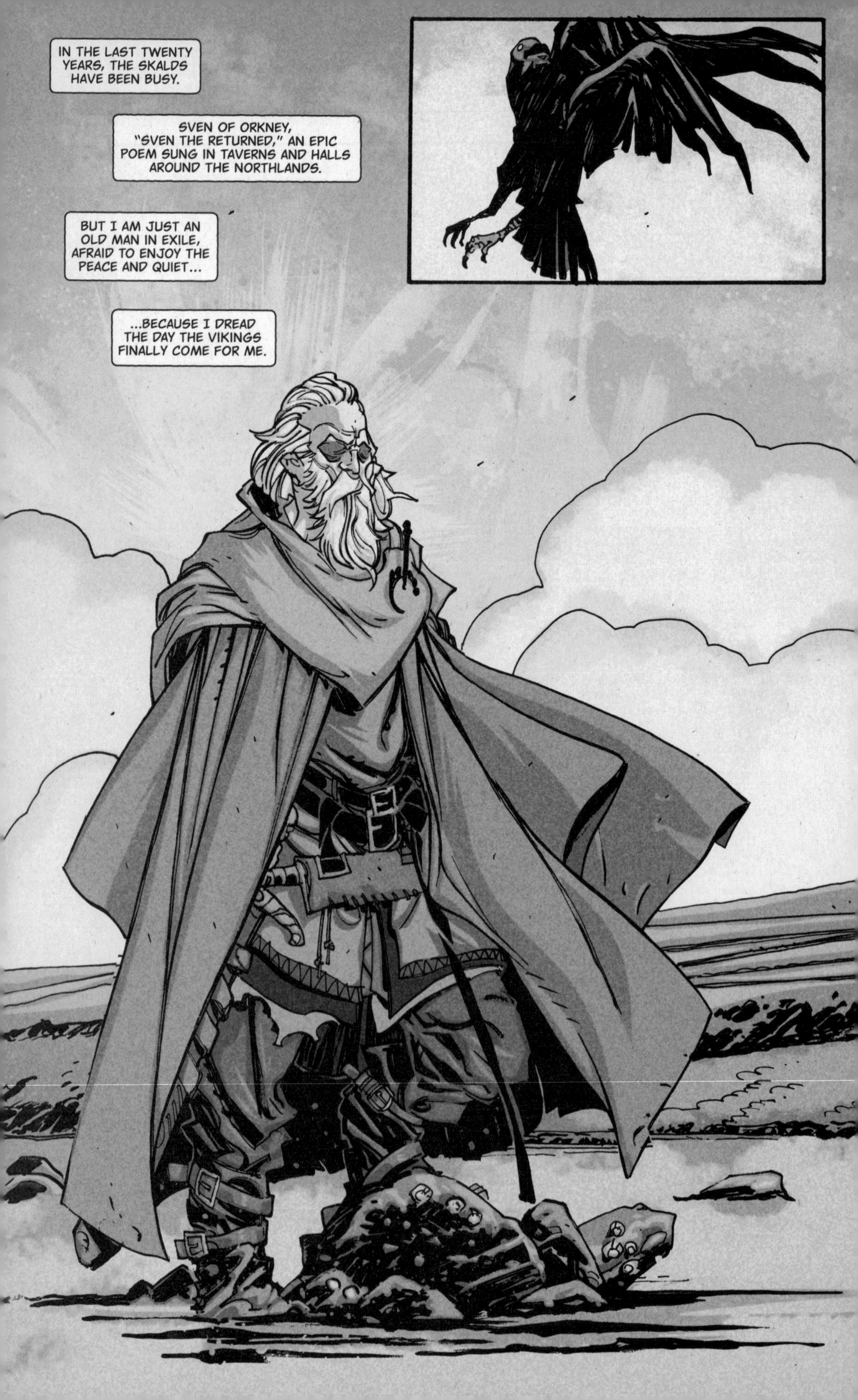
IN THE LAST TWENTY YEARS, THE SKALDS HAVE BEEN BUSY.
SVEN OF ORKNEY, "SVEN THE RETURNED," AN EPIC POEM SUNG IN TAVERNS AND HALLS AROUND THE NORTHLANDS.
BUT I AM JUST AN OLD MAN IN EXILE, AFRAID TO ENJOY THE PEACE AND QUIET...
...BECAUSE I DREAD THE DAY THE VIKINGS FINALLY COME FOR ME.

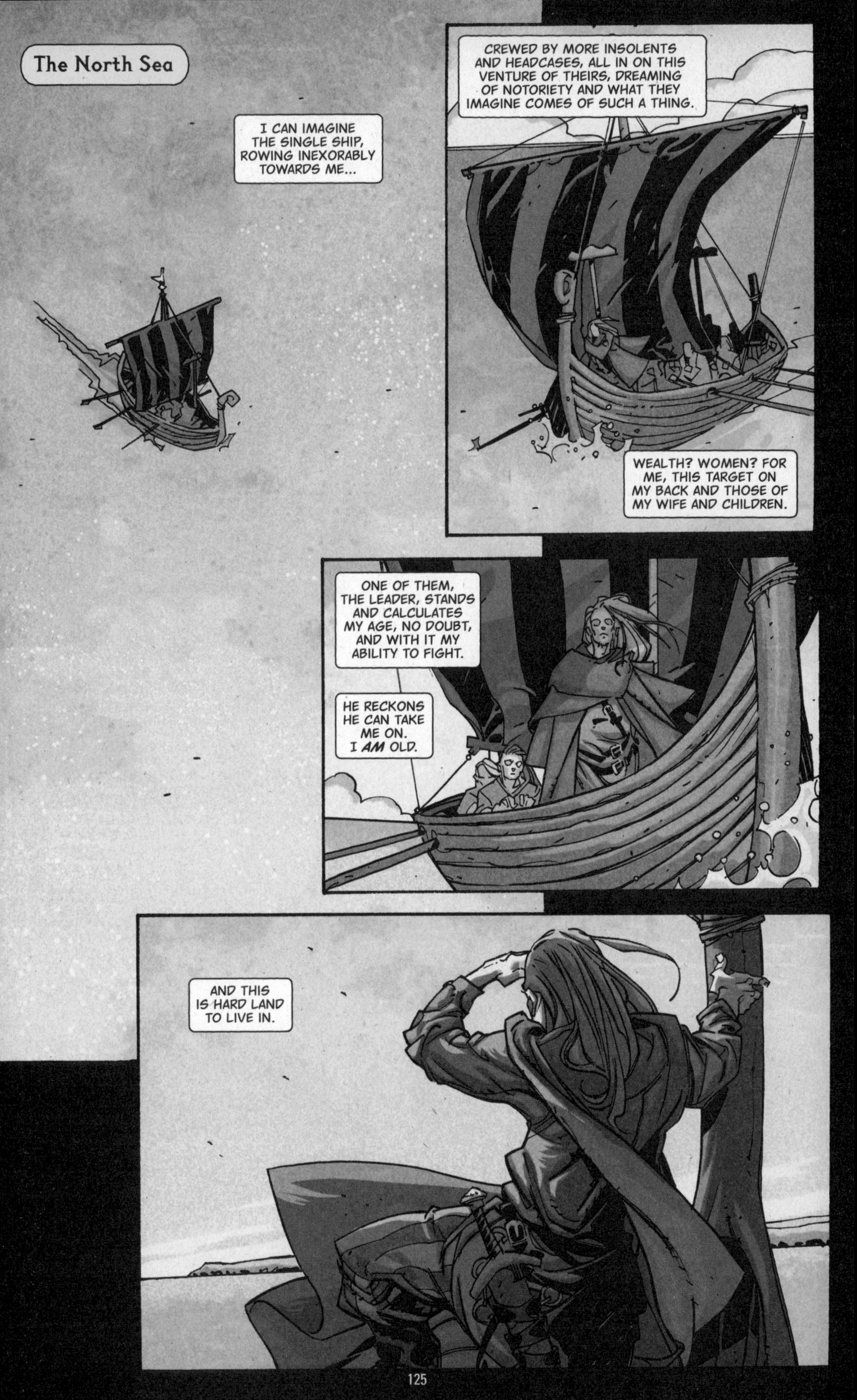
The North Sea
I CAN IMAGINE THE SINGLE SHIP, ROWING INEXORABLY TOWARDS ME...
CREWED BY MORE INSOLENTS AND HEADCASES, ALL IN ON THIS VENTURE OF THEIRS, DREAMING OF NOTORIETY AND WHAT THEY IMAGINE COMES OF SUCH A THING.
WEALTH? WOMEN? FOR ME, THIS TARGET ON MY BACK AND THOSE OF MY WIFE AND CHILDREN.
ONE OF THEM, THE LEADER, STANDS AND CALCULATES MY AGE, NO DOUBT, AND WITH IT MY ABILITY TO FIGHT.
HE RECKONS HE CAN TAKE ME ON. I AM OLD.
AND THIS IS HARD LAND TO LIVE IN.

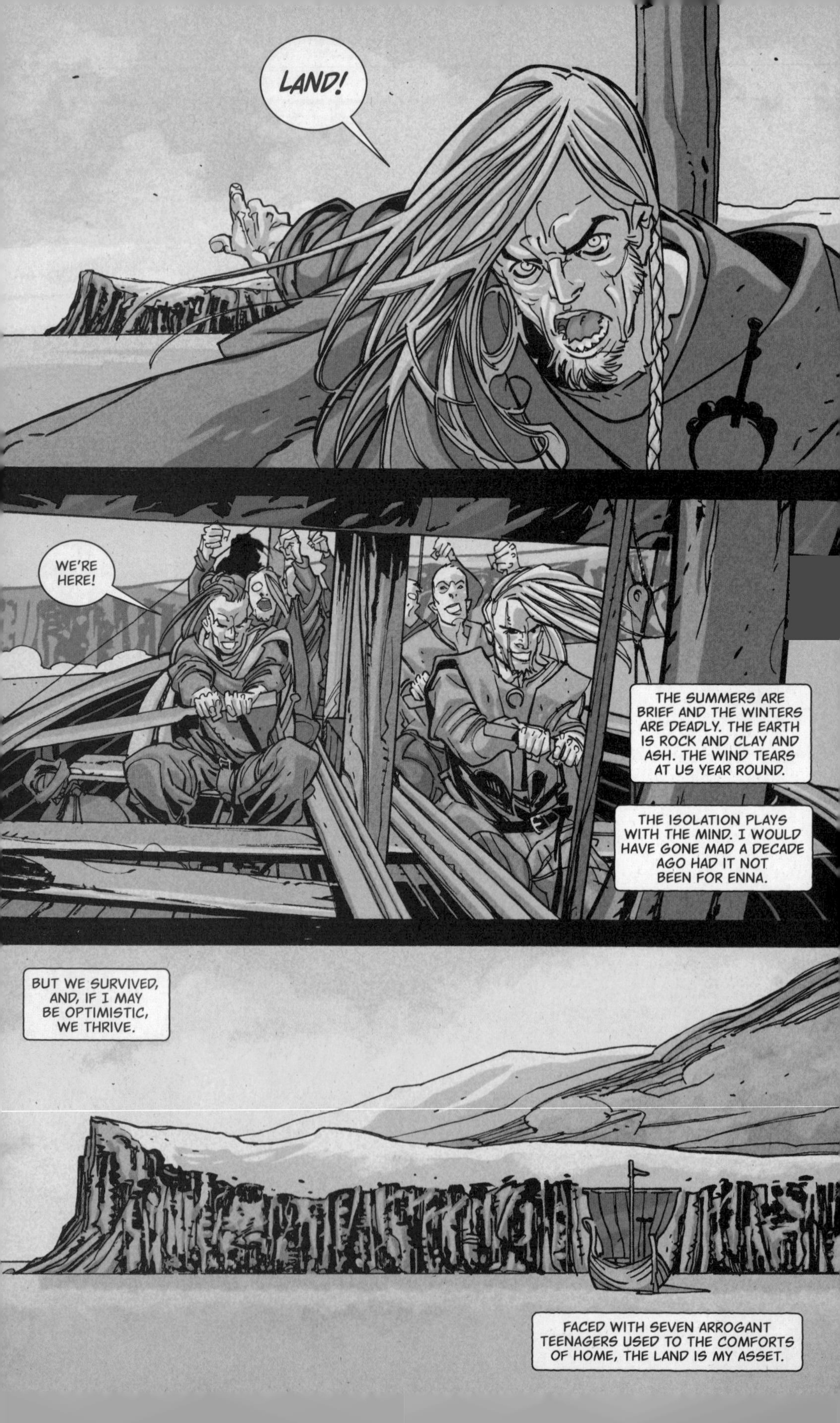
LAND!
WE'RE HERE!
THE SUMMERS ARE BRIEF AND THE WINTERS ARE DEADLY. THE EARTH IS ROCK AND CLAY AND ASH. THE WIND TEARS AT US YEAR ROUND.
THE ISOLATION PLAYS WITH THE MIND. I WOULD HAVE GONE MAD A DECADE AGO HAD IT NOT BEEN FOR ENNA.
BUT WE SURVIVED, AND, IF I MAY BE OPTIMISTIC, WE THRIVE.
FACED WITH SEVEN ARROGANT TEENAGERS USED TO THE COMFORTS OF HOME, THE LAND IS MY ASSET.

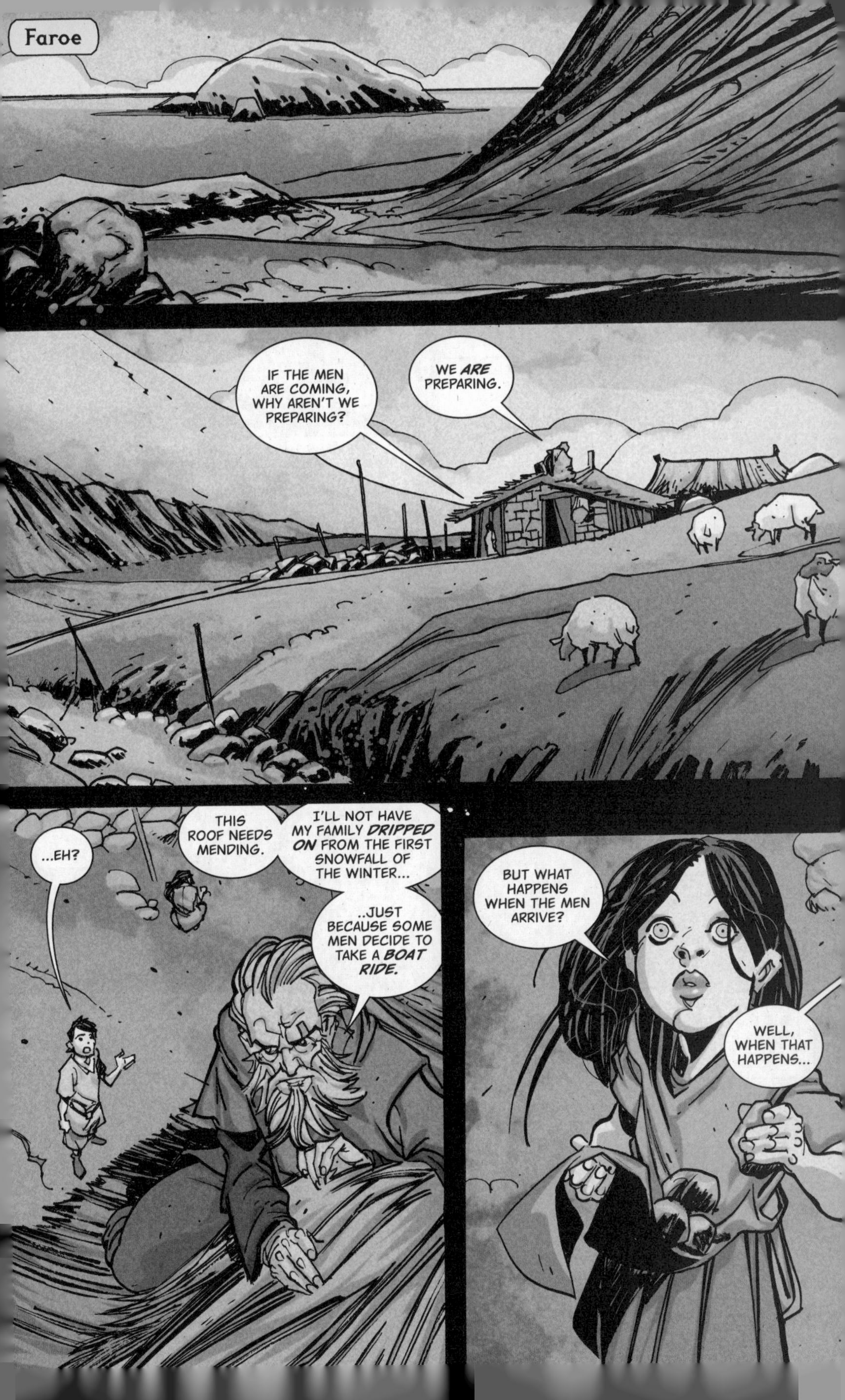
Faroe
IF THE MEN ARE COMING, WHY AREN'T WE PREPARING?
WE ARE PREPARING.
...EH?
THIS ROOF NEEDS MENDING.
I'LL NOT HAVE MY FAMILY DRIPPED ON FROM THE FIRST SNOWFALL OF THE WINTER...
..JUST BECAUSE SOME MEN DECIDE TO TAKE A BOAT RIDE.
BUT WHAT HAPPENS WHEN THE MEN ARRIVE?
WELL, WHEN THAT HAPPENS...

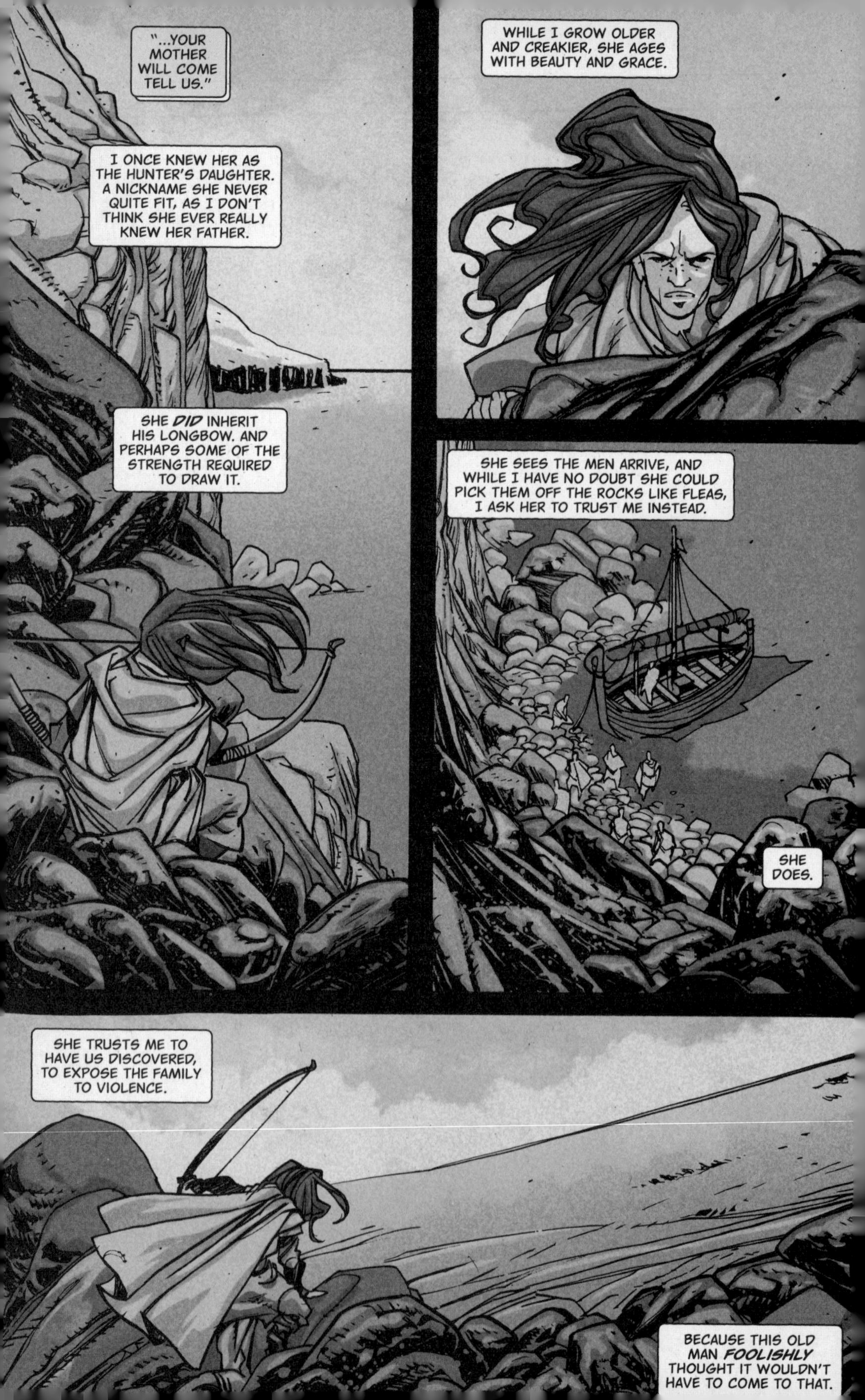
"...YOUR MOTHER WILL COME TELL US."
I ONCE KNEW HER AS THE HUNTER'S DAUGHTER. A NICKNAME SHE NEVER QUITE FIT, AS I DON'T THINK SHE EVER REALLY KNEW HER FATHER.
SHE *DID* INHERIT HIS LONGBOW. AND PERHAPS SOME OF THE STRENGTH REQUIRED TO DRAW IT.
WHILE I GROW OLDER AND CREAKIER, SHE AGES WITH BEAUTY AND GRACE.
SHE SEES THE MEN ARRIVE, AND WHILE I HAVE NO DOUBT SHE COULD PICK THEM OFF THE ROCKS LIKE FLEAS, I ASK HER TO TRUST ME INSTEAD.
SHE DOES.
SHE TRUSTS ME TO HAVE US DISCOVERED, TO EXPOSE THE FAMILY TO VIOLENCE.
BECAUSE THIS OLD MAN *FOOLISHLY* THOUGHT IT WOULDN'T HAVE TO COME TO THAT.

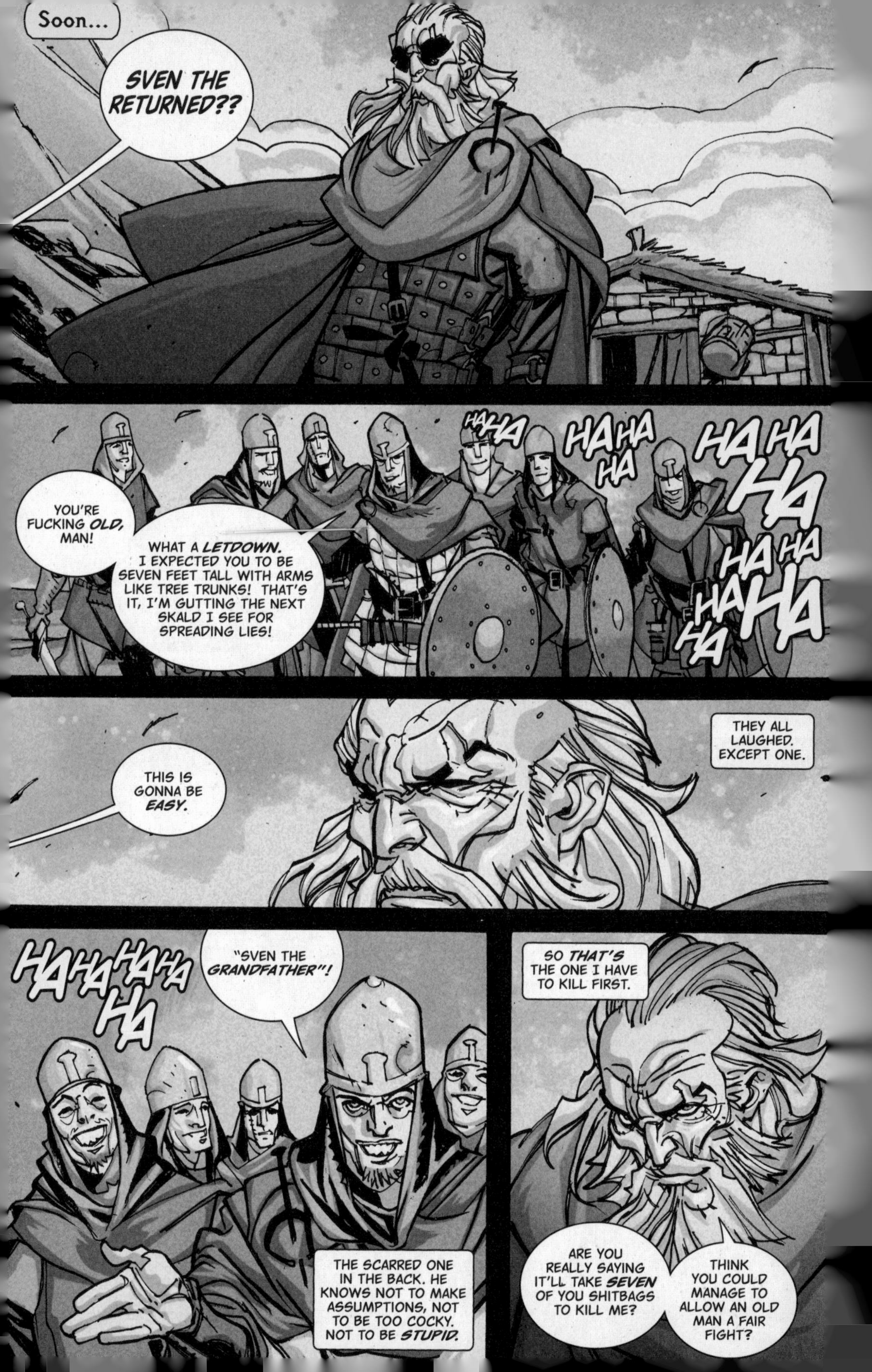
Soon...
SVEN THE RETURNED??
HA HA
HA HA HA
HA HA HA HA HA HA HA HA HA HA
YOU'RE FUCKING OLD, MAN!
WHAT A LETDOWN. I EXPECTED YOU TO BE SEVEN FEET TALL WITH ARMS LIKE TREE TRUNKS! THAT'S IT, I'M GUTTING THE NEXT SKALD I SEE FOR SPREADING LIES!
THIS IS GONNA BE EASY.
THEY ALL LAUGHED. EXCEPT ONE.
HA HA HA HA HA HA
"SVEN THE GRANDFATHER"!
THE SCARRED ONE IN THE BACK. HE KNOWS NOT TO MAKE ASSUMPTIONS, NOT TO BE TOO COCKY. NOT TO BE STUPID.
SO THAT'S THE ONE I HAVE TO KILL FIRST.
ARE YOU REALLY SAYING IT'LL TAKE SEVEN OF YOU SHITBAGS TO KILL ME?
THINK YOU COULD MANAGE TO ALLOW AN OLD MAN A FAIR FIGHT?

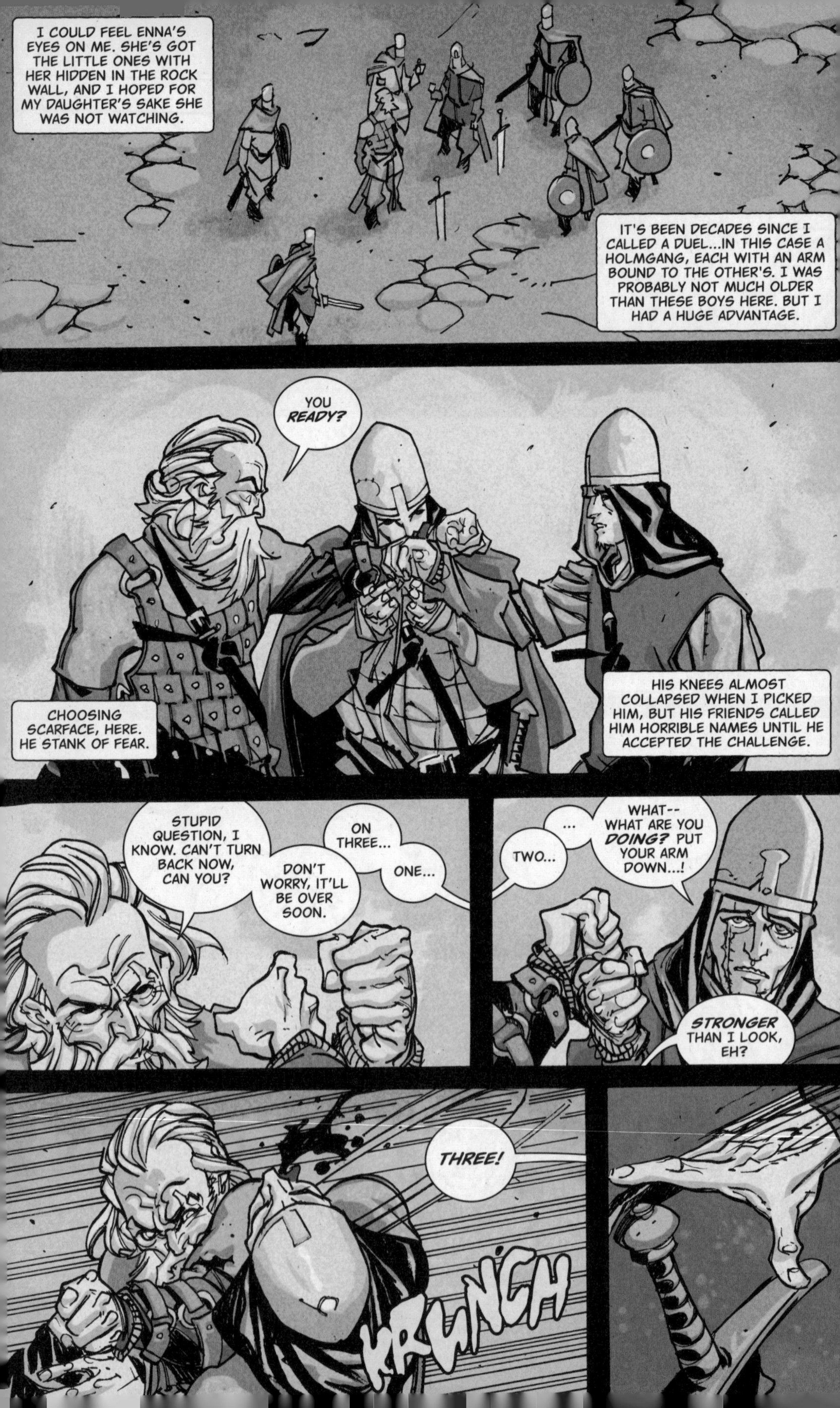
I COULD FEEL ENNA'S EYES ON ME. SHE'S GOT THE LITTLE ONES WITH HER HIDDEN IN THE ROCK WALL, AND I HOPED FOR MY DAUGHTER'S SAKE SHE WAS NOT WATCHING.
IT'S BEEN DECADES SINCE I CALLED A DUEL...IN THIS CASE A HOLMGANG, EACH WITH AN ARM BOUND TO THE OTHER'S. I WAS PROBABLY NOT MUCH OLDER THAN THESE BOYS HERE. BUT I HAD A HUGE ADVANTAGE.
YOU *READY?*
CHOOSING SCARFACE, HERE. HE STANK OF FEAR.
HIS KNEES ALMOST COLLAPSED WHEN I PICKED HIM, BUT HIS FRIENDS CALLED HIM HORRIBLE NAMES UNTIL HE ACCEPTED THE CHALLENGE.
STUPID QUESTION, I KNOW. CAN'T TURN BACK NOW, CAN YOU?
DON'T WORRY, IT'LL BE OVER SOON.
ON THREE...
ONE...
TWO...
...
WHAT-- WHAT ARE YOU *DOING?* PUT YOUR ARM DOWN...!
STRONGER THAN I LOOK, EH?
THREE!
KRUNCH

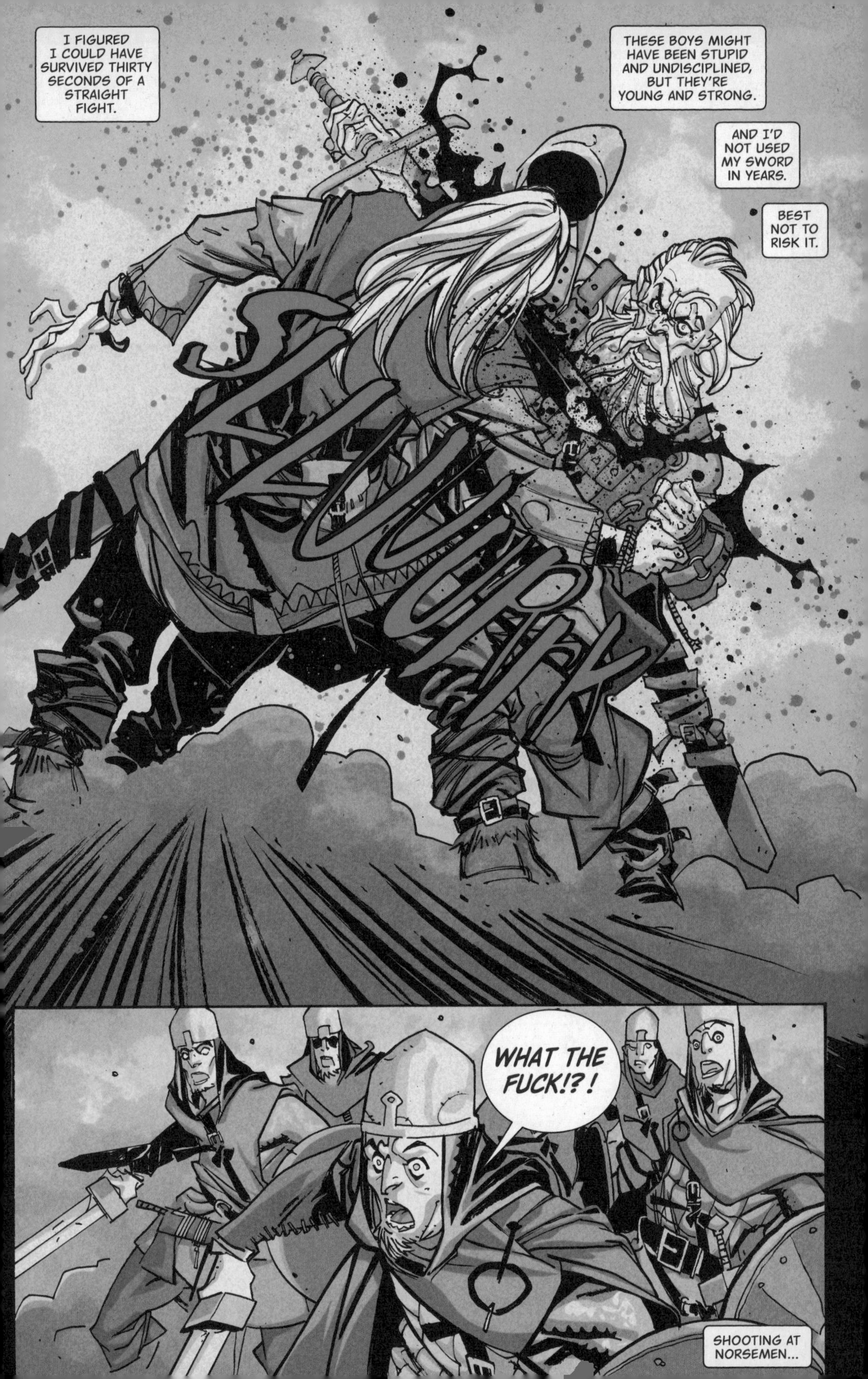
I FIGURED I COULD HAVE SURVIVED THIRTY SECONDS OF A STRAIGHT FIGHT.
THESE BOYS MIGHT HAVE BEEN STUPID AND UNDISCIPLINED, BUT THEY'RE YOUNG AND STRONG.
AND I'D NOT USED MY SWORD IN YEARS.
BEST NOT TO RISK IT.
WHAT THE FUCK!?!
SHOOTING AT NORSEMEN...

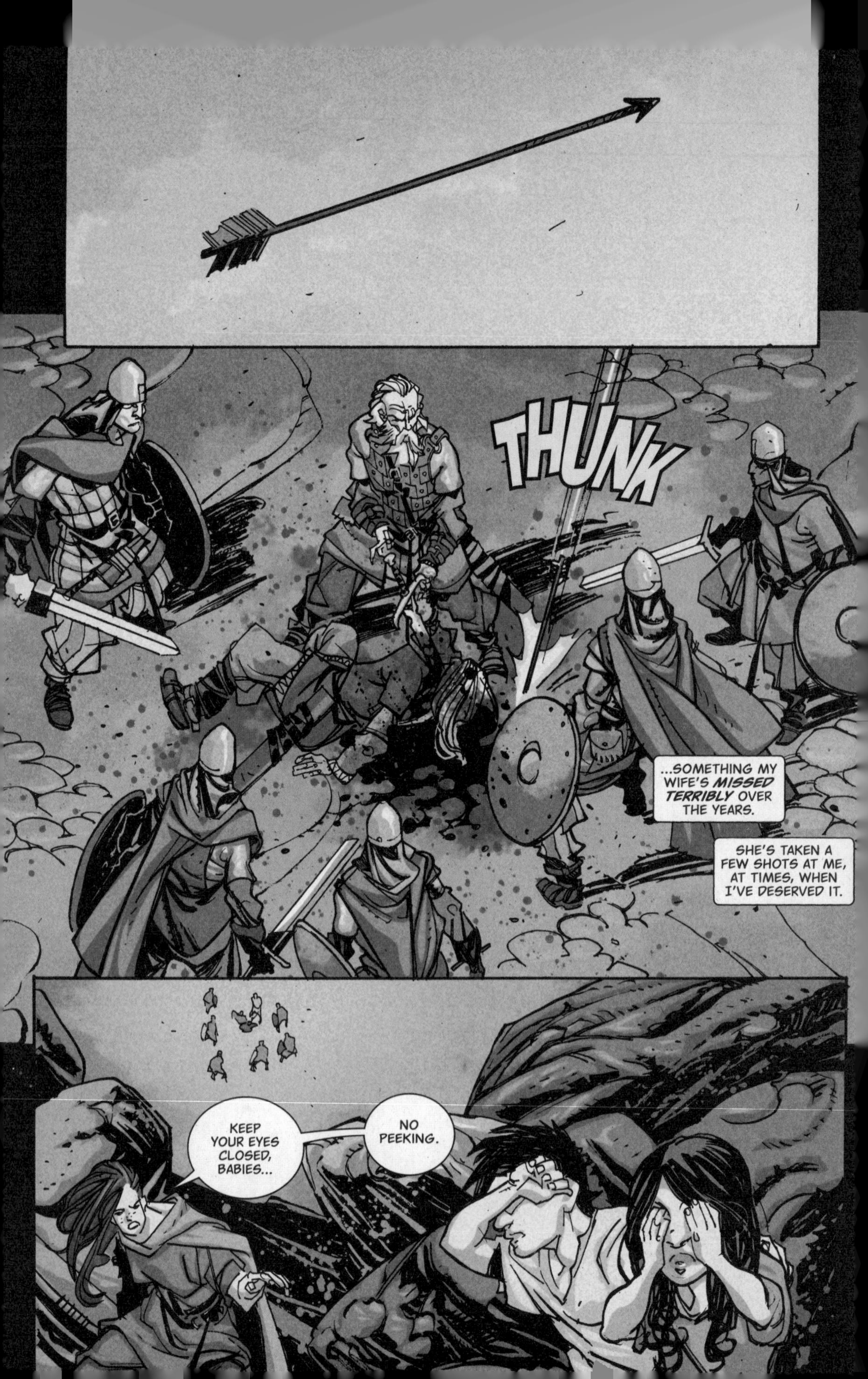
THUNK
...SOMETHING MY WIFE'S *MISSED TERRIBLY* OVER THE YEARS.
SHE'S TAKEN A FEW SHOTS AT ME, AT TIMES, WHEN I'VE DESERVED IT.
KEEP YOUR EYES CLOSED, BABIES...
NO PEEKING.

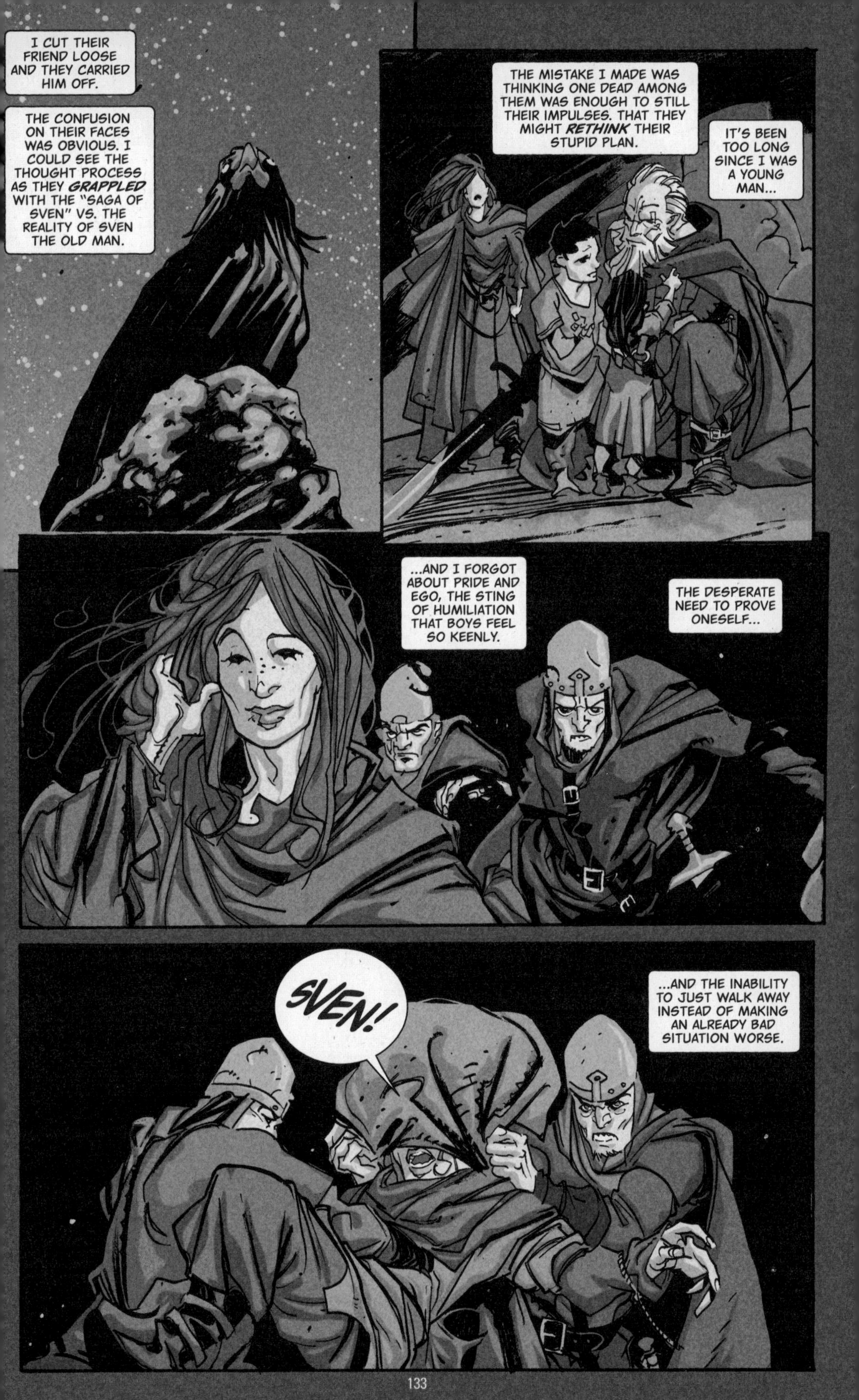

I CUT THEIR FRIEND LOOSE AND THEY CARRIED HIM OFF.
THE CONFUSION ON THEIR FACES WAS OBVIOUS. I COULD SEE THE THOUGHT PROCESS AS THEY GRAPPLED WITH THE "SAGA OF SVEN" VS. THE REALITY OF SVEN THE OLD MAN.
THE MISTAKE I MADE WAS THINKING ONE DEAD AMONG THEM WAS ENOUGH TO STILL THEIR IMPULSES. THAT THEY MIGHT RETHINK THEIR STUPID PLAN.
IT'S BEEN TOO LONG SINCE I WAS A YOUNG MAN...
...AND I FORGOT ABOUT PRIDE AND EGO, THE STING OF HUMILIATION THAT BOYS FEEL SO KEENLY.
THE DESPERATE NEED TO PROVE ONESELF...
SVEN!
...AND THE INABILITY TO JUST WALK AWAY INSTEAD OF MAKING AN ALREADY BAD SITUATION WORSE.

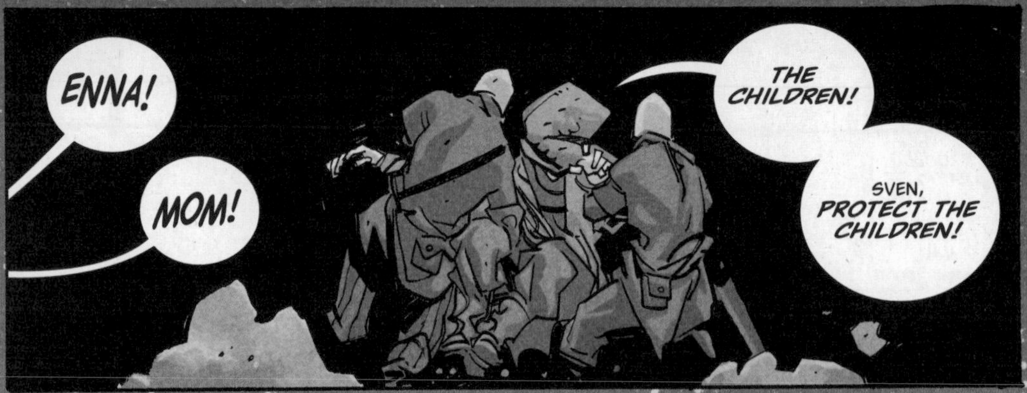
ENNA!
MOM!
THE CHILDREN!
SVEN, PROTECT THE CHILDREN!

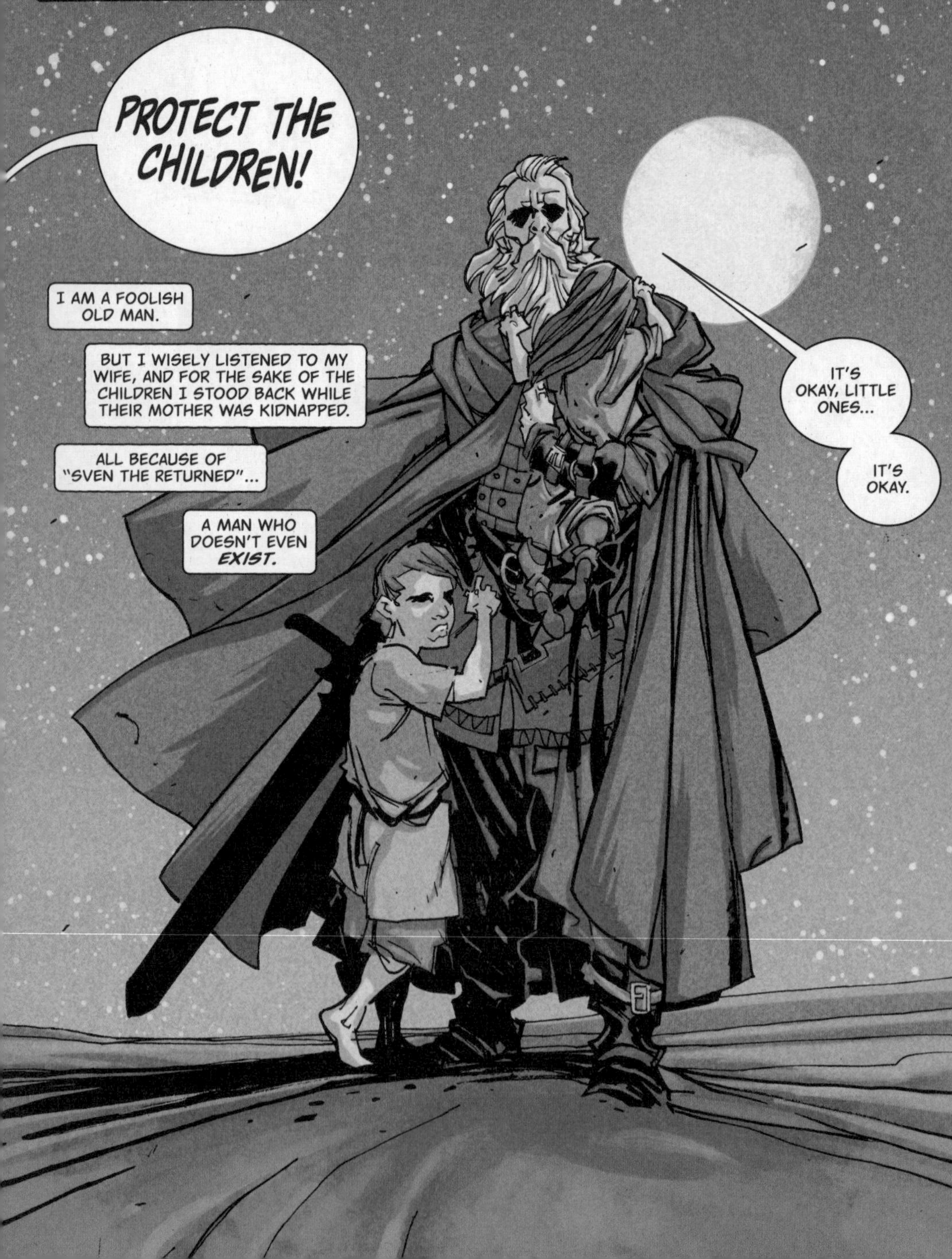
PROTECT THE CHILDREN!
I AM A FOOLISH OLD MAN.
BUT I WISELY LISTENED TO MY WIFE, AND FOR THE SAKE OF THE CHILDREN I STOOD BACK WHILE THEIR MOTHER WAS KIDNAPPED.
ALL BECAUSE OF "SVEN THE RETURNED"...
A MAN WHO DOESN'T EVEN EXIST.
IT'S OKAY, LITTLE ONES...
IT'S OKAY.

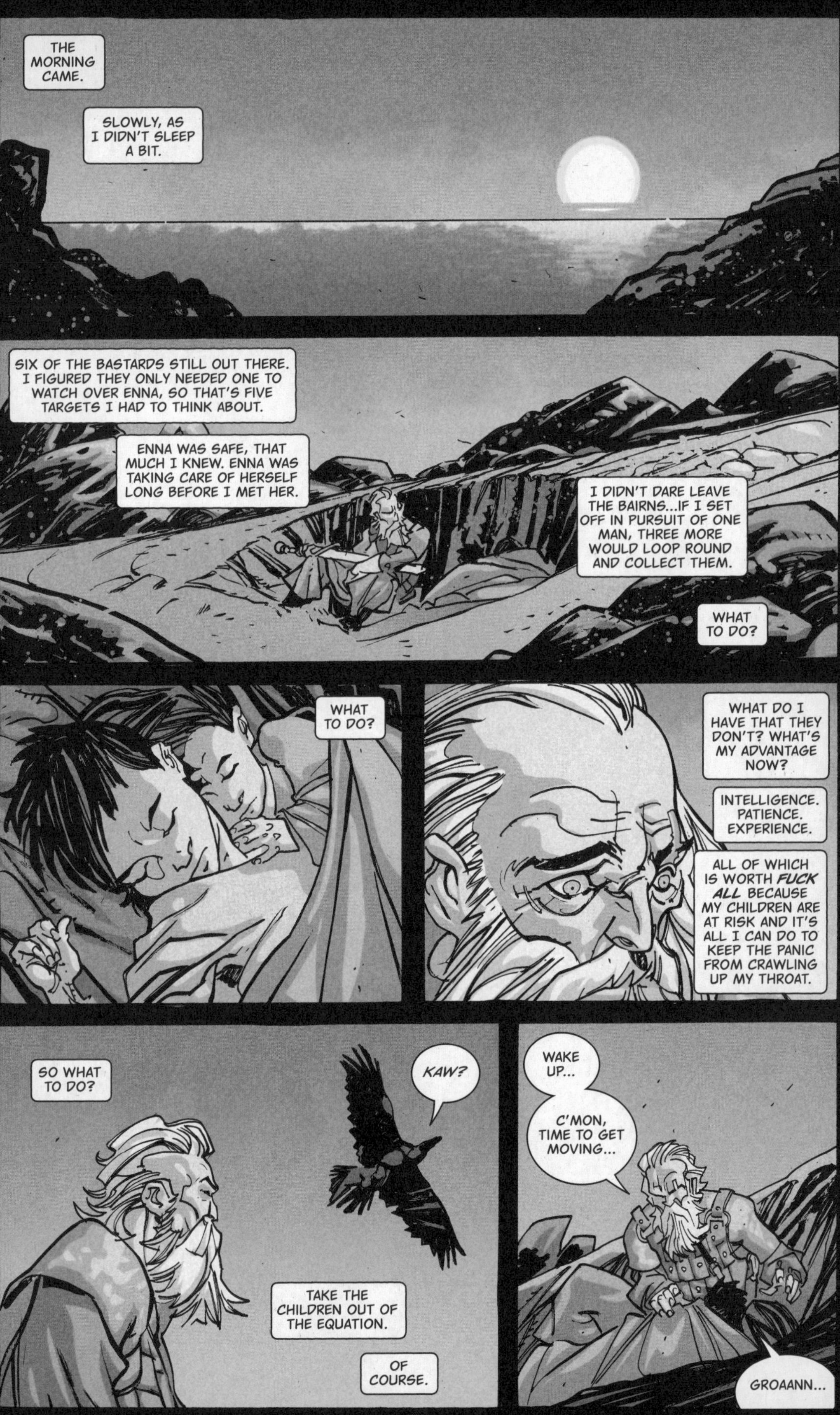
THE MORNING CAME.
SLOWLY, AS I DIDN'T SLEEP A BIT.
SIX OF THE BASTARDS STILL OUT THERE. I FIGURED THEY ONLY NEEDED ONE TO WATCH OVER ENNA, SO THAT'S FIVE TARGETS I HAD TO THINK ABOUT.
ENNA WAS SAFE, THAT MUCH I KNEW. ENNA WAS TAKING CARE OF HERSELF LONG BEFORE I MET HER.
I DIDN'T DARE LEAVE THE BAIRNS...IF I SET OFF IN PURSUIT OF ONE MAN, THREE MORE WOULD LOOP ROUND AND COLLECT THEM.
WHAT TO DO?
WHAT TO DO?
WHAT DO I HAVE THAT THEY DON'T? WHAT'S MY ADVANTAGE NOW?
INTELLIGENCE. PATIENCE. EXPERIENCE.
ALL OF WHICH IS WORTH *FUCK ALL* BECAUSE MY CHILDREN ARE AT RISK AND IT'S ALL I CAN DO TO KEEP THE PANIC FROM CRAWLING UP MY THROAT.
SO WHAT TO DO?
KAW?
TAKE THE CHILDREN OUT OF THE EQUATION.
OF COURSE.
WAKE UP...
C'MON, TIME TO GET MOVING...
GROAANN...

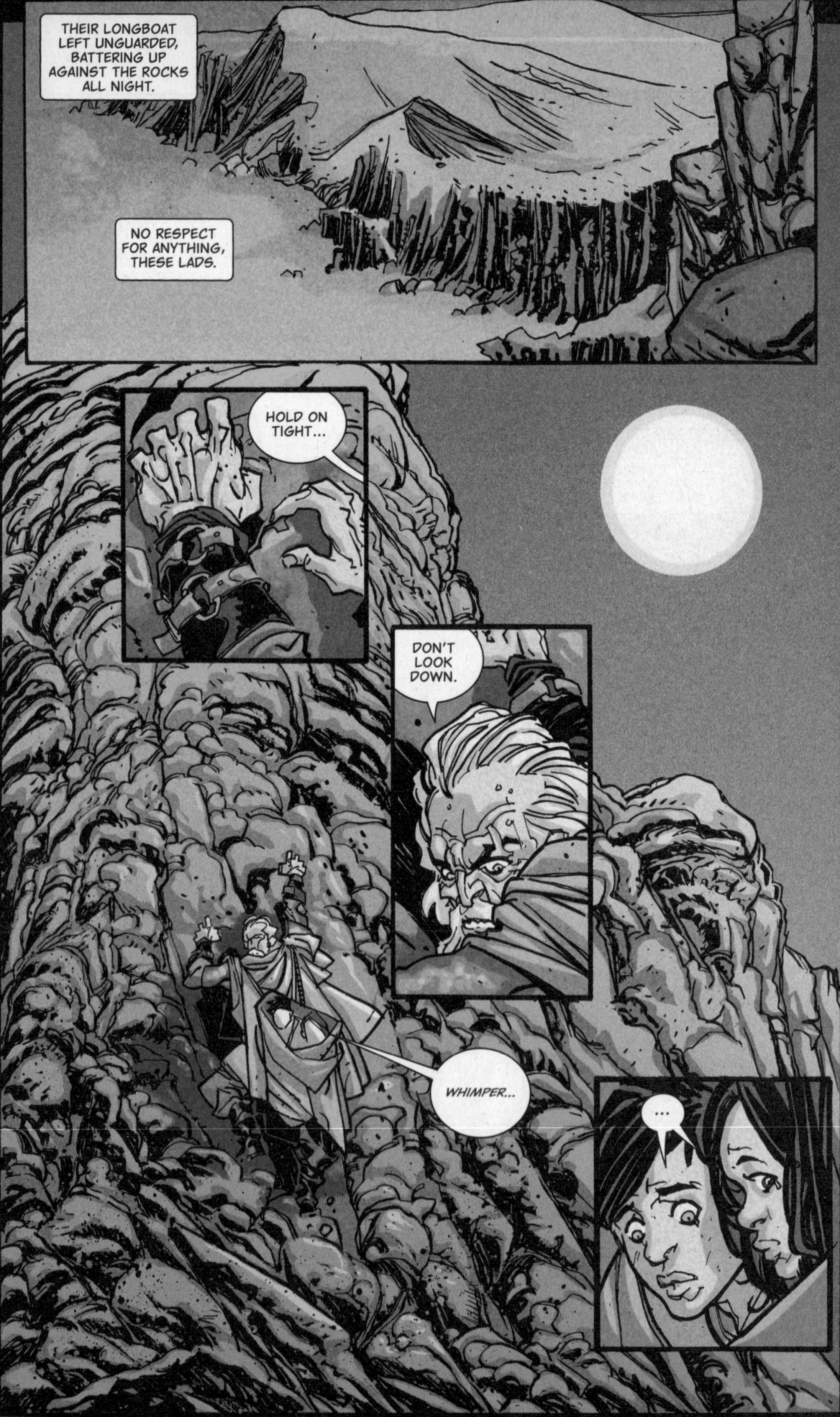
THEIR LONGBOAT LEFT UNGUARDED, BATTERING UP AGAINST THE ROCKS ALL NIGHT.
NO RESPECT FOR ANYTHING, THESE LADS.
HOLD ON TIGHT...
DON'T LOOK DOWN.
WHIMPER...
...

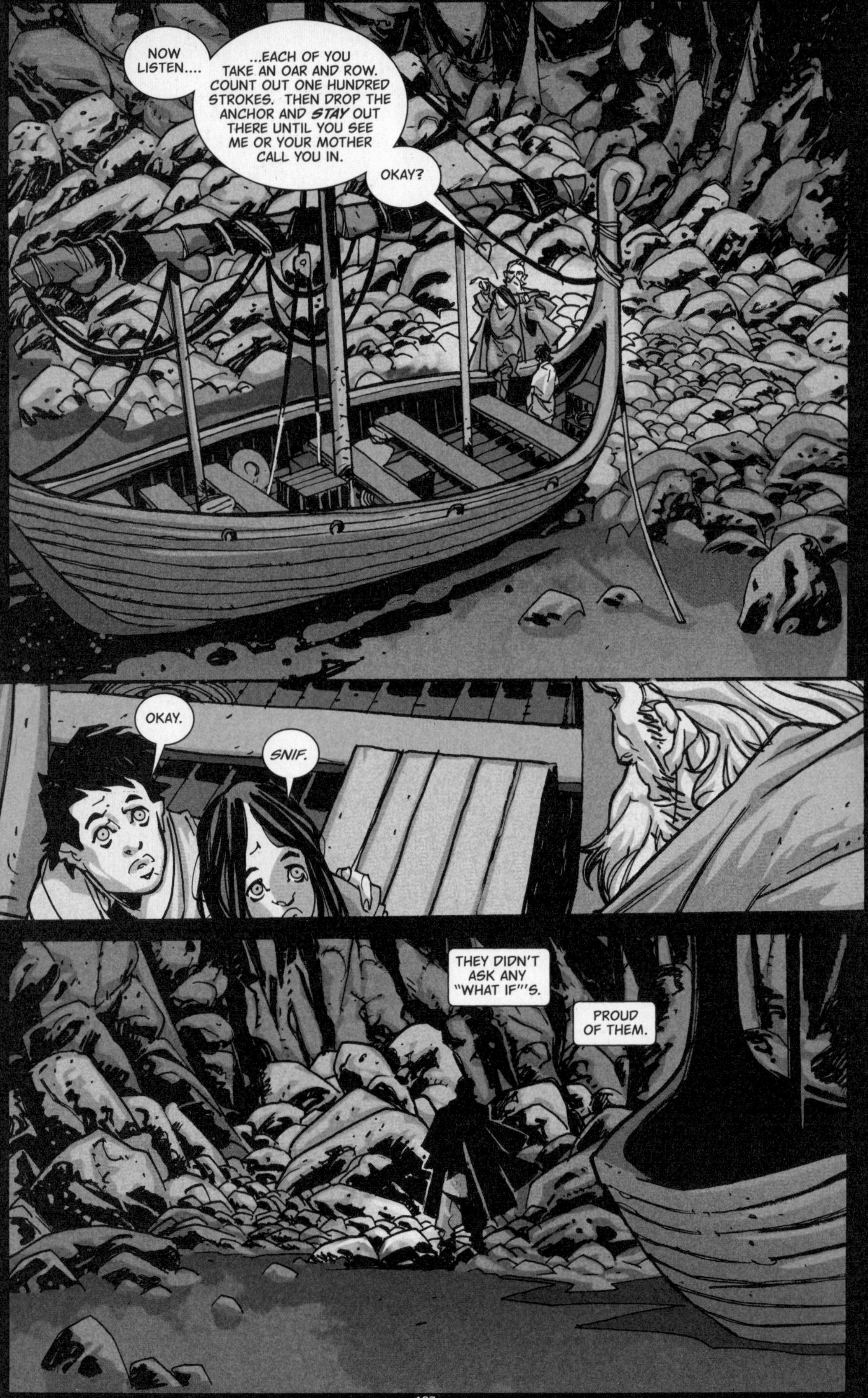
NOW LISTEN....
...EACH OF YOU TAKE AN OAR AND ROW. COUNT OUT ONE HUNDRED STROKES. THEN DROP THE ANCHOR AND STAY OUT THERE UNTIL YOU SEE ME OR YOUR MOTHER CALL YOU IN.
OKAY?
OKAY.
SNIF.
THEY DIDN'T ASK ANY "WHAT IF"'S.
PROUD OF THEM.

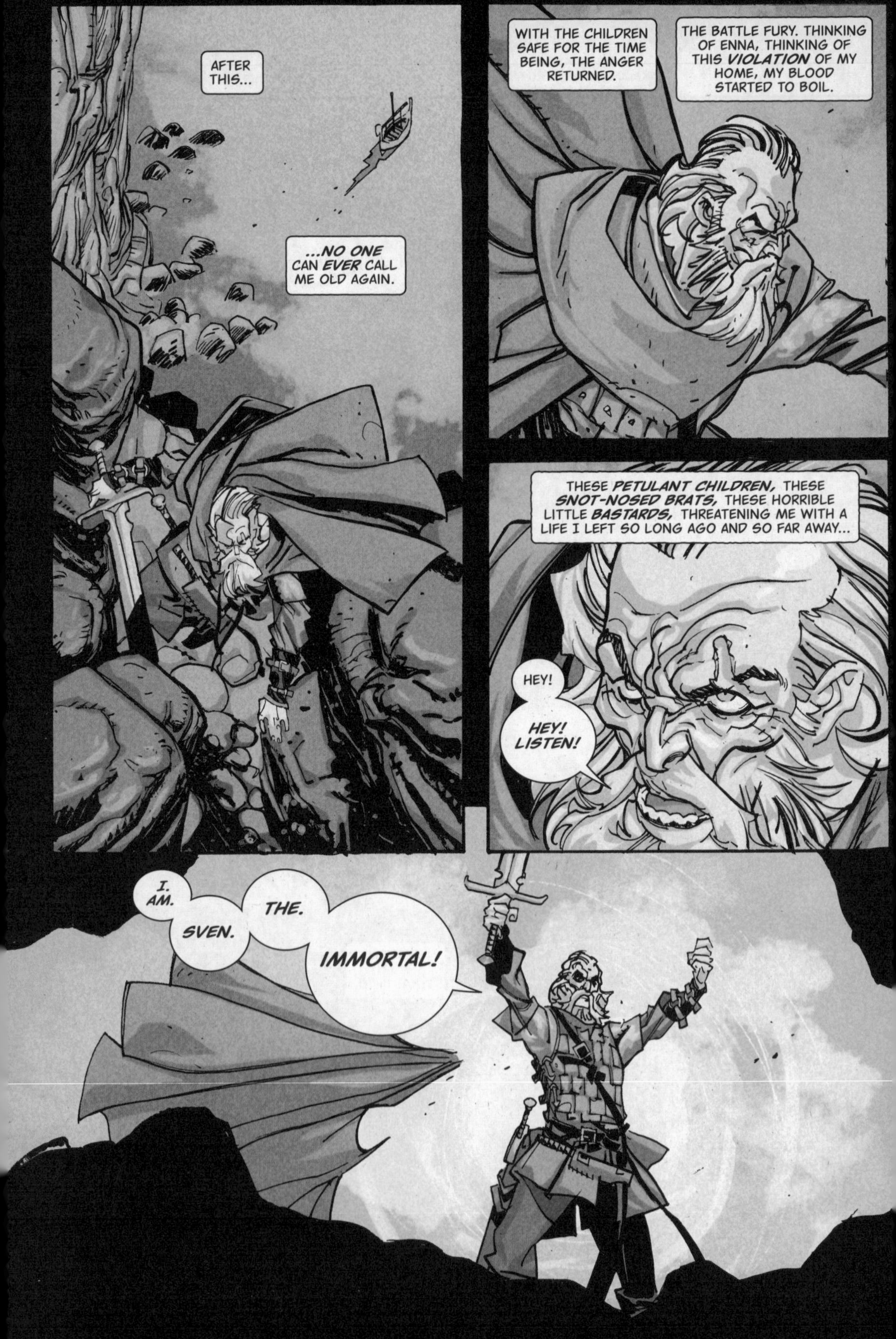
AFTER THIS...
...NO ONE CAN EVER CALL ME OLD AGAIN.
WITH THE CHILDREN SAFE FOR THE TIME BEING, THE ANGER RETURNED.
THE BATTLE FURY. THINKING OF ENNA, THINKING OF THIS VIOLATION OF MY HOME, MY BLOOD STARTED TO BOIL.
THESE PETULANT CHILDREN, THESE SNOT-NOSED BRATS, THESE HORRIBLE LITTLE BASTARDS, THREATENING ME WITH A LIFE I LEFT SO LONG AGO AND SO FAR AWAY...
HEY!
HEY! LISTEN!
I.
AM.
SVEN.
THE.
IMMORTAL!

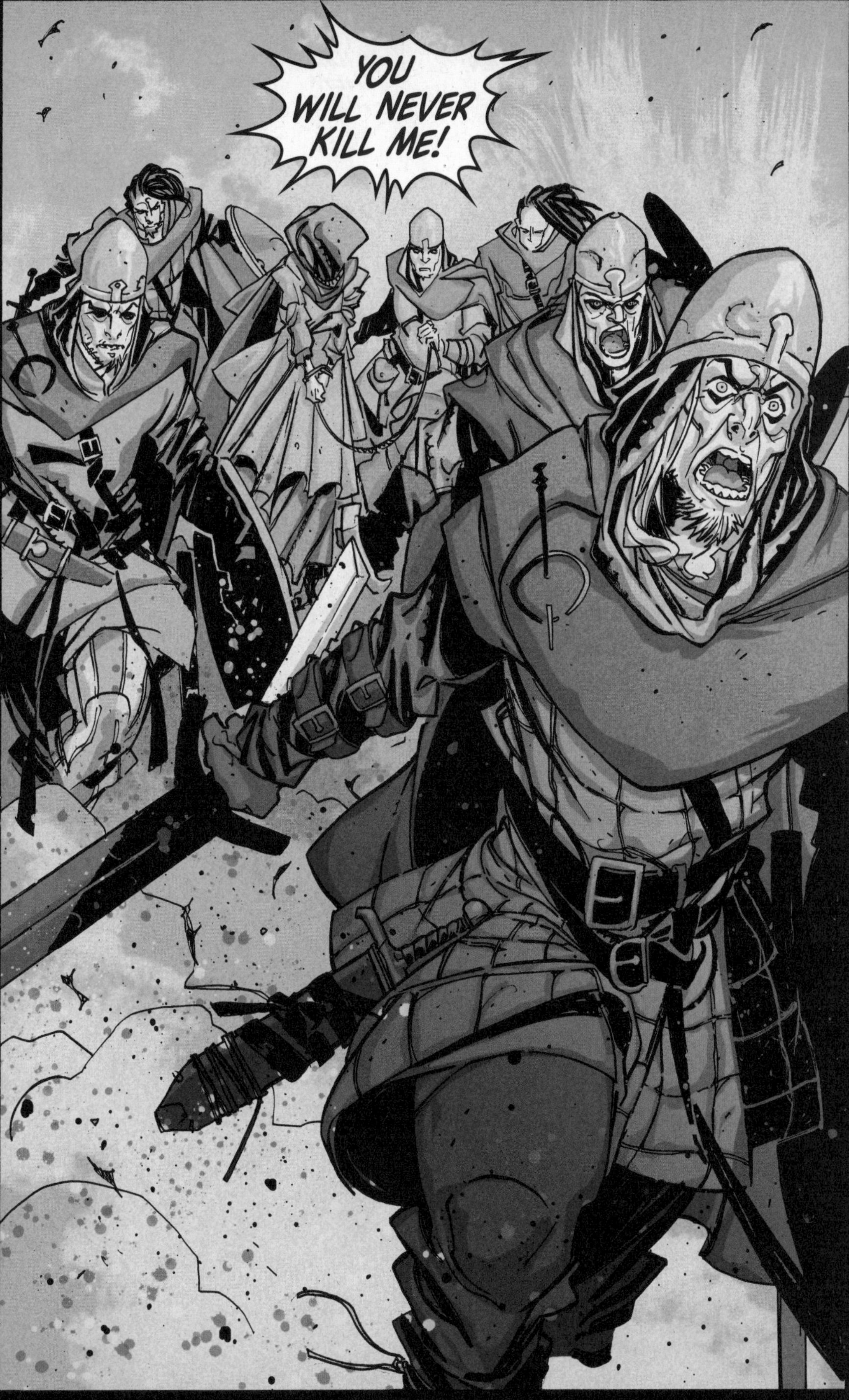
YOU WILL NEVER KILL ME!

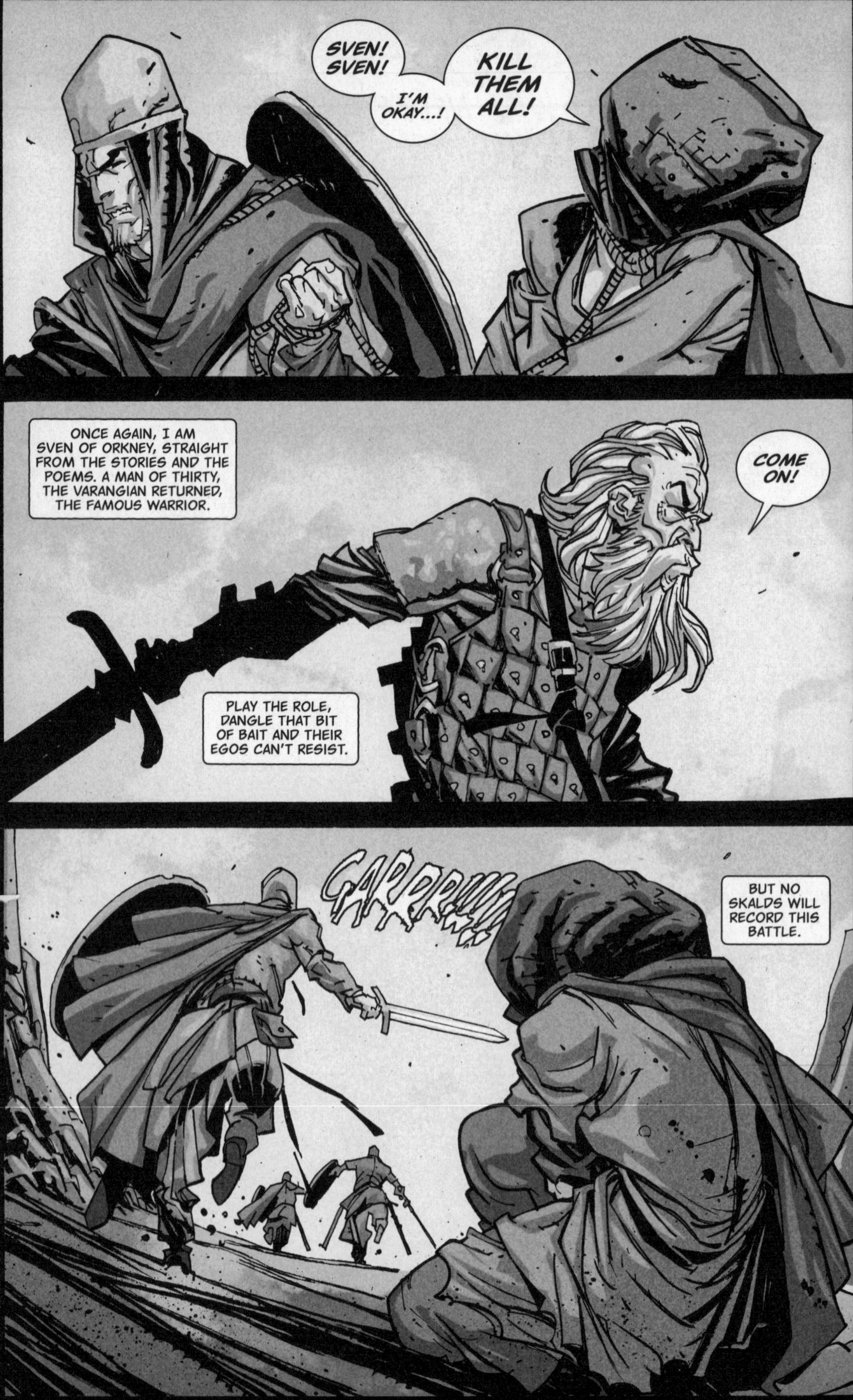

SVEN! SVEN!
I'M OKAY...!
KILL THEM ALL!
ONCE AGAIN, I AM SVEN OF ORKNEY, STRAIGHT FROM THE STORIES AND THE POEMS. A MAN OF THIRTY, THE VARANGIAN RETURNED, THE FAMOUS WARRIOR.
COME ON!
PLAY THE ROLE, DANGLE THAT BIT OF BAIT AND THEIR EGOS CAN'T RESIST.
GARRRR!!!
BUT NO SKALDS WILL RECORD THIS BATTLE.

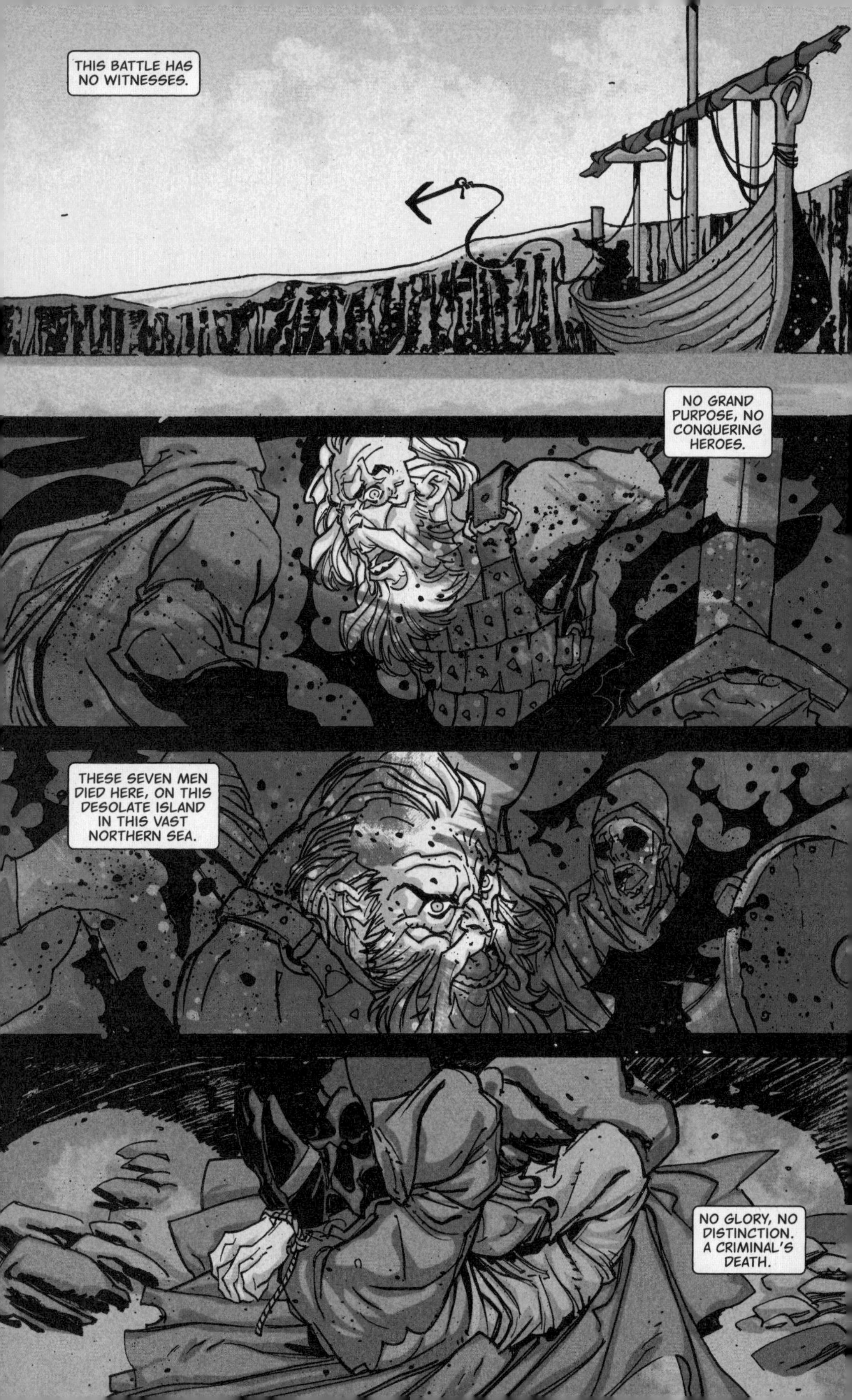
THIS BATTLE HAS NO WITNESSES.
NO GRAND PURPOSE, NO CONQUERING HEROES.
THESE SEVEN MEN DIED HERE, ON THIS DESOLATE ISLAND IN THIS VAST NORTHERN SEA.
NO GLORY, NO DISTINCTION. A CRIMINAL'S DEATH.

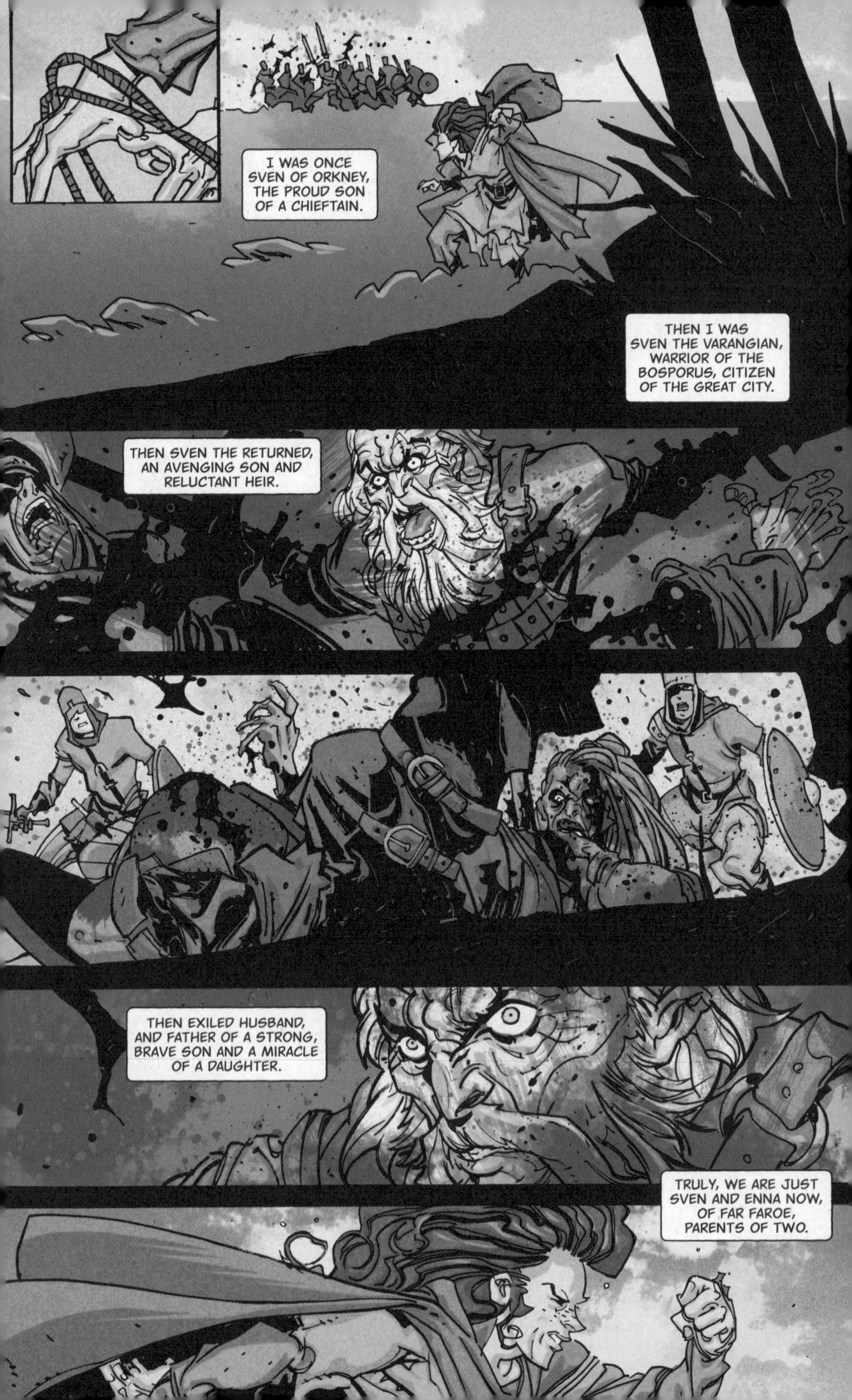
I WAS ONCE SVEN OF ORKNEY, THE PROUD SON OF A CHIEFTAIN.
THEN I WAS SVEN THE VARANGIAN, WARRIOR OF THE BOSPORUS, CITIZEN OF THE GREAT CITY.
THEN SVEN THE RETURNED, AN AVENGING SON AND RELUCTANT HEIR.
THEN EXILED HUSBAND, AND FATHER OF A STRONG, BRAVE SON AND A MIRACLE OF A DAUGHTER.
TRULY, WE ARE JUST SVEN AND ENNA NOW, OF FAR FAROE, PARENTS OF TWO.

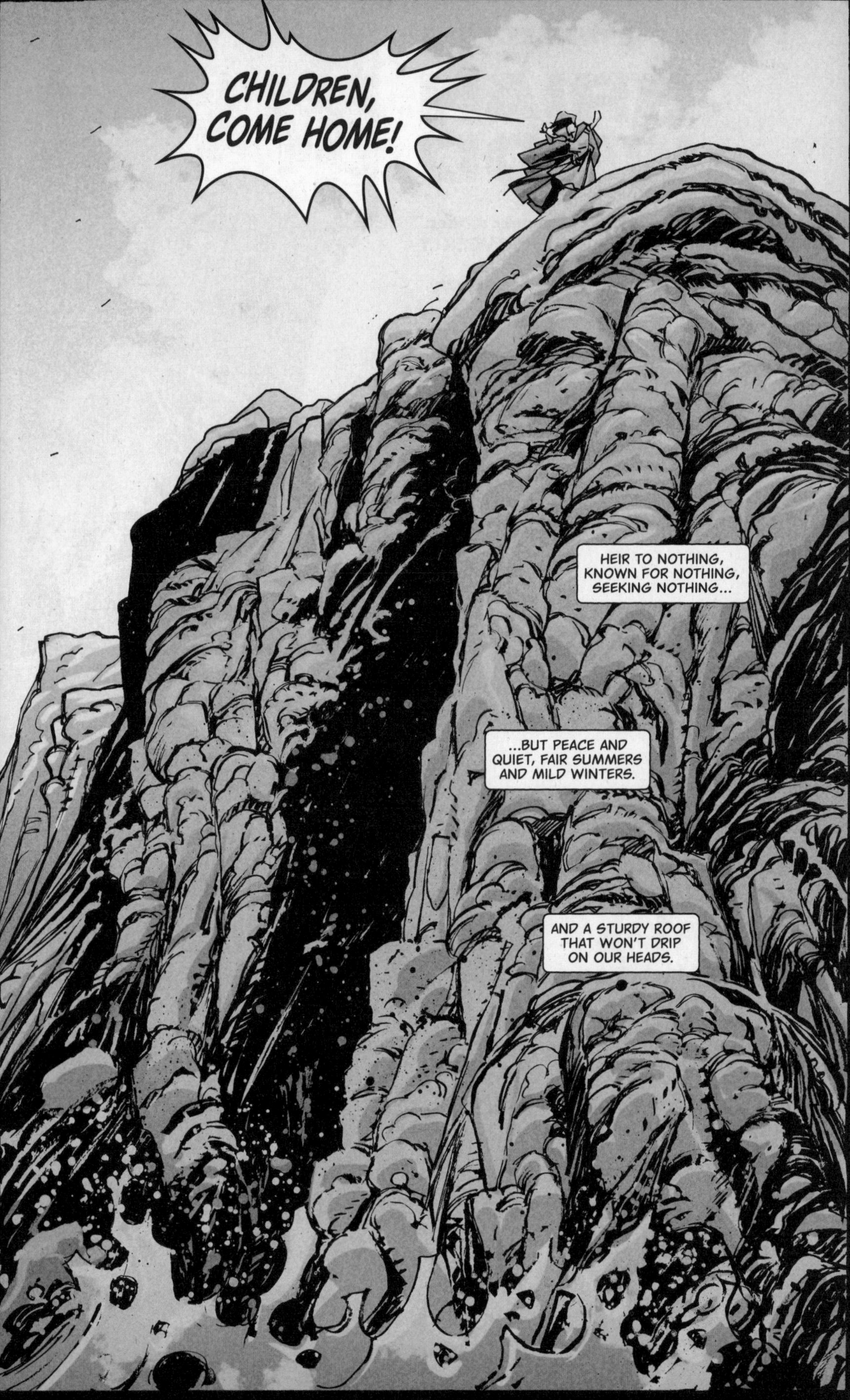
CHILDREN, COME HOME!
HEIR TO NOTHING, KNOWN FOR NOTHING, SEEKING NOTHING...
...BUT PEACE AND QUIET, FAIR SUMMERS AND MILD WINTERS.
AND A STURDY ROOF THAT WON'T DRIP ON OUR HEADS.

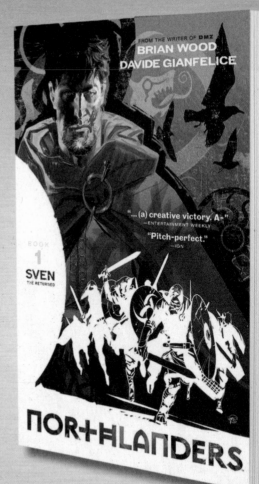
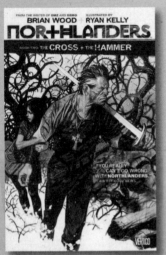
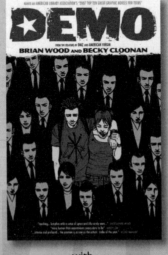